T

LIVING LIFE WITH INTENTIONALITY ONE DAY AT A TIME

A 365-DAY DEVOTIONAL

BRAD WHITE

ISBN: 978-0-578-42970-0

Dedication

I dedicate this book to my family:

- To my wife Holly who has always believed more in me than I believe in myself.
- To my two children, Cade (7) and Abi Kate (4), who have provided inspiration for many of these devotional thoughts.
- To you, my mom, my editor in chief, who spent each day editing my daily thoughts.
- To my dad and brother, thank you for your encouragement.
- Most importantly, thanks goes to the Lord who without fail daily inspired me with something to say.

FORWARD

Over a year ago, I found myself fed up with all I was seeing on social media. It seemed like each day the vast majority of what I saw was negative. I was contemplating deleting my social media accounts, but then a thought came to me. I cannot control what others are putting out there, but I can use my social media platforms for good. This spurred me on a year-long journey where I prayed each day that God would give me insight and wisdom and something to share. The pages that follow is the collection of those thoughts throughout the year.

I believe there are spiritual lessons that can be learned throughout the course of our day-to-day life. I believe God is in all things. I believe he allows us to see him in and through everyday life if only we will look. Matthew 7:7 say, "Ask and it will be given to you; seek and you will find; knock and the door will be opened to you."

Make Today Count is all about your ability to choose. I hope you will find the following daily devotions to be encouraging, enlightening, and an insightful part of your day. I pray God uses them to speak to your heart and mind.

Make today count!

Brad White, Men's Pastor
New Vision Baptist Church
brad.white@newvisionlife.com

Day 1

Happy New Year! Yesterday during lunch my family and I sat around and talked about the goals we have for the upcoming year.

Cade said he would like to read chapter books, keep learning about God, and learn how to swim better. Holly said she would like to commit to the workout routine she has started, spend more time focused on Bible journaling, and to drink 64 ounces of water a day. I have given myself a goal of completing a few writing assignments, finding a form of exercise that I truly enjoy doing, and increase my savings contributions.

The final step in establishing these goals was Holly writing them down today and posting them where we can see them. This way they are in front of us each day and can serve as a reminder of what we have committed to.

In April 2014 *Forbes Magazine* featured the article, "Why You Should Be Writing Down Your Goals." The main points of this article were to create a vision, make it measurable, set benchmarks, and celebrate success. (The article can be found at www.forbes.com.)

I believe there is something more valuable than writing your goals down. In my own strength, I don't believe I can complete any of these goals I set for myself. I need to rely on the Spirit of God for direction and clarity. Proverbs 16:3 tells us, "Commit to the Lord whatever you do, and he will establish your plans."

God did not come to just be a part of our lives, He came to be our lives so it only makes sense that we would involve Him with the goals we have set for ourselves. By committing our plans to Him, we are submitting them as an act of worship to Him and for His glory.

My challenge for you today is to commit your plans for this year to God. Submit them to Him as an act of worship. Write them down, put them somewhere you can see them, then take the steps needed each day to cross them off your list. I believe in you. With God's help, I know you can succeed!

Make this year count!

Day 2

Preparation is an ebb and flow of all of our lives. As I was driving home last night, I was thinking about preparation and saw a few things that pointed as a reminder of it. There was a fitness club advertising their summer camps, and I saw a preschool advertising for registration for next fall. At the same time, I have been planning a 10-year anniversary trip for me and Holly which is not until later this year. We plan trips, we plan for our children's education, we plan birthdays, and I'm not sure about you, but I have been in business meetings where we were preparing to prepare for the meeting. Preparation is a part of almost every area of our lives.

Where does preparation land for you when it comes to spiritual matters? Do you have a goal in mind for 10 years from now spiritually? What are the things you hope to accomplish or be a part of for Gods kingdom? I don't know about you, but my default would be to be reactionary in my spiritual life. I believe we would see a great movement of God if we put some forward thinking into what he has for us in our future. This would give us a roadmap, a game plan, to continue to shape us into who he wants us to be. 1 Peter 1:13 says, "Therefore, prepare your minds for action, keep sober in spirit, fix your hope completely on the grace to be brought to you at the revelation of Jesus Christ."

My challenge for you today is to write out your spiritual goals for the next one, five, and 10 years. These goals should be crafted after spending time in prayer and having an understanding of where you feel God is leading you. Of all the preparation that we can do, our spiritual preparation will have the greatest impact through eternity.

Make today count!

Day 3

My parents came to our home in Tennessee from Kentucky on December 26. My mom, of course, spent a lot of time baking and preparing food to bring with them. When they arrived, they brought in a rolling cooler which held the many delicious and fattening treats my mom had made for us for the week. Once they had emptied the contents of the cooler, my dad tossed the remaining ice into my yard. The next morning as I was taking the trash out, I noticed the ice was still there in perfect condition. Typically, in Tennessee, it would be unusual if ice lasted more than 24 hours. However, the extreme cold we have had for the past few weeks provided the perfect environment for the ice to remain in its solid state. The ice is thriving in this environment. It is able to be exactly what it was intended to be.

The same can be said for us. The environment we find ourselves in is either one that is conducive to our growth and allowing us to be everything we are supposed to be, or it's tearing us down. There are two ways to make sure your environment is right. The first is to move to an environment that fits what you are trying to be. The second is to work to change your current environment, in essence to be salt and light to that environment.

In Matthew 5:14-16, Jesus says, "You are the light of the world. A town built on a hill cannot be hidden. Neither do people light a lamp and put it under a bowl. Instead they put it on its stand, and it gives light to everyone in the house. In the same way, let your light shine before others, that they may see your good deeds and glorify your Father in heaven." This, my friends, is how you change your environment.

Where do you find yourself today? Are you in an environment in which you are thriving or one in which you are barely able to survive? What change do you need to make today? Do you need to move to a new environment, or can you be salt and light in the environment you are already in?

Make today count!

Day 4

So many people close to me are hurting. Divorce has ravaged marriages. Financial troubles have moved some into a place of fear. Sickness has others questioning if this is the last time they will see their loved one. We live in a broken, fallen, and mixed up world. This news in and of itself is nothing short of depressing. God gave man free will. With this free will, men have chosen to disobey and ignore him. But that is not enough to keep God from coming up with the perfect rescue plan for us.

The only way God could remedy our brokenness is by sending his Son to pay the price for our sins on the cross. John 3:16 says, "For God so loved the world, that he gave his one and only son that anyone who believes in him shall not perish but have eternal life."

Sin, simply put, is missing the mark. The mark is perfection. It doesn't matter how "good" we are. When compared to a perfect God, we have missed the mark. Romans 6:23 says, "The wages of sin is death, but the gift of God is eternal life through Christ Jesus." Here is the breakdown of this verse. Wages is what we earned for missing the mark of perfection. The gift is something we have not earned. It is simply given to us. God has given us a gift. This gift is his Son who willingly stepped in our place and took the punishment we deserved which is death, referring to eternal separation from God.

When you are given a gift, you have to open it. How does one receive God's gift? Admit to God that you have missed the mark of perfection. Believe in your heart that Jesus is the Son of God and that he died and rose again to pay your penalty.

Confess with your mouth Jesus is your Lord. The gospel of Jesus is called Good News for this very reason: anyone can be brought into right standing with God.

Will accepting this free gift make all this pain and brokenness go away? No, but what will come is a peace that passes all understanding. My challenge for you today is to go directly to the Source of love, peace, and joy. Should you have any questions about further understanding this, feel free to reach out!

Make today count!

Day 5

What is it that God has given you to accomplish? What is the great mountain he has you climbing right now? I recently felt God calling me to a mountain of my own. I have spent a significant amount of time doing research. I have also spent time developing a plan, strategy, and follow up. I spent time thinking about each and every aspect of my plan that has a need and considered who might be able to serve in those capacities. I have my action plan written down and had a few trusted peers evaluate it.

There comes a time when we are doing something we know God has called us to when we must stop. There is a point where we have done all we can humanly do to accomplish the task God has given us. We have given it our absolute best, yet something within us may feel a sense of unease. It may feel as if we are missing something. Proverbs 16:3 "Commit to the LORD whatever you do, and he will establish your plans."

Since God was the author of the idea, we must reach a point where we give it all back to him. We work as unto the Lord creating and establishing a solution and then we submit it to him. This is a lesson I need today. I have done all I can do. Now it's time to rely on him to establish the plan.

My challenge for you today is to do everything within your power to work out the plan God has called you to. Once you have done all you can do, submit it back to him.

Make today count!

Day 6

Holly has recently become quite fond of a certain type of pottery. This brand creates various types of pottery including storage containers, mugs, and plates. The interesting thing about this pottery is, in my opinion, that it looks like an unskilled potter made it. The symmetry you would expect to see in a normal coffee mug is not there. I don't really understand what all the fuss is about, but through the lens that Holly views the pottery, it is beautiful.

At times, I look at my own life and I see all of the mistakes and imperfections. I wonder how anyone, especially God, could look at my life and see it as something beautiful. 2 Corinthians 5:21 says, "God made him who had no sin to be sin for us, so that in him we might become the righteousness of God."

Simply translated, Jesus came and lived a perfect life and died for us. He bridged the gap between us and God. By doing so, when we put our faith and trust in him, God views us through the perfect lens of Jesus Christ. Where other people might see imperfections, God sees repentance and forgiveness.

My challenge for you today is not to allow Satan to let you focus on all of your imperfections, but be reminded today that God sees you through the lens of Christ.

Make today count!

Day 7

I helped a friend pack up a storage pod in preparation for a move. A few of us worked together to get this pod packed up before its departure next week. One other guy and myself organized the placement of all the items into the pod. The other two guys with muscle brought the boxes and items out to us. We were trying our best to create symmetry and weight balance. We had a vision in mind for how the boxes would be stacked to create the most ideal scenario for transportation. It seemed like every time the plan was coming together; the other guys would bring out a very obscure piece to work around to try to maintain the symmetry that we desired.

This got me thinking about how similar this is to our lives. We have a plan, an idea of how we want things to stack up. But then when we least expect it, something comes from out of the blue—an obstacle that we need to overcome or something that draws our attention away from our plan.

2 Corinthians 4:8-9 is the perfect passage to remind yourself of when these adversities and trials come. "We are hard pressed on every side, but not crushed; perplexed, but not in despair; persecuted, but not abandoned; struck down, but not destroyed." Though we can see the struggles, he has not abandoned us. He will not let us be destroyed.

My challenge for you today is to take heart when adversity comes to know that he is by your side.

Make today count!

Day 8

Every so often in the middle of the night, Abi Kate screams out for Holly or me. Last night was one of these occasions. It was probably two in the morning, and it sounded like she must have been fighting off a band of three or four thugs, one of whom must have fatally wounded her with a knife. I jumped out of my bed and promptly made my way into her room. When I entered the room, she was sitting up in her bed screaming. I said "Abi Kate, what is wrong?" She immediately stopped crying and said to me in a very sweet, gentle voice, "Can I have some water?" That's it? There's no blood loss that I need to take care of? No broken bones to attend to? Abi Kate's cry did not match the severity of the situation.

I started to think about this and realized that sometimes my cry doesn't match the severity of the situation. If I truly believe that my relationship with Jesus Christ is the only way for a person to have eternal life with God, then when I have friends who either do not believe, or I have not taken the time to tell them, I feel that I fall in the exact same boat.

Since eternity is hanging in the balance, I can think of nothing that deserves more attention. Matthew 25:31-33 says, "When the Son of Man comes in his glory, and all the angels with him, he will sit on his glorious throne. All the nations will be gathered before him, and he will separate the people one from another as a shepherd separates the sheep from the goats. He will put the sheep on his right and the goats on his left."

We have the opportunity to share the truth of Christ with those around us. It's not our responsibility to make sure that people believe and receive, it is simply our job to share. My challenge for you today is to utilize the platform God has given you to share the truth of his love.

Make today count!

Day 9

In the late 1990s,\ or early 2000, I begin playing the drums. I have a natural ability to hear a time signature in a song. With much practice and an amazing teacher, I would say I was halfway decent. James Foutch (my drum teacher) might say otherwise. The more I played for church, and the more I practiced, the better I got. Around the time I headed off for college, I started playing less and less. It has been so long now since I have played the drums, I would struggle to maintain a simple rhythm. Without nurturing this ability, it has been all but lost.

God has given each one of us different skills and talents to be used for his glory. The gifts and talents we continue to nurture and refine are the ones that we will see the most impact from and through. 1 Peter 4:10-11 says, "Each of you should use whatever gift you have received to serve others, as faithful stewards of God's grace in its various forms. If anyone speaks, they should do so as one who speaks the very words of God. If anyone serves, they should do so with the strength God provides, so that in all things God may be praised through Jesus Christ. To him be the glory and the power for ever and ever. Amen."

My challenge for you today is not to allow your talents to atrophy. Push on them, practice them, challenge them. Use your talents as an act of worship to bring God glory.

Make today count!

Day 10

My kids are both very much into speaking a language they have created. To me, it sounds like a mix of Mandarin Chinese with a slight hint of Russian, and of course, you can't forget the Martian. They will speak to each other in this language. They will speak to themselves in this language. They even try to speak it to Holly and me. Cade will come up to me from time to time speaking his special language and say something to me as if he expects me to understand. Obviously, this is an impossible task.

Prior to getting married, I believe it is very important for couples to understand each other's love language. Dr. Gary Chapman has established five love languages. He says each of us tends to feel loved primarily through one of them. The love languages are: gifts, quality time, physical touch, words of affirmation, and acts of service.

Here's a brief description of each:

GIFTS - Physical gifts given

QUALITY TIME - Devoted time set aside with the other person

PHYSICAL TOUCH - Non-sexual physical touch such as hand holding

WORDS OF AFFIRMATION - Building the other person up with your words and encouraging them

ACTS OF SERVICE - Doing little things to serve the other person (unloading the dishwasher)

Paul reminds us the importance of loving our spouse and that understanding how to speak to their love language is of significant importance. Ephesians 5:25 says, "Husbands, love your wives, just as Christ loved the church and gave himself up for her." One of these five love languages is the primary form in which you receive love by your loved one. Maybe you are a person who needs quality time to feel affirmed by the person who deeply loves you. A problem can arise when a couple has two different love languages). This is true of Holly and me. Holly's primary love language is quality time. My primary love language is words of affirmation. If Holly were only to speak to me through her primary love language and never through words of affirmation, it would sound like gibberish to me, much like Cade's gibberish. I might feel that something is missing. My challenge for you today is to strive to understand the primary love languages of those you are close with and to make every attempt to speak to them through that language so you are speaking a language they will understand.

Make today count!

Day 11

A couple of days ago Abi Kate fed our dog, Mo, a grape. This is not the first time that this has happened. I explained to her that this could make him very sick and even cause him to die. She began to sob. I said, "Why don't you say a prayer to God that Mo will be OK." Through her tear-filled eyes, she looked up at me and said, "But I don't know how to pray." This is a dilemma that many adults have felt, including Jesus' disciples.

The disciples could have asked Jesus for anything, however, they chose to ask him how to pray. His response is recorded in Matthew 6:9-13. Let's look at each part to get an understanding of how it should guide our prayer life.

Verse 9: "This, then, is how you should pray:

"'Our Father in heaven, hallowed be your name (This is where we recount God's attributes. He is holy, perfect, forgiving, merciful, etc.)

Verse 10: Your kingdom come, your will be done, on earth as it is in heaven. (We are asking for God's good, perfect, and pleasing will to reign over us in the here and now.)

Verse 11: Give us today our daily bread. (We are asking God to sustain our daily needs.)

Verse 12: And forgive us our debts, as we also have forgiven our debtors. (We are thanking God for forgiving us for all of our wrongdoings. We are forgiving those who have wronged us.)

Verse 13: And lead us not into temptation, but deliver us from the evil one. (This is where we are praying for God to guide our steps to keep us away from things that draw our fleshly desires. We are praying for God's protection and guidance over our day.)

My challenge for you today is to spend some time in prayer. Remember, the second part of prayer is listening. Prayer is a conversation.

P.S. (Mo lived to see another day!)

Make today count!

Day 12

There are noises that we can immediately discern. The sound of glass breaking, the cry of your child, or that pre-throw-up cough from kids at 2 a.m. We instinctively know these noises, and they push us into action. In a matter of seconds, we can discern the noise then take decisive steps towards rectifying or resolving the situation if needed.

Can you discern God's voice the same way that you discern glass being shattered in the middle of the night? Discerning God's voice is not an easy task. God has given us his Word as a way of hearing him speak. I believe God also speaks through other means such as through other people, dreams, music, and more. When you're trying to discern if what you heard is from God, make sure it lines up with scripture. You will never hear the voice of God tell you something that is contrary to scripture.

When you have affirmed that God has spoken something to you, the second step is that it should put you into action. Just as you respond when you hear your child crying, hearing God speak should propel you to find out where he is leading. Psalms 31:3 says, "For you are my rock and my fortress, for your namesake you will lead me and guide me." Obedience to the voice of God take us to places we could have never gotten on our own.

Make today count!

Day 13

Genesis 3 outlines the fall of Adam and Eve. When the story picks up, we see that Adam and Eve are standing underneath the tree of knowledge of good and evil having a conversation with the serpent. The tree, of course, is the one that God told them not to eat from. They put themselves in close proximity to it allowing the temptation to be great. As I was listening to a sermon last Thursday about this story, something hit me. How does our physical proximity reflect our hearts?

In my own life, the things that have pulled me away from God are things I have maintained a close physical proximity to. What are the things in your life that draw your fleshly desires? If you think about it, you would more than likely see that those things are within your grasp.

The things you maintain proximity to will reflect your heart. My challenge for you today is to choose to make your proximity close to the heart of God. Make a plan to keep away from the tree that is drawing you away from him. Scripture tells us in James 4:8a, "Draw near to God and He will draw near to you."

Make today count!

Day 14

It seems that almost anytime I'm driving the kids somewhere they are excited about going, (a friend's house, the playground, etc.) they will question the direction that I am driving. It goes something like this...

"Dad, are you sure we are going the right way?" "Dad, I don't think this is right." "Dad, the last time we came I didn't see those cows." With this type of conversation, you could turn into a crazy person. I always reassure them I know where I'm going and remind them to have faith in me. Faith is defined as complete trust in someone or something.

There times when my faith in God is lacking. I am like the little voice that is behind me questioning each step of my journey. It doesn't matter how many times in the past that God has brought me to the correct destination, I am still questioning.

Hebrews 11:1 says, "Now faith is confidence in what we hope for and assurance about what we do not see." I love those two words about things we don't see, confidence and assurance.

This is the way I want to strive to live the rest of my journey. I want to have confidence in the things God has put in my heart and assurance that He will see them through. My challenge for you today is to join me in this journey of living out a Hebrews 11:1 definition of faith.

Make today count!

Day 15

Typically at the end of the day Holly will reach over and grab my phone. She will open Instagram and scroll through my "Insta stories." I have an iPhone and so does Holly. I have Instagram and so does Holly. The interesting thing is the version of Instagram on my phone is currently up-to-date while the version on her phone is quite old. In fact, the version she has on her phone does not contain "Insta stories." This is the reason she wants to look through my phone each day. Her phone is filled up with so many pictures and text messages that the storage space is unavailable for her to download the most current version. The easy solution for this would be for her to offload all her pictures onto our computer, creating the space she needs for the download. She has the same access and capability within her phone that I have, however, she is not taking advantage of it.

We all have access to a personal and intimate relationship with the God of the universe. Some of us choose to accept and enjoy this relationship while others are either unaware of their ability to enter into this relationship or, for whatever reason, they choose not to. Ephesians 2:17-18 says, "He came and preached peace to you who were far away and peace to those who were near. For through him we both have access to the Father by one Spirit." We have access to God through Jesus Christ.

My challenge for you today is to understand the access that is offered to you. If you have already accepted it, share it with someone else!

Make today count!

Day 16

Last night I thought I had finally gotten Abi Kate to sleep. This is a constant battle every single night. The minimum number of trips back into her room averages around five. At around 10 o'clock, she came bursting out of her room sobbing saying that she had broken Candy Land. Upon further investigation, I saw that she had torn the game board completely in half. She was so upset with what had happened that I didn't even punish her for being out of her bed. Her guilt was punishment enough. Had she been in her bed like she was supposed to be, this would not have happened. The temptation to get up and play with it was just too much for her to bear.

There have been many times in my own life when if I had been doing what I was supposed to be doing, it wouldn't have led to the trouble that followed. James 1:13-16 says, "When tempted, no one should say, "God is tempting me." For God cannot be tempted by evil, nor does he tempt anyone; but each person is tempted when they are dragged away by their own evil desire and enticed. Then, after desire has conceived, it gives birth to sin; and sin, when it is full-grown, gives birth to death." We are often overtaken by our own desires.

It's easy for us to try to place the blame for poor decision making on other people or circumstances when in reality, it always comes back to the decision we have made. I firmly believe that if we keep in step with the things God has called us to, we are less likely to fall into temptation. My challenge for you today is to live out Galatians 5:16: "But I say, walk by the Spirit, and you will not gratify the desires of the flesh."

Make today count!

Day 17

We have snow today! For a child, there are only three things that I can think of that are more exciting than a snow day. These would be Christmas morning, their birthday, and a trip to Disney World.

Holly and I were busy this morning getting breakfast made, cleaning up the kitchen, then gathering all of the snow day gear. No matter how quickly this process may go, for the kids, it feels like an absolute eternity. It's human nature to be absolutely terrible at the waiting process.

Jacob, in the Old Testament, is a great example of what it looks like to be patient during a difficult time of waiting. This story is found in Genesis 29. Jacob agreed to work for Laban for seven years to have Rachel, Laban's daughter, as his wife. After seven years of work, Laban tricked Jacob and gave him his other daughter, Leah, instead. The Bible says that Leah had "weak eyes." Simply put, this meant Leah fell out of the ugly tree and hit every branch on the way down. Jacob agreed to work another seven years to be able to marry Rachel. After another seven years, Jacob was given Rachel as his wife. His patience and hard work paid off.

My challenge for you today is to model the hard work and patience of Jacob. Even when times get hard and things aren't going the way you planned, continue to work as unto the Lord.

Make today count!

Day 18

What can a single person really accomplish? In 1942, Desmond Doss joined the army during World War II. Due to his strong religious convictions, he opted not to carry a weapon. Doss enlisted as an Army Medic. He was shipped out with the rest of the 77th division to Okinawa, Japan in 1944. Doss and the rest of the 77th found themselves facing a well-fortified enemy on the top of a 350-foot ridge. The only access to the top of this ridge was a cargo net. The U.S. advanced on the top of the ridge but were quickly overrun by the Japanese. It is said that the machine gun fire was so heavy, men were actually being shot in half. The U.S. troops were given the order to retreat. Their plan was to fire motors on the top of the ridge. Doss elected to stay up top by himself for the next 12 hours to try to save as many of the wounded U.S. men as he possibly could.

In 12 hours, being fired upon by his own side, Doss single-handedly saved 75 men, one man at a time. In 1945, Doss was awarded a Medal of Honor from President Truman. Doss was one man who was fully devoted to God and God used him for something pretty incredible.

D. L. Moody said, "The world has yet to see what God can do with a man fully surrendered to Him." Matthew 16-24:25 says, "Then Jesus said to His disciples, "If anyone wishes to come after Me, he must deny himself, and take up his cross and follow Me. For whoever wishes to save his life will lose it; but whoever loses his life for My sake will find it."

My challenge for you today is to be the man or woman fully surrendered to God so His purpose can be fulfilled in you.

Make today count!

Day 19

It has been an enjoyable three days at home playing in the snow with the kids. We have had lots of quality time together. Today, I am grateful to be back at work. I always enjoy having a few days off, but by day two or three, I begin to feel like I need to be doing something productive.

God has given us work as a blessing. If you read the account in Genesis, work is actually existent pre-sin. God gave Adam things to do prior to sin entering the world. When sin entered the world, work was cursed. (See Genesis 3:16-19)

With our work, we have an opportunity to bring praise and glory to God. Colossians 3:23-24 tells us, "Whatever you do, work at it with all your heart, as working for the Lord, not for human masters, since you know that you will receive an inheritance from the Lord as a reward. It is the Lord Christ you are serving."

It's a game changer to view your work through this lens. Each encounter you have with your work is an opportunity to work for the Lord. My challenge you today is to view your work through a Colossians 3:23 lens.

Made today count!

Day 20

As I mentioned before, Abi Kate loves to feed our dog Mo. She has many different things that bring her joy. One of them is talking with our Amazon Alexa. She loves to ask Alexa all sorts of questions to hear her response. She now well knows she is not allowed to feed the dog anything other than his dog food. This morning I heard her ask, "Alexa, can dogs eat Cheerios?" Followed by "Alexa, can dogs eat apples?" This went on for several minutes with many different types of food. Some non-food items also made the list. She kept going back to one question in particular, the one we had covered over and over. "Alexa, can dogs eat grapes?"

My theory is that she continued to ask this question hoping Alexa would give a different answer. She was looking for the "all clear" to throw Mo another grape.

I've done this with God in my life. I knew there were things that were completely harmful to me, but I tried my best to justify them to God hoping he would give me an all clear. No matter how many times Abi Kate asked Alexa if the dog can eat a grape, she will always respond, "Grapes, even in small amounts, are toxic to dogs." With the Holy Spirit, no matter how many times I try to justify that which I know is contrary to scripture, he will remind me they are sin before a holy God. They are toxic to me.

Hebrews 12:1 says, "Therefore, since we are surrounded by such a great cloud of witnesses, let us throw off everything that hinders and the sin that so easily entangles. And let us run with perseverance the race marked out for us." Sin is a weight and a poison that holds us down. My challenge for you today is to stop trying to justify things you know are contrary to God's will for your life and submit them back to him.

Make today count!

Day 21

If you have small kids or have been around small kids, I'm sure you have experienced them wanting to tell you a "secret." Kids love to tell secrets. I don't know that it's the information they love as much as the fact that it requires you to get very close to the person you are confiding in. Most of the time they will pass this information through a whisper. Whispering is the most intimate form of communication. It requires close proximity between the two parties and requires the receiving party to lean in.

As you read through scripture, you can see multiple instances when God spoke. Most often, his voice was heard in a silent spot through the means of a whisper as with Moses through the burning bush, Abraham in the wilderness, and Samuel in the middle of the night, to name a few. It's interesting that of all the forms of communication God could use that he chooses the most intimate, the most personal, and the one that causes us to lean in. 1 Kings 19:11-12: "The Lord said, 'Go out and stand on the mountain in the presence of the Lord, for the Lord is about to pass by.' Then a great and powerful wind tore the mountains apart and shattered the rocks before the Lord, but the Lord was not in the wind. After the wind there was an earthquake, but the Lord was not in the earthquake. After the earthquake came a fire, but the Lord was not in the fire. And after the fire came a gentle whisper."

My challenge for you today is to identify your quiet place. This can be hard amid all of the noise that surrounds our lives. Find a place where you can be truly quiet before the Lord and wait to discern his whisper. I can guarantee that what he tells you will be worth leaning in for.

Make today count!

Day 22

This year I signed up to be the coach of Cade's five and six-year-old youth basketball team. Yesterday the Rockets took on the Hawks. In case you missed it on ESPN, the Hawks came out with a 14-8 victory. The Rockets played tough, but we just couldn't pull it out. The funny thing about coaching this age group is they have a constant need to hear my direction before they're willing to do anything. Any time one of the kids would touch the ball, the first thing they would do is look at me and wait for me to yell something to them. They would shoot the ball, then get a rebound, and I would have to scream, "Shoot again!" before they would act. This translates into some pretty poor basketball, but is an excellent model for our spiritual lives.

1 Chronicles 16:11 tells us, "Seek the LORD and His strength; Seek His face continually." What would it look like if part of our daily routine was to pause and look at our "coach?" How would it impact us if we were to seek God in prayer before we made any moves that matter? His ways are higher than ours and he is the giver of all wisdom, so it makes sense to me that we would wait for his "go."

My challenge for you today is to look at the "Coach." Allow God to order your plans and steps, and wait for his plan to unravel.

Make today count!

Day 23

Yesterday afternoon we decided to take a family walk around the neighborhood. Abi Kate loves to be the one who is in charge of walking Mo, the family dog. Cade decided to forgo his bicycle and chose to dribble his basketball for practice during the walk. The walk started off great. However, within a few minutes, Abi Kate had little to no control over the dog. Somehow Cade managed to dribble the ball directly into his face causing him to cry hysterically. Long story short, we made it halfway down our street before we decided it was probably best to just turn around.

I absolutely love how practical the book of Proverbs is. There are so many wonderful pieces of wisdom within this book. In Proverbs 13:20 the author talks about walking. No, he's not talking about family walks. He's talking about who we surround ourselves with. The verse says, "Whoever walks with the wise becomes wise, but the companion of fools will suffer harm."

Although it seems counterintuitive, it is a great reminder to walk with those who are wise. If you want to gain wisdom, spend time with people who have more wisdom than you do. My challenge for you today is to think about the people you are surrounding yourself with. If you are the wisest person in the circle, it might be time to join a new one. Make your walk a good one.

Make today count!

Day 24

Several years ago when I was a director at the downtown YMCA in Nashville, I had the privilege of meeting a man, let's call him Ron. One of my responsibilities was to sit in on interviews for part-time staff with different directors in various departments. On this particular day, I was sitting in an interview with our membership director. Ron came in well dressed, a man in his mid to late 50's, and highly overqualified for a part-time job as a membership associate at the Y. Ron had just retired from Lifeway in Nashville where he held a high-level position. This man was/is absolutely brilliant. He was not at the Y to make money for himself, but to serve people.

I have never in my life met someone who took active service and humility to the level this man did. He was kind and compassionate and was a friend to anyone who walked in the door. The paycheck he received was spent on those in need and the philanthropies the Y was involved with. This man challenged me to be a better leader every single day. If you've ever heard of the principle, "leading up," he should write a book on it.

As I was reading this morning, this passage came up. I immediately thought of Ron. Philippians 2:3-4, "Do nothing from rivalry or conceit, but in humility count others more significant than yourselves. Let each of you look not only to his own interests, but also to the interests of others." Ron is the type of person who can confidently say, "Follow me as I follow Christ."

This is the type of life and legacy I want to leave. My challenge for you today is to live out Philippians 2:3-4 and serve those around you humbly.

Make today count!

Day 25

Newton's third law of physics tells us that for every force, there is an equal and opposite force. This statement means that there are a pair of forces acting on the two interacting objects. The force put on one is equal on the other, but in the opposite direction. Flashback to physical science anyone?

Ephesians 6:12 says, "For our struggle is not against flesh and blood, but against the rulers, against the authorities, against the powers of this dark world and against the spiritual forces of evil in the heavenly realms." This scripture tells me that the same forces in the physical realm are true in the spiritual realm. If we are to pursue the things of God, then we are pushing the opposing forces away. In the same way, the opposite would be true. We need to remain steadfast and diligent about the force and energy we are putting into our spiritual growth and development.

What impact are spiritual forces having on you? Are they drawing you closer to Christ or pushing you away? My challenge for you today is to prioritize your steps to those that will move you closer to Christ.

Make today count!

Day 26

Do you hate waiting? I read a story last week about a man in Laredo, Texas, who waited for 17 days outside Best Buy for the Black Friday sales. He never mentioned exactly what he was waiting for. He did, however, mention that the highlight of his waiting experience was watching people coming into the store, watching movies on his portable DVD player, and seeing friends who brought him food during his waiting time. As I'm sure you're shocked to hear, he was the first person in line on that Black Friday morning.

In Genesis chapter 8 we see that Noah waited 105 days for the rain to stop. One hundred and five days is an incredibly long time. I pulled out a calendar and have determined that to be approximately from September 11 until Christmas Day. What we see from Noah is that he was active during his waiting process. He released different birds to see if they could find dry land.

We can become frustrated in our process of waiting on God, but what we learn from Noah is that we can actively participate in this process. Lamentations 3:25-26 says, "The LORD is good to those whose hope is in him, to the one who seeks him; it is good to wait quietly for the salvation of the LORD." We can actively participate in our waiting process through studying the word, through prayer, fasting, and through conversations with trusted community.

My challenge for you today is to work as if everything depends on you, pray as if everything depends on God, and then wait until you hear "GO" on your next move.

Make today count!

Day 27

We have so many different people/voices speaking to us throughout our day. The influence of these people and voices carry a great significance. However, the voice that impacts you the most is also the one you hear the most—yours. The truth and the lies you tell yourself permeate your heart.

Paul David Tripp in his book, "Dangerous Calling," suggests that there's not a more important person you can preach the gospel to than yourself. We should remind ourselves every day that the God of heaven is deeply in love with us and that he came and sent his Son to take our place on the cross so we could have a right standing with him.

Proverbs 4:23: "Above all else, guard your heart, for everything you do flows from it." This is a wonderful reminder about the importance of speaking truth to ourselves and allowing those truths to enter into your heart and mind. There is no greater truth we could preach to ourselves than the Gospel.

My challenge for you today is that when you find yourself questioning a tough situation or questioning your value, preach the gospel to yourself and allow its truths to radically alter the way you live your life.

Make today count!

Day 28

Words are powerful tools. They are especially powerful over those who look up to us. I don't know about your kids, but my kids have a tenancy to speak to each other in a very unkind way from time to time. They can use words that are destructive. These are not words that give life and encouragement. It's also very important for me to remember when I am correcting them that I do it in a manner that gives life. This can be hard to do when big brother makes little sister cry because he said something so mean to her.

What a gift it would be if we could all thoroughly live out Hebrews 10:24: "And let us consider how we may spur one another on toward love and good deeds." The word "spur" is defined as something that prompts or encourages.

My challenge for you today is to be a spur. Be the one who pushes and encourages others towards love and acts of service. Can you imagine the impact we could have if we lived out the remainder of our days with this verse as the foundation for which we treat one another? What a world it would be!

Make today count!

Day 29

My beautiful wife Holly has had more surgeries than any person I know. If there's a body part a person can live without, she has most likely had it removed. Here's the short list off the top of my head: appendix, gallbladder, tonsils, adenoids, and I'm sure I'm missing something else. The last time she had surgery to remove her gallbladder, I joked with David, the surgeon, (we are on a first-name basis). I asked him if we could get a two-for-one deal. I said, "If there's anything else in there that we could go ahead and take out while you're in there, that would be great." Needless to say, he thought my joke was hilarious, as did I. Holly, however, not so much.

It's amazing the body parts we can live without. But with these parts missing, it creates more strain on the other parts of the body.

In 1 Corinthians 12:14, Paul compares our physical bodies to the body of Christ, the church. The point he makes is that each one of us brings a different skill set into the church. We have gifts and talents that others do not. Together we make one complete body. If a part is missing, it will create more work on the other parts.

If you are a follower of Christ and are not plugged into a church body, my challenge for you today is to find one where your specific gifts can be used. There is a church who is looking for their missing part and that missing part may be you. For those of you who are already connected to a corporate body, do not withhold your gifts and talents. God has given them to you to bring glory to himself.

Make today count!

Day 30

My kids are constantly coming home with a new masterpiece they created at school. They are always very excited about the work they have put into these miniature Picassos. Typically, the first thing that happens when they come home with a new masterpiece is they want to display it on the refrigerator. (Side note: why is every piece that comes home from Sunday school either covered in wet glue or paint that is not dry?) Anyway, they are so proud of these masterpieces and they cannot wait to put them on display.

God is a lot like that with us. Ephesians 2:10: "For we are God's handiwork, created in Christ Jesus to do good works, which God prepared in advance for us to do." You are God's handiwork. He put time, energy, and effort into making every facet of your being. When you have days when you feel that you are not enough, may you be reminded that the God in heaven made you perfectly.

Psalms 139:13-14 says, "For you created my inmost being; you knit me together in my mother's womb. I praise you because I am fearfully and wonderfully made; your works are wonderful, I know that full well."

My challenge for you today is to remind yourself that you are God's Picasso. He is so pleased when he sees you. Find your value in who he says you are today!

Make today count!

Day 31

Each morning after I wake up, I spend some time in God's word. After that, I spend the next 30 minutes or so helping to get the kids ready for school and getting them out the door. I then go back into my room and after I spend some time in prayer and feel like God has given me something to write, I write my daily devotion. This typically takes me 10 to 20 minutes, depending on the topic. The final and most crucial step to this process is that I will either send it to my mom or to Holly to be edited.

Here is what you probably do not know about me. I have dyslexia, so for me to actually sit down and write a devotional thought each day would be incredibly difficult. My process of writing my devotional is to verbally speak the thoughts into my phone. I do my best job of editing them and then I send them off. Without this last step, this exercise would be in vain.

Ecclesiastes 4:9-10 says, "Two are better than one, because they have a good return for their labor: If either of them falls down, one can help the other up. But pity anyone who falls and has no one to help them up." It's so important that each of us have an "editor" in our life, someone who is willing to walk alongside us and help us to be the best version of ourselves.

Who is your editor? My challenge for you today is to find someone to step into that role if you do not already have someone. Allow yourself to be open to stepping into that role for someone else, should that opportunity present itself. Two are better than one.

Make today count!

Day 32

Just a few nights ago Cade went to a birthday party. He was able to win a few small trinkets from the arcade. One of these items was a very small plastic green army man, similar to the one that comes in buckets of 1000. It seems that every three days or so Abi Kate changes her new "toy affection." For whatever reason, her affection has turned towards the small green army man. The first night she cried her eyes out until her brother finally allowed her to sleep with the toy. He told her she could only have it for one night. Last night we went through the same routine of Abi Kate crying for the "small green army man." Cade was bound and determined that he was not going to let her have this army man again for another day. I took Cade aside and asked him if this is the way he would like for people to treat him. He begrudgingly said he would share it with her. I told him it doesn't mean the same if he doesn't want to share with a cheerful heart. He ended up allowing his little sister one more day with the small green army man which she fell asleep with in her hand last night.

When someone shares something with us and it feels as if they're doing so because they feel obligated, it just does not have the same meaning. However, if someone is willing to share and give out of their generosity and from the overflow of the heart, the impact is phenomenal. It's apparent to me that God has the same mindset when it comes to giving. 2 Corinthians 9:6-7 says, "The point is this: whoever sows sparingly will also reap sparingly, and whoever sows bountifully will also reap bountifully. Each one must give as he has decided in his heart, not reluctantly or under compulsion, for God loves a cheerful giver."

When we give to God, he wants us to give from the overflow of our heart where this is a joyful, cheerful, act of giving on our part. God does not need our gifts. He is the owner of all. He allows us the opportunity to trust him. My challenge for you today is to be cheerful in the gifts you give, knowing God has blessed you with everything you have.

Make today count!

Day 33

Adam and Eve had a perfect relationship in the perfect place with God. They chose the same thing we would have chosen, desiring to try to be like God knowing good from evil. This meant they ate from the tree God had instructed them not to eat from. This choice is the first sin that separated us from God.

God came down in human form through Jesus and lived a perfect life. He then took on all of the sin of the world dying a death he did not deserve on the cross for us. Three days later he defeated the grave rising from the dead. All of this to rectify the relationship between us and God.

Romans 6:23 "For the wages sin is death, but the gift of God is eternal life through Christ Jesus." Let's look at a simple breakdown of this verse.

Wages = Something we have earned (pay check)

Sin = Missing the mark (The standard is perfection which is unattainable)

Death = Eternal separation from God

but = Hold on, something is about to change

Gift = Something given to you that you don't deserve because someone loves you. You didn't earn it.

God = The giver of the gift

Eternal life = Eternity with God (heaven)

Through = The path, how you get there

Jesus = God's one and only son, willingly given as a sacrifice to bridge the gap between us and God.

If we were to put that together, it would read something like this: We have earned eternal separation for missing the mark, but hold on a second, God has offered us a free gift and the gift is heaven and you can receive it because of what Jesus did for you on the cross. Like any gift, you must open it and receive it. Scripture tells us to believe and receive. First, we admit to God that we have sinned. Second, believe in your heart that he is the son of God and that he died and rose again. Third, we must confess that Jesus is our Lord.

Romans 10:9: "If you confess with your mouth the Lord Jesus and believe in your heart that God has raised Him from the dead, you will be saved."

Maybe today you are hearing this for the first time. Maybe you've heard it but you needed to be reminded of the great love God has for you. And maybe today you heard it so you can remind someone else.

Make today count!

Day 34

Today I find myself writing with a great deal of sadness. Difficult situations are guaranteed in this broken and fallen world. It is rare for me to be at a loss for words. Today there are multiple people I know who are feeling completely broken. Everything within me wants to say something that would be comforting and would help to bring peace, but I cannot find the words. Maybe you have found yourself in a similar situation.

In the Old Testament Job suffered tremendous loss. We see in chapter two that two of his friends came to grieve with him. It's not what they said that made the difference, it's what they did not say. Scripture says they sat with him for seven days in silence. I really think this is the model as to how to care for people who are hurting so deeply. Sometimes we can try to share words of encouragement, and without knowing it, we can cause a deeper hurt. Sometimes it's best just to sit and be sad.

Psalm 34:18: "The Lord is close to the brokenhearted and saves those who are crushed in spirit." If you find yourself at a loss for words to comfort someone today, simply love them through your presence and God's love.

Make today count!

Day 35

Last night, Holly and I had a much-needed opportunity to have a date night. She told me she wanted to see a movie and she gave me the option between *The Greatest Showman* and some other movie about war. Obviously, my first inclination was the war movie, but I could tell the way that she offered me the choices that she was really leaning towards *The Greatest Showman*. I agreed with her that that's what we should go see while all along not 100% sure how it would be, seeing as how it is a musical. I was more interested in spending quality time with my wife and did not deem it necessary to get into the semantics of which movie I would prefer to watch.

I have heard quite a few people say that *The Greatest Showman* was an excellent movie, but was still unsure since I had not experienced it for myself. I have to say that I was blown away. It was an excellent movie. From the storyline to the music, it holds your attention from beginning to end. (Side note: If you have not seen this movie, you should.)

I would have continued to have questions whether this movie was any good or not until I actually experienced it on my own. I believe the same thing is true of God. There are people who are skeptics, those who are unsure if there is a God or not. The problem occurs for these folks because they have not experienced God for themselves.

Philippians 2:3-4 says, "Do nothing out of selfish ambition or vain conceit. Rather, in humility value others above yourselves, not looking to your own interests but each of you to the interests of the others." Every day we have an opportunity to be the hands and feet of Christ. Through our words and actions, we can help people to have an experience with God. When you know that the Holy Spirit is prompting you to do something or to say something to someone, those leadings could be the interaction this person has been waiting for.

My challenge for you today is to pay attention to the promptings of God's Spirit. These promptings and your interaction with them could be the catalyst that leads this person to experience God for the first time in a very real way.

Make today count!

Day 36

The small green army man I mentioned a few days ago now has a new permanent place in Abi Kate's room. Cade has decided it's best just to give this small trinket to her. This little army man is smaller than what you were probably thinking. In your mind, you're probably thinking about one like the one in the movie *Toy Story*. This one is half the size of a traditional toy army man. Its small size lends itself to being misplaced frequently. At some point during the past three days, Abi Kate has misplaced it for extended periods of time. She passionately looks for this toy until it is found.

Abi Kate's persistence in looking for this small trinket reminds me that there's nothing that will stop God from pursuing you. There's a song that has recently come out that talks about the reckless love of God. This is not reckless in the sense of being out of control. This is talking about reckless in a sense that there's nothing that can stop God's love. When you really think about what Christ did for us, it was in reckless pursuit of us. John 3:16 says, "For God so loved the word that he gave his one and only Son that whoever believes in him will not perish but have eternal life." God is in heaven where everything is perfect and he decided the best thing he could do was to come and live as a man. Then he died a death he did not deserve so we could have a right standing with God. I love the line in the song that says God leaves the 99 to find the one. This is a reference to how the shepherd would have left 99 sheep to look for one that was lost.

My challenge for you today is to know this truth without a shadow of a doubt. The God of heaven has a "never-stopping, never-ending, always and forever love for you" (as the *Jesus Storybook Bible* says it) and he would move heaven and earth to be in relationship with you.

Make today count!

Day 37

In the heart of every human being is a desire to be wanted and to be loved. This is so foundational and fundamental to our human nature that oftentimes people will seek to accomplish this through unhealthy methods. It begins as simply as when we are children willing to succumb to peer pressure simply for the approval of our friends. For most of us, this continues to play out through adulthood. We feel we must do something to gain another person's affection and affirmation.

There's a simple but profound truth found in John 3:16: "For God so loved the world that he gave his one and only Son, that whoever believes in him shall not perish but have eternal life." You can substitute "world" with your name. "For God so loved (you)." You can't earn it, and you don't deserve it. He loves you for exactly who you are. He takes great joy in you as you are his creation. When we can understand this truth of the love God has for us, it affects everything else.

Be reminded today that you are loved, you are wanted, and you are cherished.

Make today count!

Day 38

Cade is beyond excited today for a birthday party he will be attending this afternoon. This is no ordinary birthday party. This birthday party will put fathers against sons in an epic Nerf gun battle. Cade and I have been "talking trash" to each other for the past few days. I told Cade he had better be guarding himself because I was going to be coming after him. He said I needed to guard myself because he had some great plans drawn up. It will be fun to see how the battle ends.

Spiritually speaking, it is of great importance that we guard ourselves. Proverbs 4:23 says, "Above all else, guard your heart, for everything you do flows from it." From our heart, our mouth speaks. The things we allow to transcend into our heart come through in our words and actions. There's nothing more important than guarding our heart.

My challenge for you today is to be aware of the things you are allowing to penetrate your heart--and find an opportunity today to speak truth to penetrate someone else's heart.

Make today count!

Day 39

Yesterday Cade and I had an awesome time at a father-son Nerf gun party. At first, we battled the dads against the sons but quickly realized we needed to make the teams a bit fairer. There were several different Nerf guns to choose from--some small and some big. I noticed some of the guns were the actual Nerf brand while others were some type of knock off. The knock offs looked very similar, and some even had some fancier features than the actual Nerf guns. But when it came time for the battle, these knock off Nerf guns did not perform anywhere near the level of their counterpart.

In life there is real and there is counterfeit in the teaching of God's Word. We are warned in several places throughout Scripture to examine carefully the teaching we hear. If you find yourself questioning something you're hearing, it is best to go directly to the source of God's Word for clarity. 2 Timothy 4:3-4 says, "For the time will come when people will not put up with sound doctrine. Instead, to suit their own desires, they will gather around them a great number of teachers to say what their itching ears want to hear. They will turn their ears away from the truth and turn aside to myths." I believe it's pretty clear that we have reached this day and time.

People do not want to hear truth. They want to hear whatever justifies the decisions they are making. We must be careful not to fall prey to a false or easy Gospel. My challenge for you today is to practice discernment from the sources you are gathering, studying, and learning. Go directly to the Word of God as the standard where everything should be measured.

Make today count!

Day 40

Those of you who know anything about rip currents know how dangerous they can be. A rip current is a narrow channel of swift-moving water. Typically, a rip current moves from the shoreline of the beach out towards sea. They are very dangerous because swimmers can enter into them without realizing it and they begin to panic. They then begin to swim harder and harder, and eventually fatigue can set in which can lead to drowning. If you ever find yourself in a rip current, instead of swimming against it, the best thing you can do is to surrender to it. If you will let the current take you where it wants to, eventually you will come to the place where it stops and you'll be able to go to the right or to the left of it then you can make your way back to the beach with the ocean pushing waves on your back. In this instance, surrender saves.

The kingdom of God is known as an upside-down kingdom meaning the thoughts and ideas of the world are usually viewed differently. One example of this is where Jesus says if someone asks you for your cloak, you should also give them your tunic (Luke 6:30). This is contrary to the way most people would view such a request.

In Matthew 16:25, Jesus says, "For whoever wants to save their life will lose it, but whoever loses their life for me will find it." It is our surrender that will save.

Maybe today you find yourself swimming against life's current. Frustrated and fighting, you just can't seem to make it to the beach. Maybe it's time to surrender to the current. What you'll find is that surrender will lead you to a place where the waves are at your back and the beach is within reach.

Make today count!

Day 41

Today I write to you from Kentucky where I have just attended the funeral for my uncle. My uncle was an amazing man. He was full of wisdom, grace, and mercy. He will be greatly missed. Over the past few days as I have been in the funeral home, I have really done some deep reflecting. The one certainty this life holds for each one of us is death. At some point, our time will come when we will breathe our last breath.

Proverbs 27:1 says, "Do not boast about tomorrow, for you do not know what a day may bring." This passage has rung true to me over these past two days. The opportunity to set life and its busyness aside for a short period of time to gather with close friends and family has been a real joy. I believe it has been over six years since my extended family has been together. Being with them has reminded me of the importance of spending time with those you love most.

I don't believe that at the end of our lives we would ever regret turning down an opportunity to work over spending time with our family. My challenge for myself and for you today is to prioritize the things that matter the most to you right now. To my family reading this, look out for a Facebook invite. We are having a reunion this summer!

Make today count!

Day 42

This morning was another thrilling morning of five and six-year-old boys basketball. Prior to the game, I spent 15 minutes or so working with the boys on dribbling the ball down the court, making one pass, and then shooting. We had a few of the dads come out on the floor and play "defense" to give the best game type feel we could for them. We did everything we could to set them up for success prior to the actual game. Once the game began and the real pressure came, all of our preparation went out the window.

In life I have made plans to be prepared for opposition, however, sometimes these plans go right out the window when adversity strikes. Something within me defaults to crisis mode when my plans don't come together perfectly. This is when I think it is of the greatest importance that we rely on God. Psalms 46:1 says, "God is our refuge and strength, an ever-present help in time of trouble."

My challenge for us today is when times of trouble come, cry out to God and be reminded that he is our constant source of help.

Make today count!

Day 43

Like many of you, I always look forward to The Winter Olympic Games. Last night, I was watching the Men's Freestyle Snow Boarding.

This event is compiled of five sections down the mountain. The course had two sections of rails for the competitors to slide over. The last three sections were made up of enormous single jumps. These jumps were big enough that the athletes could do three or four full rotations before landing. Each snowboarder got to take three trips down the mountain and only their best score counted.

The snowboarder representing the USA found himself in 11th place going into his final run. Not letting his standing distract him, he made his final pass. He made a nearly perfect run scoring 87 points and winning the gold medal for team USA!

What an amazing lesson for us in our lives. James 1:2 tells us, "Blessed is a man who perseveres under trial; for once he has been approved, he will receive the crown of life which the Lord has promised to those who love Him." We cannot allow our failures to define us. We must push through and persevere when trials come.

Though you may have failed in something many times, don't stop. Keep pushing and keep relying on God during your time trial. Your opportunity for gold is only one run away!

Make today count!

Day 44

Happy Valentine's Day to you! My wife Holly is incredible at making any and every holiday celebration incredibly special for the kids and me. This morning we woke up to find an array of small treats with each of our names on them, and to top it off, each of the kids got a balloon. #ParentWin. Cade was incredibly excited because Holly had the foresight to buy each of us our own new Nerf gun so we could battle each other. For a six-year-old boy, it just doesn't get much better than to have the opportunity to battle Nerf guns with your dad. Today each of us felt loved through Holly's actions and gifts.

1 Corinthians 13:4-7 gives us a blueprint for understanding what love is. "Love is patient, love is kind. It does not envy, it does not boast, it is not proud. It does not dishonor others, it is not self-seeking, it is not easily angered, it keeps no record of wrongs. Love does not delight in evil but rejoices with the truth. It always protects, always trusts, always hopes, always perseveres." These attributes are much easier to read than to live. You see, love can be shown, needed, and affirmed. Ultimately, to give or to receive love, you must make the conscious choice to love. Love is a choice, not a feeling.

God has chosen to love us through Jesus. He does not force us to love him. We must choose to. My challenge for you today is to love God and others because you choose to, and let your actions and service to them flow from that love.

Make today count!

Day 45

When I worked in the aquatic industry, I had the opportunity to travel and teach aquatic safety classes. Our main goal in teaching these life-saving skills was to mitigate what we called the "danger zone." The danger zone can be explained as the time between when an incident occurred and when the EMS arrived on the scene to transport the injured person. We trained our staff to mitigate as best they could this window of time. At each facility we would have an understanding of how long it would take the EMS to arrive once 911 had been called. Most of the time it was somewhere around six minutes. These six minutes were crucial to making sure the guest was getting the best care possible until transport arrived.

Spiritually speaking, I believe we have a danger zone. I think the danger zone occurs any time we have partial knowledge about a situation but are waiting to understand the other part. For example, maybe some medical tests have been run and the first part that comes back shows something is going on, but we are waiting for further results. During this spiritual danger zone, it's easy to find ourselves filling in "truth." We make up stories that support the narrative in our head.

Today maybe you find yourself in a danger zone of sorts. My challenge for you is to meditate on the words of Romans 8:28: "And we know that in all things God works for the good of those who love him, who have been called according to his purpose." Today as you wait in your danger zone, focus on the truth of the situation and don't allow your mind to take you down the anecdotal path of what could be. Think about things that are true, lovely, and admirable (Philippians 4:8). Invite God to be part of your danger zone today.

Make today count!

Day 46

This morning I was taking Abi Kate to drop her off to play at a new friend's house. I have been to their house once before. Generally speaking, I had a pretty good idea where it was located. Just to be safe, I put the address into my GPS prior to leaving the house. As the GPS offered me my first turn, I thought, "There's no way that's right." I decided to go the direction I had planned on going knowing the general area where the house was located. Long story short, trusting my instincts failed me. I ended up turning the GPS back on which led me to my destination in a matter of moments.

I don't know about you, but there are definitely times when I find myself doing this in life. I believe I know what is best for me, and I start to try to walk it out trusting in my instinct. But then I hear God's word telling me I missed a turn. Just like I know I should trust what the GPS is telling me, I should trust completely in what God says. 2 Samuel 7:28 says, "Sovereign LORD, you are God! Your covenant is trustworthy, and you have promised these good things to your servant." We can rely on the accuracy of God's word.

Maybe today you find yourself tuning out what you know God is saying to you. What is it right now in your life you know God is calling you to--perhaps a different direction from the way you are currently walking? My challenge for you today is to evaluate whose directions you are putting more stock in.

Make today count!

Day 47

Those of you who have trained for a marathon, built a house, or restored a vehicle understand how long and arduous these tasks can be. I'm sure we all know someone who has started one of these three processes and been unable to see it to completion. Many times in life when things get difficult, the easiest option is to simply give up.

I know there are some of you reading this today who may find yourself amid some very difficult situations. It may be financial, a difficult situation with a family member, or a pending medical diagnosis. We find ourselves feeling hopeless, and the desire to give up begins to creep in. If you find yourself in this place today, I want to remind you of this scripture in Philippians 1:6: "Being confident of this, that he who began a good work in you will carry it on to completion until the day of Christ Jesus."

This passage doesn't say he MIGHT complete the work. NO--it says he WILL complete the work. During the days training to run a marathon, there are going to be days of absolute exhaustion and pain, but enduring through the process will enable you to complete the goal you have set for yourself. In the same way, these difficult life circumstances are shaping your story that God wants to use for his glory. Remind yourself today that he will complete the work he has begun in you.

Make today count!

Day 48

My kiddos, like typical brothers and sisters, get into their fair share of disagreements and fights. Once we have figured out the perpetrator of said event and that person has "served time," we ask them to apologize and ask for forgiveness from the other party when they can really mean it. We have noticed a common theme in that the person who has been wronged is overly eager for the other person to ask for their forgiveness. Typically, when Cade is the one who has been wronged, he will ask Abi Kate, "What do you need to say to me?" However, he is much slower to add any commentary when he is on the other end of the encounter.

There is something so significant about forgiving someone, regardless of whether they are aware that they have hurt you in the first place or not.

Nick Person said, "Forgiveness is the key to unlocking our freedom." I believe the more we hold unforgiveness against another person, the more we enslave ourselves. Marianne Williamson said, "Unforgiveness is like drinking poison yourself and waiting for the other person to die." Talk about a powerful visualization of the harmful effects of unforgiveness. As Christ followers, forgiveness should be second nature to us. Christ has forgiven us of much, so we should forgive others of little.

Matthew 6:14-15 says, "For if you forgive others for their transgressions, your heavenly Father will also forgive you." My challenge for you today is to forgive those who have wronged you, regardless of the level of their offense. Or perhaps today you need to forgive yourself or maybe you need to accept the forgiveness Christ offers you.

Make today count!

Day 49

Last night we celebrated Cade's seventh birthday at Chuck E. Cheese with a few of his buddies. At the end of $50 worth of tokens, the boys made their way to the prize counter where they were able to select their new treasures. The boys played their hearts out on a variety of different games to win tickets. Each of them left the counter with a handful of prizes and big smiles on their faces. The combined value of the prizes they won would probably total about $3. I believe it's the process they go through to acquire these treasures that make them so special.

There are things in life that we pursue and work after whether they be things or achievements. We, like the boys, often look at our treasures and place them where we can see them. It's so easy to become focused on the things that we acquire that we lose track of the eternal things. Matthew 6:19 reminds us, "Do not store up for yourselves treasures on earth, where moth and rust destroy, and where thieves break in and steal." This verse is not saying it's wrong to have nice things or have accolades and achievement. This verse serves as a reminder that we should keep in mind the things that will matter in eternity. The reality is that no matter how nice the things are that you have acquired, they can be compared to the boys' Chuck E. Cheese items vs. what we will experience in eternity.

My challenge for you today is to think about the things you are treasuring. Do you have a shelf with accolades and achievements you are quick to show people? Are you finding value in possessions, or are you valuing the things that will matter in eternity?

Make today count!

Day 50

I do my absolute best to keep a very clean car which is incredibly difficult to do with two small kids. Weather permitting, I try to wash my car and clean the inside every Friday. I love to use Armor All on the plastic interior. It makes it look like new. My car has a black interior and those of you who have a black interior vehicle know that it does a pretty good job hiding dust and dirt.

This morning as I was getting into my vehicle, the sun was rising off to my left. It was at the perfect height where it was shining across the front part of my car's black interior. The perfect placement of the light revealed quite a bit of dust I had apparently missed while cleaning Friday.

That's the thing about light. Light exposes. Think about operating rooms in hospital. These rooms are incredibly bright. This allows for every detail to be seen as best as possible. On the other side of the spectrum, if you think about things where you typically hear of crimes being committed or allegations of other forms of misconduct, these are typically happening where the physical lighting is low or dark.

This might seem to be a coincidence, but I think Scripture speaks to it pretty clearly. John 3:19-20 says, "This is the verdict: Light has come into the world, but people loved darkness instead of light because their deeds were evil. Everyone who does evil hates the light, and will not come into the light for fear that their deeds will be exposed."

Do you ever find yourself intentionally going to the darkness? Do you ever find yourself in a place where you were trying to keep yourself from being exposed? As Christians, Christ has called us to live our lives in His light. What are the areas today where you need the lights to be turned on?

My challenge for you today is to find a trusted friend you can open up honestly to about the dark areas in your life that you are keeping hidden. Allow Christ to redeem them.

Make today count!

Day 51

Holly is a huge fan of Bath and Body Works. A few times a year when they're having a big sale, she stocks up on an assortment of hand soaps. Last night I was washing my hands when the aroma of a new soap hit my nose. It smelled incredible. The name of the soap was "frosted eucalyptus." I've never smelled frosted eucalyptus, but I would assume that they nailed it. It's amazing to me how they are able to create smells such as butterflies in a green grassy meadow. It hits your nose and you go, "Yep, that's what they smell like." All this to say this got me thinking about the incredible design that God has made within us with our five senses.

Think about incredible sunsets you have seen over the mountains or the beach. Think about the sounds of a beautiful symphony or the laughter of a child, the taste of your favorite food, and the feeling of your favorite person holding your hand. All of these are gifts that have been given to us by God, our amazing creator. Listen to the words of David in Psalm 8"

"Lord, our Lord, how majestic is your name in all the earth! You have set your glory in the heavens. Through the praise of children and infants you have established a stronghold against your enemies, to silence the foe and the avenger. When I consider your heavens, the work of your fingers, the moon and the stars, which you have set in place, what is mankind that you are mindful of them, human beings that you care for them? You have made them a little lower than the angels and crowned them with glory and honor. You made them rulers over the works of your hands; you put everything under their feet: all flocks and herds, and the animals of the wild, the birds in the sky, and the fish in the sea, all that swim the paths of the seas. Lord, our Lord, how majestic is your name in all the earth!"

It's difficult to read this and not be taken with the all of God. My challenge for you today is to be aware of your intricate design. Take some intentional time today to thank God for the gifts he has given you.

Make today count!

Day 52

Today my son Cade turned seven. He is full of energy, life, and questions. He's kind and compassionate, and he has a giving heart that cares deeply for the needs of others. When I think about Cade, I think about prayer. When Holly was pregnant with Cade, the doctors found some things that concerned them. We were required to do a weekly ultrasound because of the size of his brain ventricles. We continued to pray over our unborn son, and at week 36, the doctor cleared us saying, "I'm not really sure how it happened, but everything is normal. You will have a healthy son." Three years later we found ourselves at the pediatrician's office where they were running tests to determine if Cade was a type I diabetic. The first initial testing looked as if that was the case. They scheduled a follow up for the next day. We gave this over to God in prayer that night. In all honesty knowing that my brother is a type I diabetic, I thought this was an exercise in vain. Upon his second round of follow up tests, every blood level and urine test came back completely normal. Again today, Holly and I find ourselves in a waiting time praying for a health concern over our son. Cade keeps me praying.

Many times, we talk about prayer as if it is a last resort. Think about how many times you've heard someone say, "I guess all we can do is pray. "I have absolutely been guilty of saying this also. But the reality is, the BEST thing we can do, regardless of other options, is pray. The ability we have to beseech the throne of the God of heaven and make our request known to him should be our first, and is our best, option. What an incredible thing it is to know God hears us when we pray to him. Jeremiah 29:12 says, "Then you will call on me and come and pray to me, and I will listen to you."

Regardless of what it is you're praying about today, whether it be something seemingly insignificant or something that seems impossible, approach God boldly. My challenge for you today is not to consider prayer a last resort but your first and best option.

Make today count!

Day 53

A few nights ago, Cade and I had the opportunity to go to a Predators hockey game with some friends. Since the game was on a school night, it was a tight window to get home and ready to go to the game. As Cade and I made our way out of the house, Holly asked me where our dog was. I told her I wasn't sure but that he was somewhere in the house. Cade and I made our way out the door and about the time we reached interstate 840, Holly called. She was quite frantic saying she had looked everywhere for the dog in the house and could not find him. Cade and I made a U-turn and headed back towards the house. On my way back to the house, I texted a few neighbors and asked if they had seen him. They had not, but they were willing to jump in and help look for him. Something inside me told me the dog was still in the house and that he was hiding. See, our dog is nine years old, and he knows that when we leave, he goes into his cage, so he has become quite skilled at hiding in the house. When I pulled back into the neighborhood, I went directly to my house. I opened the garage door and then I opened the door into our entry from the garage. Standing right there wagging his tail and jumping up and down greeting me was our dog, Mo. I called Holly and the neighbors and let them know Mo had been found. In fact, *he had never been lost.* Our perception was not reality. (After all this, Cade and I still made it to the game on time.)

I believe it is common for Christians to struggle with assurance of salvation. Satan will plant seeds of deception to make one question if they really have a saving relationship with Christ. The question is, if God holds us with his righteous right hand and no one can move the hand of God, why would Satan plant these doubts in our minds?

I think of it this way: If you don't believe you are on a sports team, you definitely will not get involved in the game. If Satan can keep you on life's bench and you take no role in sharing the love of Christ, he has won by making you an ineffective believer. John 5:24 says, "Truly, truly, I say to you, he who hears My word, and believes Him who sent Me, has eternal life, and does not come into judgment, but has passed out of death into life."

My challenge for those of you who have believed in who Christ is and have received him, be confident in the gift he has given you. It's time to get off the bench and get into the game.

Make today count!

Day 54

As the weather begins to warm up, I start to think about my yard. As many of you know, I love to work in my yard. Working with my grass is somewhat of a hobby and stress releaser for me. About a week and a half ago I applied my first treatment for spring to my yard. This specific treatment is designed to prevent crabgrass in the summer. Crabgrass begins to germinate when the weather hits around 60°, so it is imperative to put this particular compound down prior to the weather staying around that temperature. This year I used a different brand that was not only a pre-emergent but also has some fertilization mixed in. I have already begun to see the effects of the fertilizer that was mixed in. My grass is beginning to become a healthy color once again. More importantly, when the summer heat comes and the crabgrass begins to thrive, I will not be working in my yard taking care of it.

Life is full of "crabgrass." Inevitably each one of us will experience our fair share of difficult experiences in this life. The question is not *will* we have to deal with crabgrass. The question is *when* will we deal with it? In the same way that a pre-emergent gets ahead of the crabgrass sprouting, so can our times of private worship and prayer prepare us for the crabgrass of life. There will still be situations that will pop up, but petitioning them to God prior to their arrival will drastically reduce their effect on you. 1 Peter 5:7 says, "Cast all your care upon him; for he cares for you." In all the things in your life that cause you care and concern, God wants to be before them, ahead of them, and through them.

My challenge for you today is to prepare the soil of your life through private prayer and worship. Know that you can give God anything and everything you are processing. What steps do you need to make to be in front of life's crabgrass?

Make today count!

Day 55

Tuesday morning is trash pick-up day in my neck of the woods. Typically, when I get home on Monday afternoon, I roll the full trash can down to the edge of the curb then when I get home on Tuesday afternoon, I roll the empty can back to its spot. It is really quite a luxury we have here in the United States that we are able to have someone come and remove our unwanted trash and junk on a weekly basis. Can you imagine the burden that our trash would be if it was not removed?

We all have burdens that we carry. They might be fear, anxiety, or shame. God never designed for us to just continue to hold on to them. Matthew 11:28-30 says, "Come to me, all you who are weary and burdened, and I will give you rest. Take my yoke upon you and learn from me, for I am gentle and humble in heart, and you will find rest for your souls. For my yoke is easy and my burden is light."

It's an amazing thing that we have the ability to give the things we don't want to carry to the God of the universe. My challenge for you today is to release the burdens that are weighing you down.

Make today count!

Day 56

Yesterday I took advantage of an absolutely gorgeous day and worked on getting my outdoor patio ready for spring. I spent some time power-washing the concrete, cleaned the patio furniture, and reconstructed our fire pit. Our fire pit is made of stone pavers and has a fireball dropped into the middle. The bulk of the time was spent taking the pavers apart and securing them with a concrete mixture to make sure they are secure. All said and done, I worked on the patio project for approximately four hours. I felt a great sense of satisfaction when I woke up this morning to let the dog out and saw that the patio looked new.

There's something about newness that draws us. We love the smell of a new car, the excitement of having a new puppy, and the way we feel in new clothes. Here's one of the things I love about God--he loves the new. Lamentations 3:21-23 says, "Yet this I call to mind and therefore I have hope: Because of the LORD's great love we are not consumed, for his compassions never fail. They are new every morning; great is your faithfulness." God has new mercies for you today. They are the best and they are ready for you.

Regardless of how your yesterday turned out, God is ready and willing to give you his new mercy and grace for today. And guess what? He'll be ready to give them to you new again tomorrow.

Make today count!

Day 57

During the sermon yesterday, our senior pastor told a very funny story. He told about a man who came up to him and began the conversation with, "I left your church. Do you want to know why?" The man proceeded to tell our pastor that he was overly frustrated with the congestion and traffic flow of our parking lot. Our pastor said that in a moment of extreme courage, or perhaps a lack of wisdom, he responded to the man by saying, "Maybe God sent you to our church to fix the problem."

I believe he is correct. The things you notice and the things that frustrate you the most more than likely tie into the skill set God has given you. In the book of Exodus, God calls the children of Israel to build their house of worship. It's interesting how specific the detail was on the types of wood, metal, and cloth that were to be used to complete the tabernacle. In Exodus 35:10, God says, "All who are skilled among you are to come and make everything the LORD has commanded." When his tabernacle was being built, he wanted the most skilled in each one of the skilled trades to be the person to complete that task. I believe the same is true of us today. The areas He has gifted us in are the tasks we are to take on.

What are the things you see that frustrate you? What are the things you say need to be changed? How do these things line up with the natural abilities God has given you? What steps can you take today to get involved in the process of making them better, more efficient, or stronger?

Make today count!

Day 58

Last Friday there was a simulcast leadership training hosted at several churches around the country. The name of this conference was "Work as worship." The purpose of the conference was to help people understand that regardless of what their vocational role, it is to be used as an act of worship to God.

There have been times in previous jobs when I found myself frustrated with the lack of desire and poor work ethics of others. One day it hit me--these people have not been called to the same work ethic that I and other believers have been called to. As followers of Christ, we should be the hardest working, most productive employees in our various fields. Colossians 3:23 says, "Whatever you do, work at it with all your heart, as working for the Lord, not for human masters." Our work is a form of our worship to God.

My challenge for you today is to view your work as a form of worship to God. If you find yourself getting frustrated with the poor work ethic of others, utilize these opportunities as a way to let your work be a witness to who you are working for.

Make today count.

Day 59

It has been a little while since I have given myself a haircut. This morning I needed to get it taken care of. Years ago, when I actually had hair, I would have never considered cutting my own hair. Now that I permanently have what I like to refer to as my "yarmulke," I find it a much more logical and practical solution to cut my own hair. I was finishing up and was checking out the back of my hair through a mirror reflecting off of another mirror. I could see I had missed one spot. I spent the next several seconds trying to figure out how to get to it because looking through these multiple mirrors was absolutely messing with my sense of direction. I took my focus off the mirror and then was able to put the clippers in the right spot to take care of the last bit.

In the Disney movie *Up*, there is a dog that has ADD. As the dog is talking and focused on one thing, all of a sudden, he loses his focus and yells "squirrel." We are this dog. In Luke 9:62, Jesus says, "No one who puts a hand to the plow and looks back is fit for service in the kingdom of God." This idea is that of having an alternate focus. Maybe we set out pursuing the things of Christ but then the things the world has to offer beg for our attention. It is so easy for us to allow our focus to shift. We are focused on the things that will matter for eternity, but then something that is temporary draws us in.

This concept is a difficult one for us to practically live out. However, when we correctly align our focus, I believe we will see the greatest kingdom impact. My challenge for you today is to lock in your focus, look to the future, and look to the things God wants to accomplish in and through you. Fix your eyes on the author and perfector of your faith (Hebrews 12:2).

Make today count!

Day 60

Last April, Brad Ewing, David Crook, and I took a fishing trip to Hilton Head Island. Brad and I had gone the year before and were able to catch two very nice sized redfish. The expectations were very high going into this trip that we were going to catch a ton of fish. Long story short, two fishing charters, one fishing store, and many hours of fishing later, we had two very small fish to show for the effort we had put forth. We were sitting in our kayaks in a national park that was absolutely beautiful when Brad began to express his frustration about the quality of fishing. Brad's complaints didn't go over well with David, and David began to complain about Brad complaining. The two of them paddled away from each other like an old married couple in a spat at McDonald's.

This is what I've come to realize: Unmet expectations will yield to frustration, and frustration leads to complaining. When we find ourselves complaining about a situation, we are either consciously or subconsciously comparing that situation to something else. In the experience I listed above, Brad was comparing it to the previous year's fishing trip. I find myself complaining most when my kids don't get along or are ungrateful. The comparison I am making is of the times when the kids do get along and things are smooth in the house. What we have to realize is that God is sovereign over our steps. He allows some things in our lives that are frustrations for us to draw us closer to him. As the children of Israel moved through the desert, there were snakes and scorpions. If God wanted to remove them, he could have, but we see that he chose not to.

2 Corinthians 4:17: "For our light and momentary troubles are achieving for us an eternal glory that far outweighs them all." My challenge for you today is to be aware that God is sovereign over our situations. Potentially the situation that's causing you frustration is one that God is allowing to draw you closer to him. When you feel the need to complain today, change your perspective and choose gratitude.

Make today count!

Day 61

I recently received an awesome new watch. The exterior face and hand displays both glow in the dark. I knew Cade would think this was super cool so I pulled him into his room where it was dark and shut the door to show him the watch. The only problem was that the watch been covered up all day so it did not glow. I grabbed a flashlight and put it on the face of the watch for a couple of minutes then turned the lights back off. He was impressed, to say the least.

This got me thinking about our lives. We can only give out what we have received. If we have received the light from God, then it is possible for us to shine for him. But if we have been standing in the darkness, we have not been exposed to the Light, therefore, we cannot be light to anyone else. Matthew 5:16 says, "In the same way, let your light shine before others, that they may see your good deeds and glorify your Father in heaven." We can use the light that God has given us to bring glory to him.

My challenge for you today is to remember you cannot give out what you have not received. Use your light today to bring glory to God!

Make today count!

Day 62

In his book, *Wild at Heart*, John Eldridge talked about what it really means to be a true man and what authentic manhood looks like. I doubt many men have an understanding of what authentic manhood really is. He says many men go through life covering themselves with a proverbial fig leaf like the ones Adam and Eve used to cover themselves after they had sinned. Some men's fig leaf may be their identity in work, for some it is the pursuit of wealth, for others playing the role of the strong guy, or maybe even the role as a lady's man. All of these are ways we as men try to keep people from seeing our true selves.

The majority of men have a fear of being exposed. Exposed as not good enough, not smart enough, or not capable enough so we default to these different fig leaves to hide behind and to create an identity. I love the way that *The Message* breaks down Luke 12:2: "You can't keep your true self hidden forever; before long you'll be exposed. You can't hide behind a religious mask forever; sooner or later the mask will slip and your true face will be known." The reality though is that freedom comes through letting our true selves be seen.

When we open ourselves up to being known for who we truly are, we open ourselves up for growth in areas where we need it--encouragement for the things we can't do on our own. My challenge for you today is to allow people to see you without your mask on. It's time to stop hiding and be the person you are in Christ. Allow him to be your identity.

Make today count!

Day 63

I spent my morning watching church league basketball. It's inevitable that the refs, although trying their absolute best, will miss calls from time to time. In one particular game I watched, a few calls were missed and the players on both teams were getting frustrated. One player in particular got so frustrated that he ended up sitting out the rest of the game. He allowed his frustration with the officiating to keep him out of the game.

In life, it's not a matter of if "calls" will be missed or not. It is inevitable that calls are going to go against you, be missed, and someone else may advance further than you. You do not get any say in how the game of life is officiated. The option you do get is how you respond to the things that happen. Do you allow your frustration to force you to stop going, stop putting in work, or stop pursuing your dreams? Galatians 6:9 says, "Let us not become weary in doing good, for at the proper time we will reap a harvest if we do not give up." This is your reminder not to give up!

My challenge for you today is no matter how circumstances play out, choose to play.

Make today count!

Day 64

Cade got a Nintendo DS for his birthday. He was also given a couple gift cards to Toys R Us which he used to purchase Super Mario Brothers. Last night as he was playing for a little bit, he began to get frustrated because he could not pass the level. On this specific level, the object was to collect as many coins as possible in a very short amount of time while making sure to get to the end of the level before the time expired. Holly asked Cade to let her try. I was watching her play and she kept losing the level. The reason she was losing the level was because she was getting so caught up with getting all of the coins, she never made it to the end prior to the time expiring. Although it was quite humorous to watch, Holly was getting frustrated with a Nintendo game.

I began to think about how this relates to our lives. In life it is so easy to get caught up with collecting as many "gold coins" as we can. Money and things are not necessarily bad. The problem comes when they have control over you. 1 Timothy 6:10 says, "For the love of money is a root of all kinds of evil. Some people, eager for money, have wandered from the faith and pierced themselves with many griefs." In the same way Holly was getting distracted chasing the gold, we can easily find ourselves in the same predicament.

My challenge for you today is to own your things, not vice versa. Keep your focus on the eternal and do not allow yourself to get distracted with the gold of the here and now. Use your money in a way that honors and glorifies God's kingdom, not your own.

Make today count!

Day 65

Many times after my kids get into a scuffle or disagreement, we bring them together to say they are sorry, that they love each other, and then we make them "hug it out." Holly typically will tell them that they must hug for anywhere between 10-30 seconds. It is quite a sight to take in because AK adores having the chance to hug Cade for this long, but Cade typically looks like someone in nice dress clothes receiving a hug from a very large, sweaty man. The hug is intended to be the loving actions of the words behind it.

Scripture commands us to love our enemies and pray for those who persecute us (Matthew 5:44). Love is more than a feeling. It is a series of choices that has "loving actions" which follow them. When we choose love, we must also follow it with actions that align. 1 John 3:18 reminds us, "Dear children, let us not love with words or speech but with actions and in truth." Our actions should always follow our words of love.

Who is it today that you need to follow your words of love with the actions of love to? My challenge for you today is to align your words with your actions.

Make today count!

Day 66

Yesterday I had the opportunity to be in a strategy session with one of the top church leaders in the country. Practically every other sentence out of this man's mouth was solid gold. I walked away with several pages of notes and excitement to better the ministries at the church where I serve. As we were processing last night, we realized just how many steps were needed to bring us to a place where we felt God was calling us. When looking at the big picture, this could feel incredibly overwhelming. Apparently, my mind was occupied with all these thoughts because I found myself dreaming about it last night. But in my dream, I was reminded of a quote that says, "Even a 1,000-mile journey begins with the first step. "

When we, as Dr. Stephen Covey suggests, begin with the end in mind, it is easy to feel overwhelmed with all of the steps in between. But when we break the steps down into individual bite-size chunks, each task seems much more manageable.

Philippians 3:14: "I press on toward the goal for the prize of the upward call of God in Christ Jesus." I love the verbiage used here--press. When you think about pressing on, you realize it doesn't necessarily move easily. Little by little with consistent pushing, things will move forward.

My challenge for you today is to continue to push on toward the goals God has called you to. Remember, if you only move an object a centimeter, you have made progress.

Make today count!

Day 67

Have you ever found yourself in a meeting with a "dominator?" By dominator, I mean a person who overshares their opinion and point of view. In a group setting where there is a defined leader, I do think there is shared value in "group think," however, when one person dominates, the group suffers.

Yesterday I was in a small training session made up of 12 people and a leader. When I began keeping a tally over a period of 5 hours, our dominator shared 83 times.

The entire time Proverbs 17:28 kept coming to mind: "Even fools are thought wise if they keep silent, and discerning if they hold their tongues." When we find ourselves with the opportunity to learn from those who are further along than us, I think it is wise to listen. God gave us two ears and one mouth for a reason.

Today my challenge for you is to gain wisdom from someone further along than you. Sit, listen, and learn.

Make today count.

Day 68

This morning as I was working to get the kids ready for the day, I opened our laundry room closet where our garbage can is located. When I tried to shut the door, it just would not catch like it should. Upon further investigation, I found that some of the screws that connect the door hinge to the inside of the doorframe had come loose. Since these screws were not snug like they should be, it was causing the door to sag, keeping it from shutting completely. It was simply a matter of getting a screwdriver and spending 30 seconds to align the door back to the frame to fix the problem.

There have been times in my life when I feel like things just aren't coming together, and as I search for the culprit, I often focus on my own energy and effort. All the while, I do not realize I have become disconnected to God. Potentially, I have neglected time in his word, time in fellowship with other folks, or neglected seeking him through prayer. Galatians 5:25 reminds us, "If we live by the Spirit, let us also keep in step with the Spirit."

My challenge for you today is to check your alignment. Are you keeping in step with where God is moving?

Make today count!

Day 69

I make a great effort to get to know all the neighbors who live near me. We are blessed to have an amazing community around us. Over the past year and a half, I've developed a relationship with one of my neighbors who reached out to me because he was struggling. We will text back and forth and check in, and when the kids and I play outside, he often stops by to catch up. Typically, these conversations would end with prayer in the front yard. I reached out to him two days ago to check in and see how things were going. He told me that things were hard and he appreciated my prayer and concern for him. Then he asked about my family and we had a few small texts back and forth. It was extremely difficult to hear the news late yesterday afternoon that he had taken his life. I began to question if there was anything I could have done to prevent this tragedy.

Jesus' response to a question about what the greatest commandment was can be found in Matthew 22:37-40: "Jesus replied: "'Love the Lord your God with all your heart and with all your soul and with all your mind. This is the first and greatest commandment. And the second is like it: 'Love your neighbor as yourself.' All the Law and the Prophets hang on these two commandments." Neither one of these commands is easy to do, but sometimes I believe it is more difficult to love people who do not love us in return. There are so many people around us who are struggling deeply and for whatever reason, choose not to seek help. You never know how your kind words and gestures could impact someone.

My challenge for you today is just make every effort possible to love others the way you love yourself. If you find yourself in a place where you feel you have nowhere to go, know that I am more than willing to sit and listen.

Make today count!

Day 70

A couple months ago, I had arranged for my mower to be picked up for spring maintenance. Typically, this entails getting the blade sharpened, the oil changed, and making sure all of the hardware is secured. When the guy who repairs my mower showed up yesterday, I loaded my mower on his trailer. We were talking about what work needed to be done and then he pointed out something I had not noticed. I had a tire that was completely off of the rim.

In life there is extreme value in having experts in your life. These relationships matter because these people see things we miss. In my case, had I not sought out the expertise of this mower technician, I most likely would've found myself stuck in the middle of my yard with the inability to move. The wisdom of this man will give me the ability to operate my mower at its full potential. Hebrews 10:24 admonishes, "And let us consider how to stir up one another to love and good works." Having another person who can examine your life will help spur you on to the good works God has called you to.

I love the adage, "inspect what you expect." I think it's important that each of us have a person in our life who is inspecting us because of expectations we have been called to. My challenge for you today is that if you do not have this type of person in your life, find them. It will make your day count.

Make today count!

Day 71

A few nights ago, Cade and I were driving towards "Gibby's" house (his grandmother). Instead of taking our normal route, I opted for a back road. The second we got off the normal path, Cade begin to ask where in the world I was going. My first question back to him was, "Cade, do you trust me?" I reminded him of how I've never gotten him lost before, and it was not going to happen today. I reminded him who he was to me.

This morning as I was having my quiet time, I was reminded of who I am to God. Isaiah 43:1-4, "But now, God's Message, the God who made you in the first place, Jacob, the One who got you started, Israel: "Don't be afraid, I've redeemed you. I've called your name. You're mine. When you're in over your head, I'll be there with you. When you're in rough waters, you will not go down. When you're between a rock and a hard place, it won't be a dead end— Because I am GOD, your personal God, The Holy of Israel, your Savior. I paid a huge price for you: all of Egypt, with rich Cush and Seba thrown in! That's how much you mean to me! That's how much I love you! I'd sell off the whole world to get you back, trade the creation just for you." This is who you are in Christ.

Today, regardless of whether you find yourself in troubled waters or not, God's favor and love are on and over you. You are chosen!

Make today count!

Day 72

There's an older movie titled "*Envy.*" It features Ben Stiller and Jack Black as two neighbors and best friends who live very comparable lives. One day Jack Black's character has a crazy idea for a new invention. Ben Stiller's character wants nothing to do with the product. It turns out that the product was a huge success and Jack becomes a billionaire. Instead of moving out of their traditional neighborhood, Jack builds a giant mansion that literally creates a shadow over Ben's house. Ben is driven mad about the overabundance of things his best friend has acquired. Later in the movie Jack sees the amazing relationship Ben Stiller's character and his wife have together. Jack tells Ben and Ben's wife how envious he is over their relationship. Envy lives in the place where desire and want is unfilled.

This is such an important matter to God that he listed "thou shall not covet" as one of the 10 Commandments. Envy and jealousy do nothing but pull us away from thankfulness and gratitude. Proverbs 14:30 encourages us, "A heart at peace gives life to the body, but envy rots the bones." Envy does nothing but steal our joy from the inside out. As in the movie, we tend to compare the wrong way. We do not realize the things we have that we should be so thankful for.

My challenge for you today is to practice gratitude. Be aware of the blessings God has given you. When you feel envy begin to rise in your heart, remind yourself of all the good things God has given you.

Make today count!

Day 73

There's a stark contrast between exposure and influence. Exposure is the people you come in contact with throughout the course of your day and week. They could be coworkers, family, even a supervisor. As I am defining it, exposure is simply being in relationship in some form or fashion with these people. However, these relationships do not shape the lens in which you see the world. These people are not challenging you in any way. They are not pushing you towards any paradigm shifts. Your supervisor, of course, has influence over you due to the fact that they are paying you to perform certain tasks. This form of influence is superficial. If the motivation behind the influence is money, then in my opinion, it is superficial. True influence is when we want to gain something that will challenge or better us through an interaction with another person. It does not matter if the person is older or younger, if they are your subordinate, or your boss. We can open ourselves up to the influence of others whom we desire to learn from.

When we look throughout history at all of the great influencers of the world, none can compare to the influence Jesus had. We are 2,000 years past his time on earth and millions upon millions of people are still being influenced and learning from his teaching. My fear though is that many of us are just allowing ourselves to be exposed to Jesus instead of truly being influenced.

In Matthew 13, Jesus tells the parable of the sower. He then explains it to his disciples. "Listen then to what the parable of the sower means: When anyone hears the message about the kingdom and does not understand it, the evil one comes and snatches away what was sown in their heart. This is the seed sown along the path. The seed falling on rocky ground refers to someone who hears the word and at once receives it with joy. But since they have no root, they last only a short time. When trouble or persecution comes because of the word, they quickly fall away. The seed falling among the thorns refers to someone who hears the word, but the worries of this life and the deceitfulness of wealth choke the word, making it unfruitful. But the seed falling on good soil refers to someone who hears the word and understands it. This is the one who produces a crop, yielding a hundred, sixty or thirty times what was sown." You see, the exposure was the same, but the influence and outcome were different. If we have been influenced, we will bear fruit.

Have you been influenced or just exposed?

Make today count!

Day 74

Every so often Abi Kate will come out of her room and tell me there is a monster in her closet. I'll walk back into her room with her, open her closet door, and show her there is no monster. Fear is a natural part of life.

This question comes as it relates to fear--what do we do with fear? We can either allow fear to motivate us or to paralyze us. If I have a fear of getting a cavity, that would motivate me to make sure to brush my teeth well each day. If I am a small child and I believe there's a monster in my closet, that figure could paralyze me into staying in my bed with the sheets over my face. It is not an accurate statement to say that fear is a negative thing. Through our fears and weaknesses, God is made great. Isaiah 41:13 says, "For I am the LORD your God who takes hold of your right hand and says to you, Do not fear; I will help you." God says we can give him our fears.

Today you have two choices as it relates to fear. Will you allow your fears to paralyze you or motivate you? Our God is bigger than our fears. Allow him to carry them for you today.

Make today count!

Day 75

Several years ago, a hilarious clip on YouTube went viral. It's a home video clip featuring a young boy I would guess to be three years old. His mom walks up to him and asks him if he has eaten any snacks. When she puts the camera on him, he has candy sprinkles all over his face and stuck in his teeth. The little boy looks at his mom and responds, "No." She continues to ask him if he has eaten any snacks, and he continues to deny it. At the end of the video, she walks into the kitchen where there is a small can of sprinkles spilled all over the counter and maybe 25% remaining in the can. She then calls the small boy into the kitchen and asks him, "Why aren't there any more sprinkles in the can?" The boy looks her dead in the eyes and responds, "There are sprinkles in the can."

We certainly do not have to teach children how to lie. It's something we all often find a little bit too easy to do. I saw a funny quote yesterday. It read, "People couldn't believe that I had a 4.0 GPA as busy as my schedule is, but anything is possible when you lie."

On Sunday, Nick, our teaching pastor, said a 99% truth is a 100% lie. Lies can also be lived. Speaking to his disciples about the religious rulers of the day in Luke 12:2-3, Jesus said, "Watch yourselves carefully so you don't get contaminated with Pharisee yeast, Pharisee phoniness. You can't keep your true self hidden forever; before long you'll be exposed. You can't hide behind a religious mask forever; sooner or later the mask will slip and your true face will be known. You can't whisper one thing in private and preach the opposite in public; the day's coming when those whispers will be repeated all over town." It's easy for us to want to keep a religious mask covering our face. We have a deep fear of being exposed for who we really are. We are all sinners saved by grace, but none of us have come to a place of perfection, nor will we ever. Our spiritual maturity begins the day wearing our mask ends.

My challenge for you today is to stop living a lie. Put your mask down and let people see the real you.

Make today count!

Day 76

Yesterday my wife and kids went to the zoo. They always look forward to their trips to the zoo. Abi Kate loves to see all of the snakes. She's especially intrigued by the poisonous rattlesnake. What's interesting about the zoo is that there are so many animals capable of so many incredible things, but due to the environment they are in, their ability to thrive is limited.

As a Christ follower, we have God within us. This means that our potential is unlimited. As I was thinking about the animals in the zoo and the environment they find themselves in, I started thinking about the environment I am in. Is the environment you find yourself in one that's pushing you to thrive or is it holding your potential back? Within the local body of believers which you find yourself attached to, do you find yourself being pushed? Do you find yourself being spiritually challenged? Are you being held accountable? If the answer is no, then potentially you are like one of the zoo animals. Your potential is being unmet.

2 Peter 3:18: "But grow in the grace and knowledge of our Lord and Savior Jesus Christ. To him be the glory both now and to the day of eternity. Amen." My challenge for you today is to do a spiritual growth assessment. Are you being challenged, are you learning, are you being pushed to reach your full potential, and are you being held accountable? If your answer is no to any of these, it might be time to change your environment. If you are on the surface level, dive a little deeper.

Make today count!

Day 77

This morning I have been watching church league men's basketball. In the first game I watched, one team was really struggling against the other. At one point, I believe they were down almost 20 points, but during a timeout, they made one big adjustment--communication. They made a clear plan to identify the person who would be guarding, who would be screening, and to be aware when a player was left unguarded. They were a different team when they took the floor. Upon my last check, they had cut the deficit down by five. They didn't change the plays and the players on the team did not change. What changed was their communication.

One of the most important things in life, regardless of whether it is relationships with others, our jobs, or dealing with conflict, is communication. Although difficult at times, clear and direct communication can benefit us in many of the issues we will encounter in life. Colossians 4:6: "Let your speech always be gracious, seasoned with salt, so that you may know how you ought to answer each person." The easiest way to get ahead of potential problems is to clearly communicate on the front end.

Where do you find yourself struggling with your communication? What are the changes you could make today to improve it? When dealing with tough conversations, are you seasoning your speech with salt? It could make all the difference!

Make today count!

Day 78

This morning Abi Kate came into my room scratching her back. She then looked at me and said, “Dad, why does God make me itch?” In my mind, this is equivalent to the question, "Why do bad things happen to good people?" I’m reminded of a story that Dr. Ravi Zacharias tells of the man whose horse ran away. The neighbor came over to him and said, "What terrible luck you have." He responded and said, "What do I know about these things.?" Later the horse that had run away returned with five wild horses. The neighbor came over and said, "Wow, that’s great luck." He responded the same. While trying to train some of the wild horses, his youngest son was thrown off and broke his ankle. The neighbor again told him he had bad luck. Shortly after, their town was raided and every able-bodied man was captured and forced to fight in a war that was not their own. The man's son was not taken because his ankle was broken. The point of the story is that to judge the goodness of God on a single isolated incident does not give an accurate depiction of the story he is weaving together. Looking at an individual puzzle piece does not give you the picture of a 1,000-piece puzzle.

Romans 8:28 reminds us, “And we know that God causes all things to work together for good to those who love God, to those who are called according to His purpose." I understand that when we are going through difficult times, it’s hard to see the goodness of God within it. The truth is, we may never see the goodness of God in a specific situation during our lifetime. As believers in Christ, we need to trust that he is weaving together a beautiful picture.

My challenge for you today is simply this: Trust--trust that God is sovereign. Trust that although the circumstance you are currently walking through might be a tough one, that he will use it.

Make today count!

Day 79

Yesterday afternoon the kids and I spent about four hours playing outside and enjoying the nice weather. I began to push my luck on the amount of time we had been outside as both of them were beginning to get "hangry"--a beautiful mixture of hunger and anger interwoven. I don't remember the exact situation I had to correct Abi Kate for, but her response back to me was, "But I'm the boss." I informed her that she was mistaken. She responded to me, "I'm a little bit the boss." As hilarious as it is to think about a three-year old thinking she was the boss over an adult, I know there have been times in my life when I have looked at God and said, "I'm a little bit the boss."

I'm reminded of the story of the prophet Jonah. God called Jonah to go and speak to the people of Nineveh. Jonah decided that he was "a little bit the boss" and took a ship heading in the opposite direction. Jonah 1:3: "But Jonah got up to run away from the Lord by going to Tarshish. He went to the city of Joppa, where he found a ship that was going to the city of Tarshish. Jonah paid for the trip and went aboard, planning to go to Tarshish to run away from the Lord." We all know how the story ends. After Jonah was swallowed by a great fish, he decided he wasn't the boss. He did what God called him to do and lives were changed.

What are the areas in your life where you are telling God you are the boss? What is it that's keeping you from sailing your boat in the direction where he wants you to head?

Make today count!

Day 80

Yesterday Holly was working on getting a ton of laundry done. She came to me and told me \ she believed something was wrong with the dryer. It was taking an unnecessary amount of time for a load to dry. She reminded me of how old our dryer is. Holly thought it may be time for a new one.

Anyone who knows me well knows I'm not quick to go and spend money. I went to the garage, got some tools and a headlamp. After a quick survey of the dryer, I realized that the hose in the back had become partially disconnected. Within a matter of 10 minutes, the dryer was up and running and functioning as it should.

The same way the dryer was unable to function at its best, Christians who are disconnected from a local church are in the same boat. Hebrews 10:24-25 reminds us: "And let us consider how we may spur one another on toward love and good deeds, not giving up meeting together, as some are in the habit of doing, but encouraging one another--and all the more as you see the Day approaching." It's incredibly important that we are connected to a local church. Each of us has been given different skill sets that when put together allow us to function fully as God intended us to.

Today if you are a Christ follower but have not aligned yourself with a local church, my challenge is for you to find one where you can be connected and where your gifts can be utilized.

Make today count!

Day 81

Holly is on spring break this week. Today, I took the day off of work for the two of us to make a quick trip to Louisville.

We spent some time at the Louisville Slugger baseball museum and had some great food. More importantly though, we have spent intentional quality time together. Relationships, like other things in life, when fed, grow and when starved, die.

There's not a relationship that is more important for us to continue to feed than our relationship with God. Taking intentional time each and every day to grow in your knowledge of God and to better understand what he's calling you to will deepen your relationships in the other areas of your life. 2 Peter 3:18 says, "But grow in the grace and knowledge of our Lord and Savior Jesus Christ. To him be glory both now and forever! Amen."

My challenge for you today is to think about the steps you need to take to grow and strengthen your most important relationship with God. What are some ways you can grow and strengthen your secondary relationships like with your spouse today as well?

Make today count!

Day 82

Yesterday I had my first experience going to an antique mall. Holly was super excited about it as this is something she enjoys doing with her sisters and mom. I was up for going since we really had no plan for the day other than spending some quality time together.

We walked into this mall and I quickly realized it was made up of lots of people's individual booths. There was no organizational process by which people displayed their items. It truly was a "treasure hunt."

Holly was looking for a specific antique casserole dish. After looking for a good while, she was able to find some. If there is a specific item you are looking for, there is no guarantee they will have it, nor is there a guarantee that if they do have it, you will find it.

This whole process reminded me of Matthew 7:7. Jesus said, "Ask and it will be given to you; seek and you will find; knock and the door will be opened to you." Searching for God is not like searching for a specific type of milk glass vase in an antique mall. Matthew tells us we will find Jesus if we seek Him.

For those of you who are on the fence about who Jesus is to you, my question for you today is this: What is stopping you from earnestly seeking who He is? Today I am grateful for a God who desires for me to know Him personally.

Make today count!

Day 83

This morning I woke up and had over 25 emails, most of which were some form of spam. Some of them were from companies I have made a purchase through and I have ended up on their mailing list. Typically, I just quickly delete all these without looking at them, but today I decided to be intentional about unsubscribing to each of them so I would not receive any further communications. This process took me a little bit of time, but in the long run will end up saving me quite a bit of time and will help clear up my email inbox.

I started thinking about how in life I subscribe to people and ideas though media. There are certain people I allow in my life to influence and shape my thoughts and opinions. In the same way that I purged my inbox, I started thinking about evaluating the influences I am currently subscribed to. Proverbs 13:20 says, "Walk with the wise and become wise, for a companion of fools suffers harm." T. D. Jakes says, "Show me your five closest friends and I will show you your future."

My challenge for you today is to take an honest inventory of who and what you are subscribing to. Are these top five influencers leading you in the direction you want to head?

Make today count!

Day 84

Today was Abi Kate's fourth birthday party. She was insanely excited. Much work has been exerted to make the celebration happen. A, K. wanted a Trolls-themed party hosted at the gymnastics studio. Holly got the balloons, cake, and party favors organized and ready for an afternoon of fun. In our lives, it feels like we are constantly in preparation for the next season or event.

It's easy for us to forget that our life here on earth is a season of preparation for the eternity that awaits. In the book of Philippians, Paul reminds us that we should be pushing towards heaven each day. Philippians 3:14: "I press on toward the goal to win the prize for which God has called me heavenward in Christ Jesus." Today amongst all of the other preparation you are doing for your life here on earth, what preparation are you making for eternity?

My challenge for you today is to think about the ways you can impact eternity through your words, actions, and preparation here and now.

Make today count!

Day 85

It almost seems to be a certainty that each morning as I leave for work, regardless of the weather, I pass multiple people who are running or walking for exercise. When I see these people and it is 70° outside, I don't think much of it. The number of walkers/runners is always increased on these pleasant days, so the amount of dedication and determination in my mind is a bit diminished. I recall a day a few months ago when, with remnants of snow on the ground, I passed a gentleman running. When I say he was running, I mean it looked like this guy was being chased by a cheetah. His dedication and determination were quite impressive.

I was thinking about how this relates to our relationship with God. I don't know about you, but there are times in my life when I find it incredibly easy to worship God and to be in awe of him. Then there are other times when things are difficult, or I feel distant from God, and being in a state of worship is much more challenging.

If anyone on earth could claim that they were able to worship consistently day to day, it would have been Jesus' disciples who walked with him. Before Jesus left his disciples, he left them with these words in John 14:26-27: "But the Advocate, the Holy Spirit, whom the Father will send in my name, will teach you all things and will remind you of everything I have said to you. Peace I leave with you; my peace I give you. I do not give to you as the world gives. Do not let your hearts be troubled and do not be afraid." We can also take heart in these words knowing that the Spirit of God will intercede on our behalf when we find ourselves in difficult situations.

My challenge for you today, regardless of whether you find yourself in a good time or a difficult one, is to make a list of five reasons you have to worship him.

Make today count!

Day 86

Our oldest child, Cade, has one of the kindest and most generous hearts I have ever seen. There have been numerous occasions when Cade had been given a toy or piece of candy at Sunday school or at school and because his little sister did not receive anything, she will begin to cry. This is typically the point where Holly or I step in and tell her this is Cade's toy or piece of candy. On multiple occasions, Cade will say, "No, it's okay. Here, Abi Kate, you can have it." I don't remember the exact circumstance, but a couple weeks ago Abi Kate had done something that caused her to lose her treat before bed. She was crying hysterically about the consequences of her actions. Cade came up to me and said, "Dad, can I take her punishment for her?" This act of kindness deeply touched my heart.

One of my favorite scripture passages is found in Matthew 20:28: "Just as the Son of Man did not come to be served, but to serve, and to give his life as a ransom for many." When he came to serve, Jesus set the bar for what servant leadership looks like. Although he was the greatest leader of all time, he was also the greatest servant.

Each of us have found ourselves in a similar predicament as Abi Kate. Each of us have made mistakes that have led us to sin against God. Because of sin, we are separated from God and the consequence is eternity absent of his presence. Here's the crazy thing--Jesus got the OK to step in and take our consequences, dying a death he did not deserve so we could be in right standing with God. He then arose three days later proving his deity.

The consequences of our sin are the same for each of us, and the penalty for sin must be paid. My question for you today is this: Will you pay it or will you allow what Jesus did to cover you?

Make today count!

Day 87

I'm assuming that your life is similar to mine in one way: There is a lot of noise and many things competing for your attention--from emails, text messages, phone calls, kids crying, kids asking questions, your endless to-do list, and so much more. My wife Holly has gotten to the place where she struggles with silence. If she is in the house and I am not home, it is a guarantee that she will be playing music to occupy the silence. With all of this noise competing for our attention, is it any wonder why we do not feel we hear from God?

We see God speak many times in the Old Testament. The majority of these times, it comes through a still, small whisper. A whisper cannot compete, even against one person talking at a normal volume. For a whisper to be effective, other noise and distractions must be held at bay. Throughout the Gospels we see that Jesus even went and found a silent place to pray. Mark 1:35: "And rising very early in the morning, while it was still dark, he departed and went out to a desolate place, and there he prayed." To better hear from God, we must control the noise around us.

My challenge for you today is to spend 10 minutes somewhere in silence to pray and then listen to see if you can hear God's still small voice in your heart.

Make today count!

Day 88

Last night I was working on getting dinner made, Holly was working on homework with Cade, and Abi Kate was playing in her room. A few minutes went by and then I realized I hadn't seen our dog who is normally no more than 3 feet away from me at any given moment. We realized he must have gone outside when Cade and I came in after his baseball practice. Holly and I both went out and began looking for him and within a matter of two minutes, I found him hanging out outside. I brought him in and we went back to what we were doing.

My phone then began to ring. It was Nancy, one of our neighbors. I answered it and she said, "Did you find your dog?" I told her we did and began tell her what had happened. Then Nancy said, "Did you know that A. K. is outside?" It turns out that while we were frantically looking for the dog, Abi Kate decided to get her scooter and scoot up the road looking for the dog as well. We had no idea she had even left the house. Thankfully, Nancy was on a walk and began to follow Abi Kate talking with her about what she was doing. Without Nancy intervening in the situation, I can't think of any other possible endings that would be ones we would want to talk about.

Each morning part of my prayer is that God will watch over each member of my family. This has become such a consistent flow of my prayer that to be honest, I don't really think much of it when I say it. You had better believe that I will be giving this much more conscious time from now on. I understand there are times when God does not always protect us for whatever reason. Today, I am thankful that he chose to watch over Abi Kate.

In the book of Psalms 121:1-6, King David wrote about the protection God gives: "I lift up my eyes to the mountains— where does my help come from? My help comes from the LORD, the Maker of heaven and earth. He will not let your foot slip— he who watches over you will not slumber; indeed, he who watches over Israel will neither slumber nor sleep. The LORD watches over you— the LORD is your shade at your right hand."

If asking God for protection over you and your family is part of your normal prayer life, my challenge for you today is to really understand what it means that the God of heaven and earth who does not sleep or rest is your protector.

Make today count!

Day 89

As a kid, I remember taking the chance any time I could to explore the woods. My buddy Jordan used to call these "treks." There was no real objective to the trek, nothing in particular that we were looking for. We were simply searching for whatever we might find. Think about how many of the great archaeological finds have occurred. They happened because people took the opportunity to search.

I don't know about you, but when I think about searching, I don't think about searching within myself. In Psalms 139:23-24, King David said, "Search me, God, and know my heart; test me and know my anxious thoughts. See if there is any offensive way in me, and lead me in the way everlasting." This is a great prayer. This prayer is asking God to show us things that either we have hidden from God or things that are blind spots in our life. Blind spots are things you are unaware of. To pray this prayer will require humility. Because of our brokenness, it is a guarantee that what you hear back from God will sting a little, or maybe even a lot. If we want to experience true growth and if we want to truly pursue holiness, I believe this prayer is a great place to start.

My question for you today is are you willing to ask God to search you? Ask God to expose the areas in your life you are blind to. I promise, if you're willing to humble yourself and pray this prayer, God will answer it.

Make today count!

Day 90

I absolutely love springtime. Springtime, of course, means freshly cut grass, baseball, and one of my favorite things, turkey hunting. I love it when all of the trees begin to bloom with intense color. I love the temperature change and how after months of cold weather, we begin to really feel the warmth of the sunshine. You can really begin to get a sense of the new life that is coming.

When a person commits his/her life to Christ, they are given new life in Christ. 2 Corinthians 5:17 describes it this way: "Therefore if anyone is in Christ, he is a new creature; the old things passed away; behold, new things have come." When a tree is in bloom, it is obvious because of the beautiful flowers we see produced from it. So how do we know if a person is really walking in a new life from God? Galatians 5:22-23 explains the things we would see in a person who is walking in new life. "But the fruit of the Spirit is love, joy, peace, forbearance, kindness, goodness, faithfulness, gentleness and self-control. Against such things there is no law." These are the attributes and behaviors of a person who is walking in the new life God has given them.

My question for you today is this: When people see your life, do they see you walking in these attributes? Is your life revealing the new life you have been given because of Christ?

Make today count!

Day 91

Have you ever found yourself delaying to take the trash out? Maybe it was raining outside or you just simply didn't feel like making the effort. This morning I was in the kitchen helping to get the kids out the door for school. Initially when I went into the kitchen, I realized I could smell the trash. It wasn't a pleasant smell, but within a matter of minutes, my nose adjusted to the smell so much so that I didn't even notice it anymore. When Holly was heading out of the door, she said, "Oh wow, that trash stinks." This was all it took to motivate me to take it out to the garbage can. It's amazing how if you walk outside and breathe some fresh air then return to the room where you were, you notice the smell all over again.

I think sin can be the same way. You see, there was nothing in my trash that initially smelled bad. Over the course of a few days, it began to create a foul and robust odor. After a while it will begin to create a real stench. When we continue to surround ourselves with it, we become unable to notice its odor. Hebrews 12:1 reminds us, "Therefore, since we are surrounded by such a great cloud of witnesses, let us throw off everything that hinders and the sin that so easily entangles. And let us run with perseverance the race marked out for us." It's so easy for us to get wrapped up in the stench of sin. Today I am grateful for people who are in my life that pick up if my scent is off.

My question for you today is this: What is the aroma your life is giving off? Is it an aroma that has a foul stench, or is it one that is pleasing to God and draws others towards him?

Make today count!

Day 92

I've been delaying replacing a few dead trees in my yard for as long as possible. Yesterday I gave in and had some new trees installed as well as some new bushes. What's incredible to me is the growth a tree will go through from its initial planting to full maturity. One of the trees I have in my yard is an oak tree. This particular oak tree is called a pin oak. On average they are 75 feet tall when fully grown. Obviously, with a tree this large, at full maturity, it will withstand everything from being climbed on to strong storms. However, when this tree is young, it must be roped to the ground to help it grow straight and strong.

The same is true about the Christian faith. Without a strong foundation in Christ, our growth will be stunted. Colossians 2:6-7 says, "So then, just as you received Christ Jesus as Lord, continue to live your lives in him, rooted and built up in him, strengthened in the faith as you were taught, and overflowing with thankfulness." As we grow and mature in our Christian walk, it is of the utmost importance that we stay grounded in God's word and supported by other believers. God's word is the food to our soul, and the accountability and support of others helps to keep us on a straight growth path.

What is it today that is grounding you? Is your growth currently being stunted or are you blossoming?

Make today count!

Day 93

Exodus 12 details the specifics concerning the way the Israelite community celebrated Passover. God called Moses to lead the children of Israel out of captivity in Egypt into the promised land he was going to give them. Pharaoh was not on board with this plan and because of this, God sent a series of plagues to change his mind. The last and final plague was the death of the firstborn child in all of Egypt. God made a provision for his chosen people. Each family took a spotless male lamb and sacrificed it by spreading its blood over the entry of their house. When the angel of death passed over Egypt, it passed over all the houses that were covered with the blood of the lamb. Each year Jewish families still celebrate Passover. You can read the entire account in the Exodus 12.

One thing that is incredibly important for us to understand is that the Jewish calendar is based on the lunar phases of the moon. Our calendar is based on the sun. Another difference is a Jewish person would understand a day to begin at moonrise. With all that said, Jesus and his disciples were having the last supper, or as we tend to think of it, the first communion just after moonrise. This was the beginning of a new day and it was the day they were celebrating Passover. How interesting it is that the "lamb of God" was sacrificed on a cross the same day they remembered the blood of the lamb covering them from death so many years before. In the same way the Israelites took a physical lamb and covered their physical houses with its blood so the angel of death would pass over their house, we cover our house, our bodies, with the blood of Jesus so that we can pass from death to new life in him. Ephesians 1:7: "In him we have redemption through his blood, the forgiveness of our trespasses, according to the riches of his grace." God does nothing by accident. Each event in our life is carefully orchestrated to transfer back to the wonder and glory of him.

Make today count!

Day 94

The night before my 30th birthday, Holly told me to pack all of my kayak fishing gear in my kayak and have it ready to go for the first thing in the morning. We woke up and loaded up all the stuff with me not knowing where we were headed. We ended up at the house of friends who were also ready to go down the river that day. We loaded a second kayak on the top of my FJ. The guys were in my car and the girls in another. We made our way down the interstate towards the river. We weren't too far down the road when I heard a strange whooshing sound. The sound began to get stronger followed by a flash of green and a banging sound. I realized this was one of the straps on my kayak breaking loose from my kayak and it was dangling on the side of my car, slamming against it. About the time I began to apply the brakes and pull over, the back strap broke off and the kayak went tumbling down the interstate. We had to circle back and get the kayak, pick it up and load onto a new vehicle before we could make our way down to the river.

Life is like this. At times there are things we need to go back and deal with before we can move into the fullness of our next calling. Personally, I had an area of unforgiveness I carried with me for a ridiculously long time. God drew my attention to it years later. When he did, I had to go back and deal with it so he could move me forward into what he has called me to. I believe with all my heart that if I had not gone back and dealt with the unforgiveness in my life, I would not be fulfilling God's call of working in vocational ministry today. Psalms 139:23-24 says, "Search me, God, and know my heart; test me and know my anxious thoughts. See if there is any offensive way in me, and lead me in the way everlasting." King David was asking God to show him areas he needed to go back and deal with in his life. He knew he could not move forward into the way everlasting until God exposed the things that needed to be dealt with. Could I have taken my trip down the river without my kayak? Absolutely. But it would not have been the same experience. I would have either been swimming or holding onto the side of someone else's boat. For me to have the fullness of the experience, I had to go back and get my kayak.

What is it today in your life that you know you need to go back and deal with? Are you curious to see what's on the other side of you allowing God to bring healing to that situation? God wants to lead you into the way everlasting, but sometimes the first step forward is a few steps back.

Make today count!

Day 95

Psalms 149:13 says, "For you created my inmost being; you knit me together in my mother's womb." I love the visual David paints for us in this verse. When I think of someone knitting, I think of someone carefully, slowly, and purposefully bringing together individual threads to create beautiful and unique designs and patterns. Not only is there a design in a pattern when someone knits, there is also a unique purpose for their creation, whether it is a blanket or a sweater.

Many of us as believers have chosen to stay silent over the issue of abortion. There is fear of stirring up a hornet's nest of opposition. I have found myself in this majority until just recently. I've come to believe that whatever persecution might come to me, it's far less severe than the consequences of sitting idly by in silence.

Many who are pro-abortion lead with the argument that the fetus is not recognized as a life since it is dependent on the mother to survive. I would counter this argument by saying my four-year-old daughter is also dependent on her mother to survive. Left on her own, there's no way she would be able to take care of herself. This would also apply for some senior citizens and those in the hospital on breathing machines and feeding tubes. I simply will not accept this as truth. Having two children of my own, I have been able to experience the joy of watching their progression inside the womb, of hearing the heartbeat and watching them move. I heard a pastor list off some of the worst possible scenarios that one could imagine where abortion would seem like a likely option. With each one of the circumstances, whether disease, poverty, or rape, he listed individuals who fell in one of those categories but were born rather than aborted and have been beyond influential in our world.

I believe with all my heart that if you or your significant other have had an abortion, the God in heaven loves you and has plans for your life. The emotional baggage that comes with an abortion is not too much for God to redeem. My challenge for those of you who share my pro-life stance is not to place shame or guilt on anyone. It's not to act out in violence, but rather to show the love of Christ.

Make today count!

Day 96

Spring weather can be incredibly frustrating, especially here in Tennessee. We can go from a beautiful 75°-day one day to snow the next. I'm always super cautious about disconnecting my outdoor hose after I use it each time because of these drastic weather changes. This past week I connected the hose and used it to rinse off my mower. About the time I finished rinsing off the mower, it started to rain heavily. I went inside and neglected to disconnect the water hose. This morning when I woke up, we had frost and the ground was frozen. And there it was...the hose still connected to the wall. Since I was on my way to church, I decided not to even turn it on to see if the pipe ruptured inside.

The garden hose is an incredible tool for rinsing and watering things. It has a specific season in which it is most useful. If used at the wrong time and connected at the wrong time, it can cause significant damage. In the same way, there are relationships in life that are useful and beneficial for a season. However, outside of the seasons, these relationships can become toxic and harmful. There are times in life when we need to realize we need to disconnect from certain relationships. Proverbs 17:17, "A friend loves at all times, and a brother is born for a time of adversity." I believe in the same way that God moves us into relationships with people, at times he removes us from relationships.

My question for you today is, what are the relationships you feel God is moving you into, and what are the relationships you feel he is pulling you away from? Are there relationships that are becoming toxic and emptying you of your joy? Do you have people in your life who you feel connected to? Pray God will give you clarity in both of these situations so you can be connected to what he desires for you.

Make today count!

Day 97

If we are honest with ourselves, I believe all of us will admit that we have times in life when it's easy to feel a sense of entitlement. At the root of entitlement is pride. When we feel entitled in a situation, what we are really saying is that we are superior over someone or something. I know for myself, my entitlement rises up the most in my marriage. There are times when I feel Holly owes me something, typically after I have done something to serve her. An example would be if she were to go out with a friend for coffee one night, there's a high probability that I would remind her of that before making a request to hang out with one of my friends. In this scenario, I did not serve Holly out of a place of love. I was only doing it to leverage an outcome I desired in the future. My sense of entitlement is something I have to keep in check on a daily basis.

Entitlement in a marriage is one of the many things that can get your relationship heading down a destructive path quickly. Your marriage is not about your needs being met. Your marriage is about refining the impurities within you and making you more like Christ. The goal of our marriages should be to out-serve the other person with no strings attached. If we are modeling or lives after Christ, we can clearly see that he came to serve. Matthew 20:28, "Just as the Son of Man did not come to be served, but to serve, and to give his life as a ransom for many." Jesus is the perfect model of how to serve if you have every reason to feel entitled.

My challenge for you today is to serve your spouse. Serve from a place of not expecting to get anything in return, and wait to see how God blesses your marriage.

Make today count!

Day 98

When I was 14 years old I landed my first job working at Chick-Fil-A. It was a really great job that I thoroughly enjoyed. As a 14-year-old boy, being paid a physical check is great, but then when you top it with all-you-can-eat chicken sandwiches, life is pretty sweet. Prior to my 16th birthday, I made the seemingly insignificant decision to change part-time jobs. My manager at Chick-Fil-A tried everything in his power to get me to consider staying with the company long term. He even tried to sway me by telling me about the Chick-Fil-A scholarship program available for students. Although his argument was a good one, in my 16-year-old brain, I could not get girls off my mind. After passing my first lifeguarding class, I landed a job as a lifeguard at our local city pool. This small decision impacted my life in some very significant ways. Here are just a few things I would attribute to this decision that I made when I was 15 years old: meeting Holly— now my wife, choosing to get a degree in recreation business, and spending eight years working for the YMCA. Isn't it interesting how a seemingly small decision can make such a significant impact on a person's life?

Each day you make several decisions. Some insignificant decisions we make very quickly, and other more significant decisions we spend time praying about and considering the options. The less time we spend making a decision, the less serious we feel the consequences of that decision will be. I believe with all my heart that the person who develops any type of addiction does not start off with the mindset of becoming an addict. It starts with that first small decision. Each subsequent interaction with the addictive behavior or substance helps to write the person's future story. Thankfully God offers to give us wisdom if only we ask. James 1:5: "If anyone of you lacks wisdom, you should ask God, who gives generously to all without finding fault, and it will be given to you." It is such a comforting thought to know we can ask and receive wisdom from the creator of all wisdom.

Today my challenge for you is to slow down when making decisions. Think about how your immediate decisions can impact your future.

Make today count!

Day 99

I've heard others make the comment that having kids around always seems to make adventures and events more fun. If you take a kid to the zoo, their excitement level is through the roof. Have you ever been around a child when they opened presents at their birthday party? Each new gift leads to a new amount of wonder and awe. Wonder is defined as "a feeling of surprise mingled with admiration, caused by something beautiful, unexpected, unfamiliar, or inexplicable." A sense of wonder keeps us coming back and wanting more.

I think the older we become, the more likely we are to lose our sense of wonder. Do you remember the first time you saw the ocean? It's incredible and it seems to go on for days. The more you return to the ocean, the less the sense of wonder. My fear is that we can become this way with God. Deuteronomy 10:21: "He is your praise and He is your God, who has done these great and awesome things for you which your eyes have seen." I believe that over time, it is easy for us to lose our sense of wonder with God. I believe this can happen for two reasons. First, we stop pursuing new knowledge and understanding that would push us to a place of wonderment. Secondly, we ignore the sin in our lives which can cause us to minimize the wonderment of God within our own minds. Both of these are incredibly dangerous.

My challenge for you today is if you have lost your sense of the wonder of God, answer these questions honestly: Has your sin brought God down to your level? Have you stopped continuing to learn more about God to push you back into your sense of wonder? What is your next step today? Maybe it is getting involved in a study that will stretch and grow your faith. Or perhaps it is an honest conversation with a mentor about the things in your life that you are struggling with.

Make today count!

Day 100

There is a lady in my neighborhood who a most peculiar routine. She takes a walk about every day. Now, you're probably thinking that doesn't seem that odd. There are plenty of people who walk around their neighborhood. I agree—but what makes this lady's walk so peculiar is that as she walks, she pulls a large trash can behind her. She typically takes a few laps around our street then returns home. I would say that the majority of people look at her and think, "Why in the world is this woman walking dragging a trash can behind her?" But truth be told, I believe many people walk through their lives every day dragging an emotional trash can behind them.

Each of us have hurts, anxieties, and stresses that have come into our lives at one point or another. Some of us continue to shoulder those burdens each and every day. I believe that's why scripture reminds us, "Do not worry about tomorrow, for tomorrow will worry about itself. Each day has enough trouble of its own." (Matthew 6:34) If I was to equate any worry, anxiety, stress, or hurt to a physical brick, more than likely I could carry 1 or 2 bricks and continue to walk without them negatively affecting me. But if I was to carry multiple bricks, I would soon become too exhausted to continue. Jesus came to give us rest. 1 Peter 5:7 reminds us, "Cast your cares on him, because he cares for you."

I think we can all agree that lugging a trash can behind us while we walk is pretty silly. We can we also agree that it's just as silly to carry an emotional trashcan with us everywhere we go. Today Jesus has come to give you rest. Cast your cares on him today. Walk freely without your trashcan!

Make today count!

Day 101

There's nothing quite as enjoyable as watching some good quality coach pitch baseball. To see a grand slam come from what was originally really only a single always keeps me laughing. Here's how the scenario typically happens. The kid will hit the ball. It will go about 7 feet. The pitcher overthrows it to the first baseman. This is followed by 2 to 3 more overthrows which leads to a homerun or a grand slam. The result for the child who hit this ball is a deep sense of satisfaction and significance. Significance is a longing that is imbedded deep within each of us. The problem with the child who feels a deep sense of significance from this "homerun" is it has come through a false narrative.

The danger with our search for and acquisition of significance is the place in which we originally find it because we will continue to return to that place to feed from it. You can see how this could play out for a young person who has never received the sense of significance from their parents. They may seek it through other inappropriate relationships and activities. People and activities will never be able to meet our need for true significance. Trying to gain true significance from these sources is similar to eating cotton candy for dinner. It tastes sweet and is enjoyable, but as my friend Coach Burt says, satisfy your hunger. Hunger for true significance can only be found in God. As our creator, he has given us a clear design and purpose. Colossians 3:1-3 tells us, "Since, then, you have been raised with Christ, set your hearts on things above, where Christ is seated at the right hand of God. Set your minds on things above, not on earthly things." If we align our hearts to God, he will supply our significance in his purpose for us.

What is your source of significance?

Make today count!

Day 102

I had a first last night. I attended a live UFC fight. For those of you unfamiliar with UFC, these are the folks who fight in a cage with the thinnest gloves you can get and where any form of attack is pretty much fair game. Why anyone would choose this as a career is beyond me. Beyond learning that I would never want to do this, I learned that controlling your opponent's hands is the key to victory and lack of control certainly leads to a significant headache.

In UFC it is important to control your opponent's hands. When it comes to our lives spiritually, it is also important that we control our hands. Proverbs 16:27 reminds, "Idle hands are the devil's workshop; idle lips are his mouthpiece." Scripture tells us that desire happens first and is followed by sin. Sin typically involves our hands in some way, shape, or form. In Matthew 5:30a, Jesus says, "And if your right hand causes you to stumble, cut it off and throw it away." Of course, Jesus is speaking symbolically, but his point is made. The truth for us is that we should be aware of situations we allow ourselves to enter into and control our hands, using them to protect and guard our hearts and minds. Ultimately the goal is that we would use our hands to edify Christ and to build his kingdom.

What about you today? Are you controlling your hands? Are your hands being used to cause you harm or to build his Kingdom and protect your home?

Make today count!

Day 103

I believe we all fall into one of two camps: either you believe that the events in your day, week, and life are all random chance or you believe that these events are orchestrated and ordained by God. I'm sure it's no surprise to you, but I fall into the second camp. I spent the last two days at a men's conference in Missouri. Yesterday my two traveling companions and I were on our way back home when we received a notification that our flight had been delayed. We knew this delay would inevitably cause us to miss our connecting flight in Atlanta. We ended up landing in Atlanta with just 14 minutes to make our connecting flight home. Through a series of significant sprints and stair runs, we were able to get to the gate two minutes prior to departure. When we got to the gate, we realized they had already taken us off that flight and put us on a flight that was to leave five hours later. However, we were able to get back on the flight that was about to leave with just a change of our original seats. I ended up in the emergency aisle. Obviously, I was not complaining about the extra legroom. There ended up being an empty seat across the aisle from me. A lady who was seated somewhere in the back opted for the additional legroom. She and I struck up a conversation which went from small talk into a really great conversation about who Jesus was. Throughout the conversation she kept telling me how she felt like God had been trying to get her attention for a while now. Around the time the plane landed she said, "This wasn't even supposed to be my seat." I was thinking, "And I wasn't supposed to make this plane."

I wholeheartedly believe God will intervene in the small details of our life so that it can ultimately bring him glory. Jeremiah 29:11 says, "For I know the plans I have for you," declares the LORD, "plans to prosper you and not to harm you, plans to give you a hope and a future." I believe with all of my heart that the conversation this lady and I had was a God-ordained moment. When we find ourselves in these types of situations, we need to be aware of the prompting of the Holy Spirit to openly share about his love and the gift of salvation he has given us.

Maybe the next time things don't work out exactly as you had planned for them to, or maybe the next time your seat gets changed, you will see this as a divine appointment from God. Today my prayer for you is that you would be aware of the opportunities God has orchestrated in front of you to be a beacon of truth. Always be ready for a seat that wasn't supposed to be yours.

Make today count!

Day 104

I love to hunt. Spring is turkey hunting season. Turkey hunting in Middle Tennessee is excellent and one of the most effective ways to get a turkey is to set up a decoy. The decoy looks like a female turkey and attracts the large males. The decoy looks like the real thing but it is not. When a large male turkey comes near your decoy, that means dinnertime for you.

Hunters are not the only ones who use decoys. Satan loves to use decoys to lure us. He is the master of luring us to something that looks like the real thing, but the truth is, it's just a trap to destroy us. Pornography is an excellent example. It offers a false sense of intimacy. Satan falsely advertises promises he cannot keep. King David obviously experienced similar decoys in his own life. He writes in Psalms 141:9, "Keep me from the trap that they have laid for me and from the snares of evildoers!" I believe David had it right. Our best and only option is to cry out to God and to implore him to keep us from falling prey to Satan's traps.

My challenge for you today is to be aware of the decoys that have been laid in front of you. Ask God to give you strength to stay away from them and to be given the ability to clearly recognize them.

Make today count!

Day 105

What are your plans for today? What are the things you hope to accomplish? I believe each one of us lives with a desire for clear purpose and direction. For me, there's nothing quite as satisfying as drawing a line through the last item on my to-do list.

Regardless of what is ahead for you today, the words in Colossians can provide great clarity for the challenges and opportunities you may face today. "And whatever you do, whether in word or deed, do it all in the name of the Lord Jesus, giving thanks to God the Father through him." (Colossians 3:17) If we were to move about our day and operate out of a clear understanding of this scripture, I believe we would experience a new level of clarity and satisfaction. When we do everything to the glory of God, we are offering even the most mundane tasks up as an act of worship to Him. What if we were to approach taking out the trash as an act of worship? What if our frame of mind was to ask ourselves how we could glorify God through how all we do? This could be a real paradigm shift in the way you approach every activity of your day.

My challenge for you today is to operate out of a Colossians 3:17 mind frame.

Make today count!

Day 106

I was super grateful for the opportunity last night to take Holly on a late Valentine's date to see the musical *Wicked.* (Quick side note: If you have not seen this musical, it is well worth your time.) Seated just one row ahead of us was a couple I am assuming were a husband and wife in their mid-late 30's. Those of you who have been to Broadway-style performances know what typical etiquette looks like at these productions. It is customary to applaud after each song and expected that if the performance was excellent, there will be a standing ovation at the end with thunderous applause and cheering. I don't really feel like I am stepping out on a limb when I say that these two were probably the biggest fans of *Wicked* on the face of the earth. After each musical number, the lady would erupt with loud "whoop woos" over and over. I'm pretty sure people working in office buildings downtown could have heard her. Her husband had the most distinguished clap I have ever heard. It was a clean, crisp popping sound. His clap put others to shame. It was not only the decibel range that he could create, but the cadence in which he clapped it. This man would clap at least eight times between a normal person's claps. There was no question at all that these two were deeply and emotionally invested in this performance. These people were passionate about this musical. If I had to guess, each of them probably owns the soundtrack, a T-shirt, the hat, and maybe even the scarf to go with it.

I was thinking about these two folks and how evident their love and passion for *Wicked* was. No one within earshot would have had any doubt of it. I would say most of us have something we could identify as a passion in our life. For some of us it may be a particular sports team. For others it might be a particular activity or hobby. If you were to do some honest reflection, what would those closest to you say you are passionate about? Would your life point people to Christ or to something else? Matthew 5:16 encourages us, "Let your light so shine before men, that they may see your good works, and glorify your Father which is in heaven." Our lives should be lived in such a way that they show our passion and love for Christ and point others to him.

I have some questions for you to meditate on today. First, if you did the exercise in self reflection, who or what would others say you're passionate about? Does your passion line up with what you want it to be and what you want people to know you for?

Make today count!

Day 107

The story is told of a young farmer in Indiana who was standing in his corn fields looking up at the sky. On this particular day, he saw three very clear and distinct clouds. The first looked like the letter G. The second looked like the letter P, and the third looked like the letter C. He sat and thought about it for a minute, and came up with the idea that this must mean "Go Preach Christ," so he rushed to his local deacon body at his church and told them he has been called to preach from the pulpit. With a great deal of reluctance, they allowed the young farmer to take the pulpit that Sunday morning. After an hour of the most incoherent, irrelevant, and most biblically inaccurate sermon that anyone had ever heard, the eldest of the deacons walked up to the young would-be preacher, and said, "I'm pretty sure that GPC means "Go Plant Corn!"

When God calls us to something, he will give us clarity of the call and he will also equip us for the call. The first chapter of the book of Joshua details God's call to Joshua to take over the leadership of the children of Israel. Moses, the greatest leader in history to that point, had just died. Joshua was now in charge of taking 1.2 million people into the land that God had promised them. There was one enormous battle that stood between them and the land God had promised them. Joshua had been commanded to have courage by God. He had been given victory before the battle ever took place. In Joshua 1:9 we read God's command to Joshua: "Have I not commanded you? Be strong and courageous. Do not be frightened, and do not be dismayed, for the Lord your God is with you wherever you go." God's call comes with clarity, equipping, and a command to courage.

My question for you today is this: What is God calling you to have courage in? Maybe it's to take a stand in a situation. Maybe it is to share his love with someone close to you but far from God. God has given you victory, but you must step into the battle.

Make today count!

Day 108

Today is good Friday. It's the day we remember Jesus' crucifixion and physical death. It seems odd that we refer today as "good." The brutal crucifixion of an innocent man seems far from good. The Romans were experts when it came to crucifixion. From what history tells us, crucifixion would have been the most brutal way someone could possibly be executed. Prior to actually being nailed to the cross, they would have been whipped 39 times. The whip tore skin and flesh away. The number 39 was chosen because after 40 times, most people would die just from the beating. Jesus was then nailed to a cross. Keep in mind that his back was torn open from all the lashes and each time he needed to take a breath, he had to slide himself up a rugged cross. Eventually suffocation is what causes death during a crucifixion. This is a horrendous way to die.

We refer to today as good because Jesus stood in our place taking the punishment we deserve for our sin. But without Sunday, the day he rose from the dead, Friday would not be referred to as a good day. Sunday is what proved he was God. It's what proves that what he did on the cross for us paid our penalty in full. Isaiah 53:3-5 says, "We despised him and rejected him; he endured suffering and pain. No one would even look at him—we ignored him as if he were nothing. But he endured the suffering that should have been ours, the pain that we should have borne. All the while we thought his suffering was punishment sent by God. But because of our sins, he was wounded and beaten because of the evil we did. We are healed by the punishment he suffered and made whole by the blows he received." The gospel is this, that he stood in our place so we could have right standing with God. This is why today is Good Friday.

Make today count!

Day 109

Failure is an inevitable part of life. Each of us have experienced and will experience our fair share. Michael Jordan, arguably the greatest basketball player who has ever lived, failed to make his high school basketball team. He did not allow this failure to define him. Instead, he allowed it to push him to a place of extreme discipline. During this time, he worked hard to refine and hone his craft which is the reason he is a household name today.

There's a quote that says that if you have never failed at anything then you have never tried anything. I believe that is true. As we learn how to ride a bike, hit a baseball, or learn to cook, we will inevitably face failure along the way. Thomas Edison, when he failed to successfully make a lightbulb, was questioned about his failure. He responded and said, "I now know several thousand ways a lightbulb cannot be made." Proverbs 24:16 reminds us, "The righteous may fall seven times but still get up, but the wicked will stumble into trouble." It's not a question of whether it will happen, it's a question of how will you respond to it.

There are many names in history we will never know. These are the names of people who attempted something, they failed at it, then they gave up. Don't allow your failures to define you. As Pastor Craig Groeschel says, "Failure is an event, never a person." My challenge for you today is to continue to push forward despite your failure.

Make today count!

Day 110

I'm sure that many of you, like me, have had a car accident that was not your fault. It's always super helpful in those situations if there is a reliable witness to stay on the scene to validate your account of what happened. A reliable witness is the difference between you or the other driver paying your deductible. In our litigious society, one reliable witness is really all you need to settle your case.

Can you imagine if you had a car accident and you had 500 witnesses? Talk about an opened and closed case. Scripture tells us that the third day after Jesus' death, he rose. Note for those of you who are skeptics, if this was all it said, it would be quite difficult to believe. But scripture goes on to tell us that he showed himself to over 500 people. In 1 Corinthians 15:6 Paul is writing a letter after Jesus' death and resurrection and he writes, "He appeared to more than five hundred of the brothers and sisters at the same time, most of whom are still living, though some have fallen asleep." What he is saying here is "these witnesses are still alive. If you don't believe me, ask them for yourself."

Pastor Brady shared this quote from Charles Colson. Charles was one of the men involved in the Watergate scandal. "Look what he has to say. I know the resurrection is a fact, and Watergate proved it to me. How? Because 12 men testified they had seen Jesus raised from the dead, then they proclaimed that truth for 40 years, never once denying it. Every one was beaten, tortured, stoned, and put in prison. They would not have endured that if it weren't true. Watergate embroiled 12 of the most powerful men in the world--and they couldn't keep a lie for three weeks. You're telling me 12 apostles could keep a lie for 40 years? Absolutely impossible."

"And he said to them, "Do not be alarmed. You seek Jesus of Nazareth, who was crucified. He has risen; he is not here. See the place where they laid him." (Mark 16:6) Today the debt is paid, the tomb is empty. The Savior of the universe is waiting to come into a personal relationship with you. He is risen! Happy Easter!

Make today count!

Day 111

Yesterday afternoon was a very full day for our family. Cade is in a school play. They had a long rehearsal yesterday afternoon. We also had some friends who just had a baby, so Holly decided to drop Cade off at practice and then head to the hospital to see our friends. That left Little Miss and me at home. We made it through several rounds of different board games and puzzles before my little ball of energy couldn't take it anymore. She got somewhat of a running start and jumped right on top of me. She began to tell me she was going to "get me." Our wrestling match was fun and successful for about three minutes. Somewhere around the three-minute mark, I felt a sharp pain in my arm. This turned out to be A.K.'s top left tooth. After spending some quality time in time out, we discussed the situation. I talked about how biting was never OK. A little later, Holly called to check in on us. A.K. asked if she could talk to her, so I handed her the phone. She began to tell Holly what happened even though I told her it was OK to keep it between us. Then she called her grandma on FaceTime and confessed to her. The second that Cade got home from play practice, she told him what happened. If that doesn't prove that confession is good for the soul, I don't know what does.

James 5:16 says, "Therefore confess your sins to each other and pray for each other so that you may be healed. The prayer of a righteous person is powerful and effective." We often feel unsettled until we have confessed to another person. Confession to other people is beneficial for gaining accountability in whatever your area of weakness is. In my own life, there have been many times when until I have confessed something to a trusted friend, I have not felt completely free from the burden. Because of what Christ has done for us, we do not need someone to intercede for our confession. We can go straight to the God of the universe. When Christ died on the cross for us, he covered all of our sins. This means we are approaching his throne from a place of thankfulness for the forgiveness already offered us. When we confess our sin, we are agreeing with God on what our sin is.

If there something you need to bring before God in confession, quickly agree with him on it then find a trusted companion you can confide in and let them know what's going on in your life so they can help point you towards Christ.

Make today count!

Day 112

One of my favorite treats is a cookie sandwich from Julia's bakery. I was reminded of a story via a Facebook memory just the other day. One evening last year I desperately wanted a Julia's cookie sandwich. Unfortunately, Julia's is on the opposite side of town so I made the decision to head to a grocery store near my house to pick one up. I walked in and headed to the bakery section. To my delight, there was one cookie sandwich with a tag on it that said, "manager's special." At this point, I felt like God was smiling down on me. I made my purchase and headed home. Holly and I were sitting on the couch watching a movie as I prepared to indulge in this small piece of heaven. As I took my first bite, I felt something in my mouth, a texture that my mind did not agree with. I put my finger in my mouth and pulled out what I swear was nothing short of a 4-foot long hair. OK—maybe I'm exaggerating a little bit about the length of the hair, but you get the idea. Here's the moral of the story: compromise will always cost you.

Compromise can occur in so many different areas of our lives. We can compromise our integrity with a business deal, compromise our marriage to gratify a momentary physical desire, compromise our physical well-being by making poor health choices, and even compromise our financial stability with quick get-rich schemes. In Romans 13:14, Paul says, "But put on the Lord Jesus Christ, and make no provision for the flesh in regard to its lusts." Making a provision for your flesh is compromise. As Christians, we have been called to live an uncompromised life.

What are the areas in your life today in which you find yourself compromising? What are the steps you need to take today to live in an uncompromised life? When we live a life where we are unwilling to compromise our beliefs, values, and integrity, we will point people towards Christ.

Make today count!

Day 113

I'm sure you have heard it said, "God will not give you more than you can handle." I'm pretty sure that until I was around 20 years old, I believed this was found somewhere in the Bible. I was shocked when I intentionally went looking for this passage and could not find it. The reason I couldn't find it is because, well, it is not in there. This phrase has become very commonly used and is a very dangerous Christian cliché that we tell people who are journeying through a difficult time in life.

I have found myself to be guilty of being the person who has said this to another person. I have also been the recipient of it. It feels good to say and to hear. The problem is it is biblically inaccurate. I believe the opposite is true. Oftentimes God will give us exceedingly more than we can handle. When we find ourselves in these situations, we have to draw strength from him and depend on him. If you haven't already experienced a time in your life when you felt you had been given more than you can handle, I can assure you it's coming. I'm not sure if God sends or if he simply allows the storms in life. I am absolutely sure though that he works through them. In Romans 8:28, Paul says, "And we know that for those who love God all things work together for good, for those who are called according to his purpose." Nowhere does this verse say this will be easy. In fact, I believe it will be difficult, but we must remember who is ultimately in control and that he is weaving together a larger picture than we can see.

My question for you is this: When life comes and gives you more than you can handle, where will you turn?

Make today count!

Day 114

For several nights in a row last week, Cade was fearful while he was in his bed trying to go to sleep. For Cade to come out of his room at any point after he's gone to bed is extremely unusual. This child could sleep through a tornado. A typical night goes something like this: brush teeth, say prayers, hug goodnight, lights off, asleep within 3 to 4 minutes. But last week something was making him experience a great sense of fear and this fear was driving him out of his room. After coming out of his room for the third time, I decided it was time for us to pray together again. I raised my hands in the air and prayed in Jesus' name that he would provide peace and calm over Cade's room. I'm assuming that at some point during this prayer Cade opened his eyes. I opened my eyes just prior to saying amen and noticed that his hands were also in the air. Cade and I never discussed this, but I believe he realized by doing this we were submitting the situation to God. We were recognizing that it was out of our hands.

I believe four posture during prayer is as important, if not even more important, than the words we say.

Jesus modeled a posture of prayer right before he went to the cross. In Matthew we see Jesus in the garden prior to his arrest facedown before the presence of his father. Matthew 26:39: "Going a little farther, he fell with his face to the ground and prayed, "My Father, if it is possible, may this cup be taken from me. Yet not as I will, but as you will." Louis Giglio refers to this as the "posture of possibility." He explains that in this posture we are humbled before the God of the universe. What an example it is for us to draw from in our private and personal prayer life, approaching God in a posture of humility, the posture of possibility.

When is the last time you truly humbled yourself with your posture as you approached the throne of God? Satan has this crazy way of shrinking God down and building us up. My challenge for you today is to spend your private prayer time in a posture of humility knowing your place and honoring God for his.

Make today count!

Day 115

As far back as my memory serves me, this has been the rainiest April we have had. We have had very few days of consecutive sunshine. I have heard several people joke about how this must be what it's like to live in Seattle. I am grateful this morning for some significant sunshine. By the looks of the forecast, we shouldn't have any storms in the near future. But here's the thing about the rain and storms—they make things grow.

In the same way, the trials of life can be incredibly frustrating. It can be difficult when we feel like we are in a constant storm. During life's storms, our faith is strengthened. Just like the roots of grass grow and are deepened due to the storm, so is our relationship with Christ and our relationship with the other people who walk through the storm with us. James 1:3 says, "For you know that when your faith is tested, your endurance has a chance to grow." Instead of viewing these trials as a storm, view them as an opportunity to grow.

My challenge for you today, regardless if you are in the middle of the storm or if you are basking in the sunshine, don't lose sight of who planted you. Today if you are in the midst of the storm, know the sunshine is coming!

Make today count!

Day 116

There are certain noises that naturally draw our attention: when you hear a police siren while you're driving a vehicle, if you have a small baby and you begin to hear the cry, or a firework busting open on the 4th of July. Not only do these sounds draw our attention, but we are able to immediately put context to them and the origin.

I have a sound that does just this for me, and it seems to only happen in the middle of the night. It's the sound of my dog coughing right before he gets sick. I can be dead asleep but will gain immediate clarity and origin when I hear this noise. It puts me into immediate action. I grab the dog as fast as possible and toss him off the bed.

I know that the majority of us desire to discern God's voice. We desire to hear His voice and have clarity of what He desires for us. The question becomes, "What do we do when we hear Him calling?" In 1 Samuel, the story of the boy Samuel is detailed. God calls him in the middle of the night multiple times. However, Samuel thinks it is his teacher, Eli.

The third time that this happens we see how Eli responds in 3:8-9 "A third time the Lord called, "Samuel!" And Samuel got up and went to Eli and said, "Here I am; you called me." Then Eli realized that the Lord was calling the boy, so Eli told Samuel, "Go and lie down, and if He calls you, say, 'Speak, Lord, for your servant is listening.'" So Samuel went and lay down in his place."

What I have found to be true in my whole life, and it seems rooted in the Scriptures, is that God is not one to compete with the noise in our lives. He speaks when we are quiet. Just as Samuel and Eli had difficulty identifying the voice of God, I believe the same is easily true of us. When we do recognize the origin of the voice, we must move into action.

My challenge for you today is to allow yourself the opportunity to hear from God. Set aside time where you can be quiet before him. When you hear His voice, take action!

Make today count!

Day 117

I'm pretty particular about my car. As a guy with two young kids, I would put my car's cleanliness up against anyone else who is in a situation similar to mine. I usually wash my car at least once a week. It has actually become part of my and Abi Kate's Friday date. Two days ago, I decided it made the most financial sense for me to join a wash club at the car wash. For a flat monthly fee, you are allowed unlimited use of the car wash. Today marks the third day I have been enrolled in this unlimited wash club. I have already washed my car twice and I can't guarantee you that I won't make it three for three today. There's something about having an incredibly clean car, and the best part is the price has already been paid.

Because Christ has paid the penalty for our sins, we have unlimited access to God. I can honestly say there are times when I don't take full advantage of this wonderful privilege. Hebrews 10:19-21 says, "Therefore, brothers and sisters, since we have confidence to enter the Most Holy Place by the blood of Jesus, by a new and living way opened for us through the curtain, that is, his body, and since we have a great priest over the house of God." The most holy place is in reference to where the high priest made sacrifices for the people. He was the only person allowed to enter the Holy of Holies. When Jesus died, he created direct access for us to God. There was no longer a need to go through a priest. We have the unbelievable ability to access the God of the universe immediately, directly, and unlimited times.

I can promise you that I'm going to take full advantage of my unlimited access to the car wash. My question for you today is, are you going to leverage the unlimited access you have to God?

Make today count!

Day 118

Holly has come down with what we believe to be the flu. She is awaiting the official diagnosis today. I decided the best option for me last night was to sleep on the couch just in case our diagnosis was correct. Around 2:30 in the morning, I heard Abi Kate's door open and she came around the corner of the living room and sprinted into the darkness to put her cup on the kitchen counter. She then sprinted back towards my bedroom.

I don't know about you, but I can remember in great detail being scared of the dark as a kid. Any time I would have to cross a dark area, I would run as hard as I could to get it over with as quick as possible. I stood up and came behind Abi Kate and asked what she needed. She said she needed some water. I begin to make my way towards the kitchen in the dark. When I looked behind me, I saw Abi Kate walking calmly behind me. She wasn't sprinting and she had no fear because her father was in front of her.

I believe it to be a safe assumption to say that as adults, fear of the dark probably is not a very prevalent fear. I do think, however, that many of us fear a different type of darkness—death. I was thinking about how the situation last night relates to our spiritual lives. We have the ability to face darkness because our father has already gone ahead of us. Jesus' death and resurrection provided a way for us to walk into the kitchen without fear. Deuteronomy 31:8: "The LORD is the one who goes ahead of you; He will be with you He will not fail you or forsake you. Do not fear or be dismayed." With your father ahead of you, you have nothing to fear.

Today if you find yourself with a fear of what's to come, I would encourage you to know that your father is ahead of you. John 3:16: "For God so loved the world that he gave his one and only son, that anyone who believes in him will not perish but have eternal life."

Make today count!

Day 119

Yesterday afternoon was absolutely beautiful. The kids and I decided to take a scoot around the neighborhood. They each have scooters, and I like to ride my longboard. The first part of our track was slightly uphill, then once we turned the corner, the second part of our trip was primarily slightly downhill. I looked over at Cade as we were beginning the downhill and he had one foot on his brake, and with the other foot, he was pushing on the road as hard as he could. I explained to him that if he would take his foot off the brake, with good pushes, he could coast down the hill without doing anything but standing on his scooter. Once he discovered this, it made his trip down the hill much more enjoyable.

This made me think about how many of us operate in our spiritual lives. We are in a personal relationship with Christ, but something within us leads us to believe we must work to earn this free gift that has already been given to us. It's just like keeping your foot on the brake of a scooter while going downhill and trying to pedal yourself. Salvation is a free gift that we cannot earn or deserve. It is really an exercise in vain to try to do enough good deeds to stand as worthy before God.

In a letter Paul wrote to the church at Ephesus he said, "For it is by grace you have been saved, through faith—and this is not from yourselves, it is the gift of God—not by works, so that no one can boast." Our deeds should point others to Christ, but on their own they cannot make us worthy to stand before him.

Today if you are in a personal relationship with Christ, you can put both feet on the scooter. What he did was enough. Allow your good deeds to flow from the excess love he has given you.

Make today count!

Day 120

I had a first yesterday. I got to ride in a bright red convertible Ferrari. This thing was absolutely unbelievable. I was told the exhaust on the car was worth around $25,000. This car cost more than my house. To hear the sound of the exhaust as we went through a tunnel was unbelievable. It was incredibly loud, and the thing is, we weren't even driving fast. I believe this car has somewhere around 500 horse power. The speedometer topped out around 240 mph. I believe the highest speed limit in the area we drove around in was 40 miles per hour. We might have hit 55 at one point. A Ferrari is not made for roads that have low speed limits. This thing is made to be driven on the autobahn or on a race track where it can really be opened up.

Each one of us has lost a close loved one to death. Death is ridiculously hard to grasp. There's something about death that just doesn't feel right. It's like we were meant for more. Philippians 3:20 adds truth to this statement: "But our citizenship is in heaven. And we eagerly await a savior from there, the Lord Jesus Christ." We are meant to be in eternity with God forever but because of sin, death has come on the scene. Our lives here are like driving a Ferrari in a 30 mile per hour zone. We were meant for so much more.

Today I hope this scripture serves as a reminder that we are not meant to make our treasures here on Earth. Let's strive for things that will matter in eternity.

Make today count!

Day 121

Without a doubt my grandmother was one of the biggest influences on my life. She was a godly woman with a bit of Southern sass. She was never shy about making her opinion known. She had the heart of a servant and the mind of a leader. She had deep care and concern for each member of her family. She instilled deep roots of faith and prayer into my life. She was confident in her relationship with God. She prayed fervently over each one of her children and grandchildren. She has left a Godly legacy that will continue to far outlive her life. I know that my sentiment about my grandmother is shared by many others in my family.

Legacies are not made overnight. Legacies are in the small decisions that we make each and every day. Legacies are not made by impulse. Legacies are made by consistency. Day after day striving and pushing. I love how Dr. Stephen Covey says it: "Begin with the end in mind." Think about the legacy you want to leave and work backwards from there. Proverbs 13:22 says, "A good person leaves an inheritance for their children's children, but a sinner's wealth is stored up for the righteous."

The question today is how do you want to be remembered? If we are to begin with the end in mind and work backwards, this will help to influence the decisions and habits we focus on today. What step do you need to take today to begin to leave the legacy you desire?

Make today count!

Day 122

As a kid, I remember going to Opryland quite a few times. I could never bring myself to ride any of the big rides like The Hangman. About as far as I would go was the Screaming Delta Demon. It was on an eighth-grade trip to Williamsburg, Virginia, with my school that I finally overcame my fear of rides. My friend Jonathan talked me into riding a rollercoaster where your feet dangle and it does all sorts of flips and corkscrews. I was absolutely scared to death as we began to take off, but as soon as we were in motion, I realized I had been missing out on something amazing. To this day, I still love roller coasters.

I believe fear has the ability to move us into one of two places—back to the familiar or into a place of faith. The day my friend convinced me to get on the roller coaster moved me into a place of faith. Had I chosen to sit on the sidelines, I would have gone back to what I had known as familiar, watching people ride rollercoasters instead of being on the rollercoaster myself.

Hebrews 11:1 says, "Now faith is the assurance of things hoped for, the conviction of things not seen." Taking steps of faith is almost a guarantee that you're taking steps into the unknown. But that's where trust in God comes into the picture.

Where are you currently allowing your fear to push you back into what is familiar and comfortable? What will it take for you to take the step of faith you know God has called you to? When God calls you to take a step of faith, you can know that big things are on the other side of it.

Make today count!

Day 123

Yesterday I was helping a buddy move some things at his house. A few of the neighbors stopped by to say hello to him since they had not seen him in a little while. An older gentleman came over and began to chat with us. At some point during the conversation, someone started explaining a new form of technology that had recently been released. The older gentleman responded and said, "My days of learning are over." For some reason his comment struck me. This man was probably in his mid to late 70's. I'm sure that through the course of the years, this man has gained some incredible knowledge and wisdom. However, I highly doubt he has learned everything there is to learn. I started thinking about how I hope that when I am his age, I still have the desire to learn new things and challenge myself to be the best version of myself possible.

Solomon, an Old Testament king, was given the choice of anything in the world that he wanted. He chose wisdom. He was said to be so wise that kings and queens from far and wide would come to sit underneath his teaching. Proverbs 15:14, "The discerning heart seeks knowledge, but the mouth of a fool feeds on folly." As followers of Christ, I believe we should have the desire to acquire as much knowledge as we can. When we look at the life of Jesus, scripture says he grew in wisdom and in stature and in favor with God and man.

How are you being challenged today? What book are you reading? Who are you meeting with who is making you wiser?

Make today count!

Day 124

Yesterday my kids were given a pretty awesome gift. A good friend of mine gave them a go-cart. They were beyond excited about it as you can imagine. The go-cart had not been run in a few years so it required a little bit of work to get it up and running. All four of the tires were deflated. My friend suggested infusing them with tire slime prior to inflating them. I had never used this tire slime before. The way it works is the gel is pumped into the deflated tire then the tire is filled with air. If there are any small holes in the tire or if the tire gets a hole in the future, this gel will automatically fill in those spots keeping the tire inflated.

In life each of us will experience times when we have a "flat." Things will come up unexpectedly. Problems will arise without any notice. If we are not filled with the right things, these problems will deflate us. Hebrews 4:12 says, "For the word of God is living and active, sharper than any two-edged sword, piercing to the division of the soul and the spirit, of the joints and the marrow, and discerning the thoughts and intentions of the heart." We need to fill our minds and hearts with the Word of God so that when punctures (problems) come, we will be sustained.

What are you filling yourself with? Are you surrounding yourself with a community that is deepening your roots in Christ? When life comes and you experience a puncture, will you be deflated or will you be able to continue rolling?

Make today count!

Day 125

I got to spend some time recently with a high-capacity leader. This person is incredibly motivational and inspirational. He has set his life's work to lead others to reach their potential. He came to me to discuss a difficult situation which we both agreed that regardless of how he decided to move forward, would be a hinge point for the rest of his life. This person is someone who has committed himself to live a life of integrity, so the decision was made with integrity at the forefront. The decision carried very heavy, very real consequences, but my friend chose to keep his integrity, regardless of the cost.

Many of us have ambitious plans for our future. We aspire to affect change in the lives of others. We are very cautious about the public person we present to others, all the while not realizing that the private man will eventually come forward. To live a life of integrity is not the easiest path to take. However, if we desire to be a person of high moral character and have the respect of others, it is absolutely necessary. Proverbs 11:3 states, "The integrity of the upright guides them, but the unfaithful are destroyed by their duplicity." Scripture is clear that integrity should guide the private man.

Your integrity, or lack of, will guide you privately. My question for you today is this: Does your private integrity align with your public person? What steps do you need to take today to better align these two aspects of your life?

Make today count!

Day 126

I have been working on getting the kids' go-cart up and running. Since it has been a few years since it has been fired, a few things needed to be done to it. We replaced the engine belt, installed a new battery, made sure the tires were properly inflated, and did a few other minor routine maintenance items. However, for some reason, we just could not get it started. Pull after pull, no luck. Upon further inspection, it appears that the carburetor was flooding and a replacement was needed. I have a friend who is very gifted when it comes to working with small engines. I called him to help me acquire the correct replacement part. He said before we bought one, he would swing by and take a quick look at it to make sure it didn't just need a simple cleaning. He came by yesterday and within a matter of five minutes, the go-cart was up and running. The culprit was a tiny bit of build up within the inside of the carburetor. Once it was sprayed with some cleaner, the engine started right up. This small amount of junk made the entire cart immobile. Once it was removed, the cart was zipping up and down the streets with no problem.

There was a time in my life when I carried hidden sin with me. It was my own private struggle that I believed was not affecting anyone else, and honestly, at the time, I couldn't even see how it was affecting me. Hidden sin is like the small amount of junk that was keeping the go-cart from working properly. It seemed small and hidden and unseen by people. However, the consequences of having these hidden areas in your life are catastrophic. I believe hidden sin can immobilize us to advance the kingdom of God and step into the calling he has for us. It limits our effectiveness. Proverbs 28:13: "He who conceals his transgressions will not prosper, but he who confesses and forsakes them will find compassion." Keeping our sin hidden will immobilize us. It is only when we are free from the burden of it that we are able to operate fully in the capacity God has laid out for us.

Today are you carrying around some hidden sin that is holding you back? What are the steps you need to take today to get yourself freed up and mobilized?

Make today count!

Day 127

With the go-cart up and running, the kids were anxious to take their first rides. We had talked over and over about the importance of safety while riding the cart. I made sure they had their helmets on and were strapped in with a seatbelt. I took each of them around the block a few times and they absolutely loved it. When we got done riding for the day, we pulled back into the garage and parked the car for the night. Cade looked up at me and said, "Hey, Dad, why don't you have to wear a helmet?" His question struck me because I had ingrained it into their heads that they should never be on the go-cart without wearing a helmet. My actions carried far more significance than my words.

I believe this is an important lesson for us to remember in our daily lives. People are watching our actions, the way we live our lives, more than hearing the words that come from our mouths. After the apostle Paul visited Crete, he wrote these words in Titus 1:16: "They profess to know God, but they deny him by their works. They are detestable, disobedient, unfit for any good work." For us to claim the things of God yet live a life contrary to the words coming out of our mouths only pushes people further away from the kingdom. Today what are your actions saying that your words or not?

My challenge for you today is to make sure your actions line up with your words. Don't be like me getting called out by your kids for your hypocrisy. (Side note: My helmet has been ordered and is on its way.)

Make today count!

Day 128

There is a pretty common theme in my household every morning: Abi Kate will do something to aggravate Cade. Cade will then tell me in detail everything that happened. And then this will repeat about 4,000 more times. Abi Kate is the one who antagonizes and Cade is the tattle-teller. Both have their contributing factors to the problem, but what tends to happen is that Cade begins to tattle-tale about things that aren't actually a problem. "Hey Dad, Abi Kate just said she's hungry." I believe kids tattle-tale to try to find favor with the authority figure to whom they are relaying the information. Tattle-telling drives me absolutely crazy. I would say this typically starts in early childhood, but then we move on to something far more malicious—gossip.

Gossip is really about us feeling like we have something over another person. It gives us a feeling of power and being in the know. Similar to tattle-telling, we use this gossip to attempt to gain favor with others. As Christians we often disguise gossip as a "prayer request." Proverbs 11:13 reminds us, "A gossip betrays a confidence, but a trustworthy person keeps a secret." Boiled down, gossip is a sin of pride. We allow our ego to take priority over someone else's confidentiality

My question for you today is this: Are you a person others know will keep their issues confidential? As Christ followers, we should strive to be people who are trustworthy in all walks of life.

Make today count!

Day 129

Three years ago I planted a tree in my front yard. For some reason, it began to lean forward significantly. To straighten it, I put a few stakes in the ground and attached rope higher up to anchor the tree. As the tree has continued to grow, the tree has begun to lose its forward lean. With the anchoring and the tension from the ropes on the ground, its path of trajectory has been corrected.

This is an important concept for our lives. As we continue to grow and mature, it's important that we have people who are observing our lives to see if we are pointing in the right direction. At times, the process of having someone move in to shape us can be painful. When they recognize that we need to be pulled in a different direction, it can be difficult on us and it can be difficult on them as well. Those of us who desire to follow Christ know the importance of having people who have walked the path in front of us to lead, guide, and to correct us. Proverbs 9:9: "Give instruction to a wise man, and he will be still wiser; teach a righteous man, and he will increase in learning." I believe it is important that we are on both sides of this process. First that we are being guided by someone who is further along than we are, and secondly that we are imparting wisdom and guidance to others.

The question today is, "Who is shaping you and who are you shaping?"

Make today count!

Day 130

As a kid, I remember taking the chance any time I could to explore the woods. My buddy Jordan used to call these "treks." There was no real objective to the trek, nothing in particular that we were looking for. We were simply searching for whatever we might find. Think about how many of the great archaeological finds have occurred. They happened because people took the opportunity to search.

I don't know about you, but when I think about searching, I don't think about searching within myself. In Psalms 139:23-24, King David said, "Search me, God, and know my heart; test me and know my anxious thoughts. See if there is any offensive way in me, and lead me in the way everlasting." This is a great prayer. This prayer is asking God to show us things that either we have hidden from God or things that are blind spots in our life. Blind spots are things you are unaware of. To pray this prayer will require humility. Because of our brokenness, it is a guarantee that what you hear back from God will sting a little, or maybe even a lot. If we want to experience true growth and if we want to truly pursue holiness, I believe this prayer is a great place to start.

My question for you today is are you willing to ask God to search you? Ask God to expose the areas in your life you are blind to. I promise, if you're willing to humble yourself and pray this prayer, God will answer it.

Make today count!

Day 131

To say that I have two amazing women in my life would be a drastic understatement. I am blessed beyond measure to have my mom and Holly—two strong, Godly women who encourage and support me.

I can remember from a very early age that if I needed to find my mom in the morning, she would be in her room praying over my brother and me without fail. She demonstrated what it was to have tremendous faith and trust in the power of God. She continually pushed Jared and me back to Christ in each and every situation, regardless of how much it annoyed us at the time. If you don't believe that my mom is a saint, keep in mind that she homeschooled me for one whole year and we both lived to tell about it. I believe without a doubt that I am who I am today because of the way she challenged me and prayed over me.

God knew exactly what he was doing when he gave me Holly. She has the ability to see things in me that I cannot see within myself. She has been my rock during difficult times and consistently points me back to truth. Holly is quite possibly the most selfless person on the face of the earth. She is constantly thinking of others ahead of her needs. She wants to make sure that everyone else is taken care of before considering her own needs. One area that I know I am not the best in is having mercy. This is an area Holly thrives in. She can empathize with an individual's situation and care for their needs in a way I could not even fathom. She is an amazing mom, and she has an incredible way of making special occasions even better with her special touches. I'm so grateful to have her in my life.

Proverbs 31:14-30 describes these two wonderful women. "She is like the merchant ships, bringing her food from afar. She gets up while it is still night; she provides food for her family and portions for her female servants. She considers a field and buys it; out of her earnings she plants a vineyard. She sets about her work vigorously; her arms are strong for her tasks. She sees that her trading is profitable, and her lamp does not go out at night. In her hand she holds the distaff and grasps the spindle with her fingers. She opens her arms to the poor and extends her hands to the needy. When it snows, she has no fear for her household; for all of them are clothed in scarlet. She makes coverings for her bed; she is clothed in fine linen and purple. Her husband is respected at the city gate, where he takes his seat among the elders of the land. She makes linen garments and sells them, and supplies the merchants with sashes. She is clothed with strength and dignity; she can laugh at the days to come. She speaks with wisdom, and faithful instruction is on her tongue. She watches over the affairs of her household and does not eat the bread of idleness. Her children arise and call her blessed; her husband also, and he praises her: "Many women do noble things, but you surpass them all." Charm is deceptive, and beauty is fleeting; but a woman who fears the LORD is to be praised."

Happy Mother's Day!

Make today count!

Day 132

Abi Kate is a huge fan of playing hard-to-get with me. I'll ask her to come give me a hug and she'll run the opposite direction. I'll ask her to snuggle with me on the couch and she says, "No, you sit on the other couch." She constantly makes me work for her affection. Last night I asked her if she wanted to lay on the couch with me while she was watching her movie and she said no. And then she said, "I want a new daddy." This was a new level of playing hard-to-get so I decided to flip the script on her. I said, "OK, that sounds good. I'm going to get my stuff and your new daddy will be here in a little bit." She said "OK, bye." My plan had backfired. At this point, I had to pretend like I was actually going to leave to see what she would do. She ran up to me right before I got to the door and said, "I do want you to be my daddy, but I also want another daddy. I want two daddies." I told her I would not be sharing my daddy responsibilities and privileges with anyone else and that if she wanted me, I was her only choice. To get to the end of the story, we had a wrestling match and ended the night with a big, long hug. She sure keeps life entertaining, that's for sure.

This experience shed light on one of God's Commandments. In Exodus 20:3 God says, "You should have no other gods before me." I have always known this, but this incident gave me a new understanding of it. Abigail is my child. I don't want anyone else playing the role of her father. I am her father, no one else is, and even though she's four, her telling me that she wants another dad made me feel jealous. Scripture tells us God is a jealous God. He doesn't want us to put anything ahead of him because we are his.

In our day and age, I don't think we are prone to making and worshipping physical gods. I believe our proclivity is to worship other things—maybe our children, maybe our work, and maybe even our hobbies.

Be honest with yourself—have you put anything ahead of God? Is he the object of your time and affection?

Make today count!

Day 133

Last night I had a really fun fishing trip with my mother-in-law. This was my gift to her for Mother's Day. She loves to fish but rarely gets to go, so I thought that would be a great gift for her. We had a great time and caught lots of fish. Instead of taking my normal path to get the kayaks out of the water and loaded back up into the vehicle, my friend Brad told me about an easier and better path than the one I had been using. The problem came as it was dark when I got off the water, which meant I was unable to see the landmarks he had told me about so I attempted to create my own path through some pretty thick woods. This proved to be a pretty poor idea considering the number of thorn bushes, poison ivy plants, and spider webs I came in contact with. Upon further investigation, I found the clear-cut path. This path provided room for me to walk and see. The path was not perfectly smooth. The path had some rocky spots, but compared to the other path I had been taking, it was easy.

Jesus has given us clear commandments by which to live and operate. When we operate within the confines of his laws, our path is much easier. When we choose to forge our own path, it is similar to me trying to get through the thick woods. We get bumps, bruises, and sometimes even poison ivy. We push and fight convinced that our paths will work out but, in the end, it only leads to destruction. Jesus, speaking in Luke 11:28, said, "Blessed rather are those who hear the word of God and obey it." If we put into action what we know God is calling us to, Scripture says we will be blessed. That doesn't mean our paths will be perfect. It means our paths will be much easier.

My question for you today is this: Do you find yourself rebelling against the things you know God has called you to? Are you forging your own path? Do you keep finding yourself getting hurt, stuck, or frustrated? There is another path, the path of obedience. Will you walk it?

Make today count!

Day 134

Abi Kate is just a few short months away from going to her "brother's school." Cade is greatly enjoying the ability he has to prepare her for all the things that await her at Providence Christian Academy. This morning I came into the kitchen as they were eating breakfast and they were having an in-depth conversation about all of the exciting things that will happen in kindergarten. Abi Kate was planning in great detail the things she would do on all the incredible "field trips" she would be taking. Her excitement level was almost uncontrollable. She cannot wait to be at her "brother's school."

I believe most of us think about our future. We have plans for ourselves that we hope will fall into place. Frustration tends to creep in when we are unable to successfully complete the plans we have set for ourselves. This can create a lot of frustration. Oftentimes I have taken my frustrations to God. I find myself saying things like, "God, why isn't this working out?" "God, why can't I get the money together to make this happen?"

I believe the problem exists because we forget to involve God on the front end of the planning process. We generate plans we deem best instead of praying and asking him to guide us to what he wants to complete in and through us. The writer of Proverbs has a simple solution to avoiding the frustration that comes when plans fail. Proverbs 16:3 reminds us to "Commit to the LORD whatever you do, and he will establish your plans." God's plans will prevail. It's just a matter of when/if we choose to submit ourselves to them.

Today maybe you have found that what you're striving for is keeping you stuck and frustrated and no matter what you do, you just can't seem to make it work. My question for you is this: "Are these your plans or his plans?" Invite him into the process of planning your next steps and watch to see how his purposes will prevail.

Make today count!

Day 135

From the beginning of this week through the rest of the week, the weather forecast is nothing short of grim. They are predicting a 90% chance for heavy rain and thunderstorms. Thus far, the weather forecast could not have been more incorrect. It has been beautiful and 85 degrees every day. A friend of mine had a camping trip planned, but he canceled it due to the impending forecast. He altered his plans due to what he was told would happen.

I believe this is also true for many of us when it comes to our theological beliefs or our understanding of God. Many times, we are swayed by the latest and greatest thought from people in prominent positions. The Bible warns us against this in Matthew 7:15: "Watch out for false prophets. They come to you in sheep's clothing, but inwardly they are ferocious wolves." Before we are deceived, we should check the things we hear to see if they line up with scripture.

It's an incredible thing to have the opportunity to learn from other people. God has gifted many people to draw us closer to himself, but we must be wise to make sure what we are hearing lines up so we are not led astray.

Make today count!

Day 136

Abi Kate is an incredibly mischievous child. If left alone for even the shortest amount of time, I can almost guarantee you she will have gotten into something. Yesterday I was loading some things up in my car. She was in the garage. When I turned back around to look in the garage, she had climbed up the side of one of my shelves. The other thing I failed to mention is she is a very good climber. If she can get a foothold on something, there's no telling what she will end up doing. A foothold is what gives her access.

God has already defeated Satan. He is a defeated foe, yet we find ourselves falling into temptation. The short reason for this is we have given him a foothold or access into an area of our life. Ephesians 4:26-27 says, "In your anger do not sin. Do not let the sun go down while you are still angry, and do not give the devil a foothold." Let me give you a practical example of this. If I struggle with gluttony, the best place for me to have a Bible study probably is not at Julia's Bakery. The only time Satan wins victories over us is when we allow him access. The Bible says we are more than conquerors in Christ, but we must remain close to Christ for this to be true.

What areas do you find yourself falling prey to temptation? Strategically think through what access you are giving up that is costing you victory in this area. Like Abi Kate, a foothold is all he needs.

Make today count!

Day 137

Yesterday was a super busy day. We had church and then immediately following church, Holly had to get ready for Providence Academy's high school graduation which left me picking up groceries, making lunches, and entertaining the kids. After lunch we decided to go outside and fill up their kiddie pool and have a water gun fight. When I say "we" had a water gun fight, I mean we, all of us. We were all in our swimsuits soaked to the bone. My neighbor across the street from me was hosting a high school graduation party for her daughter to which we had been invited. I didn't feel right about going to a high school graduation party considering the fact that we were not really presentable for this type of occasion. My neighbor, Nancy, saw us playing outside and basically walked the kids into her house to make sure they got some of the treats from the party. We did not necessarily fit in with the rest of the folks there. We were far more casual (and wet) than the rest of the partygoers. The thing is, it didn't matter. We had been ushered in and given access by the host.

The same is true for us spiritually. We have been invited to come into a relationship with God and to experience eternity with him. We may feel as if we are unworthy to receive this invitation based on our situations, past mistakes, and other places we have defined our worth and identity. Ephesians 2:4-9 says, "But God, being rich in mercy, because of the great love with which he loved us, even when we were dead in our trespasses, made us alive together with Christ—by grace you have been saved— and raised us up with him and seated us with him in the heavenly places in Christ Jesus, so that in the coming ages he might show the immeasurable riches of his grace in kindness toward us in Christ Jesus. For by grace you have been saved through faith. And this is not your own doing; it is the gift of God." When the host pursues you to come to a party, you come. This is the invitation God has for you today—with your wet clothes, swimsuit, and messy hair.

My question for you today is, "Will you accept the invitation he has offered you?"

Make today count!

Day 138

A few years back I had the opportunity to trade a guy swim lessons for golf lessons. He was a very experienced golfer who had played through college. At the time, I was working for the YMCA and had the opportunity to play in quite a few golf tournaments. We went out to the course and began our day of play. Within just a few short minutes, he was able to ascertain my biggest problem. It wasn't my swing. It wasn't my ability to keep my head down. It was the way I was lining up. When I approached a tee box, I would look at the flag however far away. I would make my best adjustment then hit the ball. Many times, I would find myself hitting the ball in the wrong direction. It was because I was focused on the target that was way too far away. He showed me how to place something small about 20 feet in front of me that lined up with the flagstick on the green. From there, when I set my feet, I would look 20 feet out to the ball marker or tee I had set to line myself up to. This allowed me to hit the ball the direction I was aiming for. This short intermediate target made all the difference.

What are the goals you are trying to reach? Most likely they will take some time to attain. So today, the question is, "What are the intermediate targets you need to hit to eventually lead you to your long-term goal? Currently, one of my goals is completing a 365-day devotional book. I don't think it would be possible for me to write 365 quality devotions in one day. However, I can write one devotion a day for 365 days. This is my intermediate target. 2 Chronicles 5:17: "But as for you, be strong and do not give up, for your work will be rewarded." Any goal that's worth reaching will require some persistence and time. Stick with it so you will see the fulfillment of the goal.

Today what are the goals God has put on your heart and mind? What are the intermediate targets you can aim for today to set you on the path of completing that which you have set out to do?

Make today count!

Day 139

The first car I ever owned was a five-speed Mitsubishi Eclipse. This car is the only manual-transmission car I have ever owned. It was a lot of fun to drive. I can remember one thing I did quite often. I would get the car up to a decent rate of speed (I use the word "decent" because I know my mom is reading this) to see just how far I could go keeping the car in neutral. Even now, from time to time. I find myself trying to coast into my driveway from the end of my street. When your car is in neutral, it is subject to the kinetic energy being put on it along with the slope of the terrain on which it is driving. For example, if your car is parked on a hill and you put it in neutral, it will begin to roll backwards. The result of what happens in neutral depends on what was happening right before neutral and the effects of the outside terrain.

In life, it's easy for us to go into neutral, or auto pilot, in our work, in our spiritual life, and in leading our family. When we fail to operate our life "in gear," the results will be left up to external circumstances and our last internal push. In all matters in our life, we must continue to aggressively drive towards our ambitions. Putting life on coast will not be the most effective means to reach your goals in separate areas. In Philippians 3:14, Paul reminds his readers, "I press on toward the goal to win the prize for which God has called me heavenward in Christ Jesus." Living a life that is pressing on is living a life that is in drive.

Today have you found yourself coasting in neutral? What do you need to do today to put your life in drive? My challenge for you today is to push!

Make today count!

Day 140

I'm on staff with a guy at church whose is also named Brad. Many of the staff order products from the same companies, so you can see how there could be confusion between two Brad's at the same workplace. We have an awesome men's weekend fishing trip/Bible study coming up next April. I have been investigating different swag options for this event and put in an order for a really cool hat I thought might be a good option as one of the gifts for the guys. Last night as I was browsing through Facebook, I saw that my friend Brad had posted a picture of the hat I had requested a sample of. His post read something like this: "I'm not sure who sent me this hat, but I absolutely love it! Thank you so much!" I didn't have any choice but to burst his bubble and let him know the hat was actually supposed to go to me. By claiming the same name, Brad ended up with a pretty sweet hat. This is the problem of having the same name.

Through what Christ did on the cross, we have the ability to claim his name. John 20:31 says, "But these have been written so that you may believe that Jesus is the Christ, the Son of God; and that believing you may have life in His name." This is our best and only option for standing before a holy and perfect God. By claiming his name, we are claiming the right to eternal life with him.

Whose name are you claiming today? Are you claiming his or your own?

Make today count!

Day 141

Another school year has come and gone, the progression of which can be measured through a number of avenues. I love to see everyone's first-day-of-school versus last-day-of-school photos. In most cases, it's pretty clear which is which. Children grow in stature. Cade came home with an end-of-year summary notebook. This is the accumulation of all the things he has learned this year. These pictures and pieces of paper are a physical representation of the mental progress made over the course of the last school year. The second book Cade brought home was his Bible notebook. These are all of the Bible stories and verses they have learned throughout the past year. My hope is that these verses penetrate his heart.

It's so easy for us to gauge progress at the end of each school year with our students, but what does progress look like for us?

We know very little about Jesus from his childhood to the beginning of his ministry. One of the few verses we find regarding this time in his life reveals somewhat of an end-of-year progress report. Luke 2:52 says, "And Jesus grew in wisdom and stature, and in favor with God and man." As adults, I would say the majority of us do not take a yearly assessment where we actually look back to see all the things and ways we have learned or progressed. I don't think we should ever reach a point where we say our growth is finished. I believe God has given us the capacity to learn and create, and these things are given to us so we can in turn worship God for the gifts he has given us.

How are you growing in wisdom and knowledge today? What is a challenge you could give yourself over the next 30 days to sharpen your mind and your understanding of God?

Make today count!

Day 142

Last night we had an awesome event at church that happens twice a year, called "Man Church." This particular one was themed around a car cruise in. We had several amazing vehicles on site for guys to check out.

A good friend of mine is one of the managers at Nissan and was able to acquire one of the new Nissans GTR's. This car retails in the neighborhood of $140,000. It's a sports car that has the ability to set you back in your seat when the gas pedal is hammered. I got to go for a test drive in it last night and was so impressed with how intelligent this car is.

If this car is put into a manual transmission mode, and the driver makes a mistake, the car will automatically put itself into automatic mode to correct for the driver's missed gear changes. The computer will make corrections as soon as the driver makes a mistake so the engine is not ruined. Simple truth, the computer is much smarter than the driver.

I don't think there's a single person who would be operating this $140,000 vehicle that would be upset with the computer if it shifted into automatic transmission while they were driving it. The driver would understand that the computer made this change to keep them from the disaster that could be ahead.

Oftentimes we get frustrated when God keeps something from us. We feel we have something under control and then God, in His sovereignty, changes it. Then, on the other side of the coin, when God doesn't take something from us and destruction comes, we ask God why He would allow that to happen.

The sovereignty of God is something we will not completely grasp until we are on the other side of this life. Why God chooses to intervene in certain circumstances and not in others is a difficult thing to understand. Psalm 135:6: "Whatever the Lord pleases, he does, in heaven and on earth, in the seas and all deeps." God will do what he wants to do regardless if we understand or not.

Today many of you are dealing with situations where you feel God should or should not have intervened. As a child of God, you must trust that just like the computer on the GTR is smarter than the driver, God is smarter than you. Your best interest, your Holiness are at his discretion.

Make Today count!

Day 143

School has come to an end and family vacation has come upon us. We decided to spend this week with my brother and his family in Florida. It is truly the perfect destination for us. We get to see family, we're close to the beach, and we're close to all the various attractions Florida has to offer. As you all know, it takes quite a bit of work to get prepared to go on vacation, but the importance of spending some time away out of the normal routine is something we hold dear. It's important for all of us to get outside our normal routine in some capacity to allow our hearts and minds to be rejuvenated so we can come back to work refreshed and ready to bring our best each day.

As important as it is for us to take time to physically rest, the same is even true when it comes to spiritual matters. It's so easy for us to continue to carry our burdens and stress on our own. In Matthew 11:28 Jesus says, "Come to me, all who labor and are heavy laden, and I will give you rest. Take my yoke upon you, and learn from me, for I am gentle and lowly in heart, and you will find rest for your souls. For my yoke is easy, and my burden is light." Jesus came to give us spiritual rest. We can bring our load to him and rest in the fact that he can bear it.

Today do you find yourself needing rest? Maybe you need physical rest. I would suggest you take a day to get away alone and spend some time with God to do something you enjoy doing. Maybe you need spiritual rest. Take it to the God of the universe who wants to bear your burdens.

Make today count!

Day 144

Since I was a small child, the weekend of Memorial Day has marked the official kickoff to summer. As a child, I never really gave much thought to the holiday itself. Honestly, I just assumed it was a barbecue to let everybody know school was out and the pool was filled. As an adult, I now reflect on this holiday in a completely new manner. My sister-in-law has a sign in her home that reads, "Home of the free, because of the brave." This is so fitting for this holiday as we remember the ultimate sacrifice so many paid for our freedom. It is because of their sacrifice we are free to enjoy all the privileges we hold so dear. John 15:13 reminds us, "Greater love has no one than this: to lay down one's life for one's friends."

The freedom we have in Christ comes through Christ. His sacrifice yielded our freedom from sin and freedom from an eternity separated from him. Ephesians 1:7-8 says, "Because of the sacrifice of the Messiah, his blood poured out on the altar of the cross, we're a free people—free of penalties and punishments chalked up by all our misdeeds. And not just barely free either. Abundantly free!" Not only are we free, but we have an abundance of freedom. Abundance is defined as existing or available in large quantities; plentiful. Christ offers us life to the full.

Today we have so many reasons to be thankful. As Americans, we have been given so many amazing freedoms that are not to be taken lightly. As followers of Christ, we've been given freedom that not only affects us here on earth but will extend into eternity. How are you using your freedoms today?

Make today count!

Day 145

Oftentimes when making commitments, they are easier to keep on the front end but become increasingly difficult as time passes. I have made a commitment to write 365 devotions in 365 days. I started this process last October. There are days when it is very easy for me to keep this commitment because I have an idea that is clear. On other days, it can be incredibly difficult. I found that the first and best tip to me keeping this commitment is to ask God to give me wisdom and clarity each day as I consider what to write about. Like so many other things, I believe the commitments we make and keep are acts of worship given to God one step at a time.

In second Timothy 4:7, Paul says, "I have fought the good fight, I have finished the race, I have kept the faith." Each of us should aspire to say that whatever we have made commitments to do, we push through to see them to completion. What are things you have committed to today? How have you done keeping these commitments? What are the next steps you need to take to bring them to completion?

My challenge for you today is to list three things you have committed to do over the next 30 days. This will serve as a quick reminder each day to help you take the daily steps needed to see them through.

Make today count!

Day 146

For weeks now Holly and I have been planning a trip to Legoland with our kids, my brother, his wife, and his two boys. We've really been excited about it and have kept it a secret from both sets of children. My son Cade absolutely loves Legos and we knew he would probably be the most excited about where we were going. We woke up early this morning and told them we were going to "Muscle Beach" just to throw them off and to explain the long car ride. As we began to drive, the rain began to fall. The closer we got, the harder it rained. We made it to the park and the kids' excitement level was unmatched. Unfortunately, the rain did not let up. Because of the rain, many of the attractions were closed, but we huddled together and made the decision to make the best of the time we had to share together. The weather didn't change, but our outlook did, and it ended up being a great day filled with great memories. Sometimes you can't change the external weather, but you can change the internal weather.

Paul, the writer of the majority of the New Testament, had an internal perspective that was impossible to shake due to outside circumstances. Many of his letters were written while he was in prison and what we see is that he writes them with a great amount of joy and thanksgiving. Paul wrote in Philemon 1:1, "I Paul, a prisoner of Christ Jesus, and Timothy our brother," then in verse 3 he says, "Grace and peace to you from God our Father and the Lord Jesus Christ." He's clearly not letting his external circumstances dictate his internal joy. Joy is a choice. Many times, in life it's very easy to allow the external weather to dictate our internal response. The fact is that you have the choice to control your thoughts and attitude.

Today if you're being honest with yourself, do you allow external circumstances to dictate your internal attitudes and behaviors? What adjustments can you make to find joy in your current situation?

Make today count!

Day 147

Legoland has an area devoted to giving kids the opportunity to do things in a protective environment that they would otherwise not get the chance to do. They have one experience called driving school and another experience called boating school. Driving school has mini vehicles. The kids watch a short video about how to operate the vehicle and learn the rules of the road. The roadway is lined with traffic lights, stop signs, and even a traffic circle. This experience allows them to experience what it's really like to drive in a controlled environment. In the boating school, the boat begins on the track, but within about 30 feet of getting into the boat, the child is completely in control. The boats have rubberized bumpers on them so if the child makes a mistake, they will bump right off the rail and continue to progress down the river. The kids absolutely loved this opportunity to get hands on with some typically adult opportunities.

I believe there's a strong takeaway for each of us who are parenting young children. It's important that we spend time with our kids letting them into our world and helping them understand how things work and why we do the things we do. Oftentimes my kids will sit next to me in the morning while I'm writing my morning devotion or come in the door while I am reading my Bible. Allowing them to sit in definitely makes both of these things more difficult, but it is helping to shape who they will become in the future. This applies to spiritual and non-spiritual matters. If you're good at working on cars, by allowing your children to sit and work with you, you are pouring into them and investing in them. Proverbs 22:6 reminds us, "Train up a child in the way he should go; even when he is old, he will not depart from it." Each child has particular bents and talents. It is our job to help them navigate these as they grow up, but more importantly, we are teaching them about God's great and redeeming love.

Today if you are doing a self evaluation, would you say you are doing a good job providing your child "Legoland opportunities?" Are you pushing your child to become the best version of themselves they can be? And are you pointing them to the maker of heaven and earth?

Make today count!

Day 148

We spent our day yesterday at the beach. We borrowed a few boogie boards from my nephews to ride the waves. Cade had never really tried to ride the waves on his own before. For those of you who have never boogie boarded, it is a wide board about the length of a child's torso. If you wait until the waves are about to crash then jump out in front of them as they crash, it will take you for a ride as long as you can stay on the board. The key to catching a good wave is timing it right before it begins to crash. Cade was having a difficult time understanding the concept of when to jump out. If you jump too early, the wave will simply roll over you. If you jump too late, you will miss it altogether. For the maximum ride, you have to time your jump right as the wave crashes. By the end of the day, he had it figured out. He even rode one wave all the way into the shoreline.

Timing is everything. Many times in life we are waiting for God to move or lead us in a situation. If you're anything like me, you're always questioning the right time to take a step or a leap of faith. Galatians 5:25 encourages us, "Since we live by the Spirit, let us also keep in step with the spirit." This visual aid of keeping in step with the Spirit shows us that our timing needs to be in step with God's. When God moves, we need to move. We don't jump before or after. We must keep in step. If God has called you to do something, you will have a confirmation and the clarity of the call. You will know when it's time to take your step.

Today are you waiting on a "wave?" Continue to seek God for his discernment and direction. You'll see the white tops coming and you'll know when to jump.

Make today count!

Day 149

Lately, for whatever reason, I've been walking with several couples who are considering divorce. Some of these couples have children and others do not. I see many similarities between these couples.

The biggest commonality is that the majority of the time the individuals are very good at pointing out the faults of their partner. It is so easy for them to see the shortcomings the other party brings to the table. However, it is much more difficult for them to see how they are contributing to the issues in the marriage.

There are some situations where one party is the sole contributor (infidelity, abuse, etc.), but in most situations, both parties have contributed to the issues that have risen to the surface. Another thing that seems to be universal between these couples is that they often say they don't "feel" in love anymore. The thought that love is a feeling is a fallacy. Love is a choice.

Marriage was designed for our holiness, as a way to shape us to be more like Christ. Marriage is not about what we can receive, but what we can give. There's no question that marriage can be incredibly difficult at times.

I believe it is very important for us to remember that we have made a covenant between our spouse, ourselves, and God. When we don't feel the feelings of love, we must choose love. God is very clear on his stance on divorce. Malachi 2:16 says, "God hates divorce."

I use an analogy in premarital counseling explaining that divorce is like this . . . taking two separate pieces of paper, putting super glue on each of them, sticking the two pieces together, and letting them dry completely. After the two pages are completely dry and stuck together, trying to separate the two pieces and make them two individual pieces again would be an exercise in vain as each piece would have shards of paper from the other attached to it. Neither piece would be completely whole. This is what divorce does to families. I know many of you come from divorced homes or have walked through a divorce. I understand the hardships and difficulties you have gone through, as I have walked with several families who have gone through this process. My cry today for those of you who are married and contemplating divorce is to take divorce off the table. Set your pride to the side and see where you are contributing to the problems. As the two of you individually seek God and become closer to God, He will start to heal the wounds and bring you closer together.

My challenge for you today is to choose love. Choose the vow you have taken before God, your family, and friends.

Make today count!

Day 150

Holly and I seriously began dating when I was a sophomore in college. One night we were hanging out in her dorm room when this strange feeling overtook me. It was a deep fear, an unexplainable worry. Looking back now, I can identify this as God helping me realize this was my future wife. I had never been in a serious relationship prior to Holly, so I didn't really know how it was supposed to look or what to do. My anxiety got so bad I began to feel sick and actually did get sick at her dorm. I went back to my house feeling this terrible sense of panic. At the time, I had just transitioned back to Tennessee from Indiana so I was living with my parents for a few months before I got a place with a couple buddies. I got home and went to bed and woke up in the middle of the night with the greatest sense of uncontrollable fear I have ever experienced in my life. This panic attack (later identified) was just one of many that would come over me in the next year and a half.

According to the American Anxiety and Depression Association, 18.1% of the U.S. population struggles with anxiety so there's no doubt in my mind that many of you reading this have or are experiencing what I am talking about. Anxiety is defined as a "feeling of worry, nervousness, or unease, typically about an imminent event or something with an uncertain outcome." After visits with the doctor, some prescription medicine, and some counseling with my dad, we were able to identify the root of my fear which was the fear of commitment. Identifying the source of the anxiety is the first step in finding relief. I continued to struggle with anxiety attacks even after I had identified the source. My ultimate relief in anxiety did not come until I stopped keeping the matter private and went public with my church body during a time of prayer and asked them to pray over me. This is an incredibly humbling thing to do as none of us want to admit we do not have it all together, but not until I was willing to completely give up my unfound fears and concerns was I finally able to live on the other side of panic attacks.

1 Peter 5:6-8 encourages us, "Humble yourselves, therefore, under God's mighty hand, that he may lift you up in due time. Cast all your anxiety on him because he cares for you. Be alert and of sober mind. Your

enemy the devil prowls around like a roaring lion looking for someone to devour." Our God wants to carry our worries and he has the ability to carry them because he carries tomorrow. He is ahead of them. He is behind them.

If you are struggling with anxiety, my prayer for you today is to stop living in silence about it. Seek help, seek the source, and seek the Lord. The things in your future won't control you when you know God is already present in the days to come.

Make today count!

Day 151

Year after year, I can't seem to escape that first summer sunburn. Spending the bulk of my working career in outdoor pool environments, my skin has definitely had its fair share of exposure to the sun. Typically in the summer, I have a nice golden-brown look—not counting the first week of summer. This is where I wear my lobster about-to-be-boiled look. As those of you who have had a good sunburn know, taking a shower is a burning reminder that you did not put on enough sunscreen. Once a sunburn has occurred, the best option is to treat it with topical lotions and to be sure to apply plenty of sunscreen until the burn has subsided. For some reason, I just can't learn to put on enough sunscreen at the beginning of the summer.

I think of sunburns like making a mistake. The mistake will have natural consequences that go along with it. Typically, there is a solution to help repair the mistake that was made. For example, if I told a lie to cover something up, then the solution to unravel the mistake would be to come forward with the truth. The problem is that once the burn has healed, we tend to forget about it and we find ourselves tempted to put ourselves back in the same situation the burn put us in in the first place. In Romans 7:15, Paul clearly articulates the struggle we all have: "For I do not understand my own actions. For I do not do what I want, but I do the very thing I hate." Wisdom is allowing these burns to serve as a marker in our memory to keep us from allowing them to happen again.

Today my challenge for you is to think back on some of the ways you have burnt yourself because of your selfish desires and you chose to sin. Set it aside as a marker in your mind so you do not repeat the very thing that cost you this hurt to begin with.

Make today count!

Day 152

I am an incredibly vivid dreamer at night. Most mornings I can recall with great detail the dream I had that night. Some mornings I awaken convinced for a short while that whatever I just dreamed actually happened. Two nights ago, I had the most vivid dream about being at the Smoothie King inside the downtown YMCA ordering my favorite smoothie, the banana boat with peanut butter. It's been a long time since I've had this smoothie. After getting ready the next morning, I took a non-typical route to the church to make sure I could stop by where?? You guessed—Smoothie King. I picked up a delicious banana boat with peanut butter. It was every bit as delicious as my dream reminded me it would be.

My question for you today is this: Where are your dreams driving you? I believe God has put within each of us various skills and abilities. Our particular set of skills align with the way we think to solve the problems in the dreams we will chase after. Proverbs 21:5: "The plans of the diligent lead surely to abundance." When we pursue the dreams God has given us with diligence, he will bless them.

Where are your dreams driving you today? What are the steps you need to take in order to move closer towards the dream God has laid on your heart?

Make today count!

Day 153

Cade and Abigail have been eagerly anticipating building the Lego sets they purchased while we were at Legoland last week. Abi Kate got a small Beauty and the Beast set. There is no way she would be able to put the set together on her own. She needed help, and Holly and I thought the best person for the job was our Lego master builder, Cade. Cade patiently sat with his sister explaining piece by piece the correct order the Legos needed to be placed in order to bring the picture on the front of the box to life. With Cade's help, Abigail was able to assemble her Beauty and the Beast set and she enjoyed playing with it for the rest of the night.

This picture is a great visual of life. All of us will reach a point in our lives where we do not have the solution. We will reach a point in our life where we have to rely on the strength and wisdom of others. Galatians 6:2 says, "Carry each other's burdens, and in this you will fulfill the law of Christ." I believe the different circumstances in our lives we personally have to walk through are opportunities for us to then walk alongside another individual as they go through a similar trial.

Today you could find yourself in one of two places in this message. Maybe today you need to hear you have something valuable to share with people who have walked through the same hurts you have experienced and come through. Have the courage to share what God taught you and lend a listening ear. Some of you have found yourself stuck today like Abigail. You can't "build" what's in front of you on your own. It's time to humble yourself and find someone who can help you pick up the pieces and put them together.

Make today count!

Day 154

In our fast-paced, immediate access world we live in, it's easy to become addicted to staying busy. Many of us do not know how to handle down time. We look to our phones for social media to fill our voids and we will create new projects for ourselves that don't necessarily need to be done. Many times, I've heard people say, "Well, I would do that, but I'm just too busy." The reality is that much of the busyness we experience we put on ourselves. These additional responsibilities create unnecessary stress in our lives.

I assume you are l like me in that many times when I'm reading the Bible, I will read a verse and realize that it's a new thought to me, as if I had never read it before. I ran across this verse this morning: "But Jesus often withdrew to lonely places and prayed" (Luke 5:16). We understand the word "often" to mean with frequency. Jesus understood the importance of taking time to be alone in prayer and to allow himself rest. Maybe you are thinking, "Brad, of course we should be taking time alone frequently." There's no question that taking time alone with God in the morning should be an important part of your day. What I am actually talking about is when the tension mounts and the busyness sets in, we should pause and take time to get quiet.

If you're being honest with yourself, are you addicted to busyness? Are you taking time to fill your soul and mind through prayer and quietness alone with God?

Make today count!

Day 155

This morning I'm preparing to take the kids for their six-month dental checkup. Something about going to the dentist makes me feel obligated to brush their teeth just a little better than normal. I guess internally somewhere down deep I believe that if they were to have some type a cavity or something, this extra 35 seconds of brushing should do the trick. All of us are smart enough to know that cavities happen over time. A trip to the dentist reminds us of the importance of brushing. An extra 30 seconds of brushing right before seeing the dentist isn't going to do anything except maybe improve one's breath.

I think we tend to try to do the same thing with God. Our default tends to be based on what we do. We tend to do an extra good deed, say an extra prayer, or toss an extra $20 into the offering plate, as if any of these things are going to improve our standing with God. Ephesians 2:8 reminds us, "For it is by grace you have been saved, through faith--and this is not from yourselves, it is the gift of God." We cannot "brush our teeth" enough to stand perfect before a holy God. It is not about our works; it is all about his grace.

Today do you find yourself trying to "brush your teeth" so to speak to keep a right standing with God? God does not love you based on your works. God loves you because he made you, even with all those Oreo crumbs in your mouth.

Make today count!

Day 156

Cade and Abigail are both really enjoying swimming this summer. Cade has gotten to the place where he has a pretty good freestyle stroke. Where he struggles is taking a breath on the side then putting his face back in and continuing to swim. After working with him for about 35 minutes or so yesterday, he was able to swim across a large section of the pool. The depth of the pool was 3'6" where we had been swimming and it began to get pretty crowded, so we decided to move to the far end of the pool. On this end of the pool, Cade was unable to touch the bottom which caused him a great deal of fear. It took me having a conversation with him. I encouraged him that the depth of the water was not relevant to the ability he had. After some convincing, he got in and swam even further than he had on the more shallow end. He had grown comfortable in the shallow end. When we remain comfortable, we can easily fall into complacency. With Cade's newfound swimming abilities, many new opportunities will be available for him at the pool. He'll be able to enjoy all it has to offer including slides and diving boards.

It's easy for us to become complacent in a comfortable setting within our lives. We grow used to a routine and the way we are serving and being used. When new opportunities arise that push us into the "deep end," we tend to give all the reasons why we're not ready.

Philippians 4:13 is one of the first power verses I remember memorizing as a child. It says, "I can do all things through Christ who gives me strength." We have the power, skills, and abilities God has given us to do the things he has called us to. If God has called you to step out into a new area of the "pool," then take that step knowing he has equipped you. Don't allow your comfort to hold you hostage to complacency. God has more for you in the deep end.

Make today count!

Day 157

There's no question that it's our job as parents to teach our children a multitude of things. The further I go along in parenting; I realize our kids probably teach us just as much as we teach them. Yesterday my two nephews came over to play with my kids. They are between my kids in age. My nephew Aiden was playing with Abigail when they began to have a disagreement about whose turn it was with a particular toy. Abigail had been playing with this toy and it was now Aiden's turn. Abigail then tried her best to keep the toy away from Aiden, but after a little convincing, she shared the toy with him. Aiden told Abi Kate he forgave her then asked her if she wanted to go play trucks on the patio. My sister-in-law looked at me and said, "And just like that, everything's fine."

I think the ability children have to truly forgive is something we as adults can learn from. I believe we tend to fall more in the camp of reminding the person how they offended us or we go and talk about it with other people rather than forgiving the offense. Forgiveness is incredible. Jesus seemed to understand this would be a tough principal for us to grasp. In Matthew 5:39 Jesus says, "I tell you, do not resist an evil person. If anyone slaps you on the right cheek, turn to them the other cheek also." This is completely contrary to the way we operate. If someone slaps us in the face, we're going to slap them back in self-defense then sue them for assault. From the pure heart of a child, we see the type of forgiveness Jesus taught. If only we could extend the forgiveness we desire to receive.

Who is it you need to forgive today? Christ has forgiven you much. Should you not also forgive others for the things they have done to you? I'll leave you with a question: How is your unwillingness to forgive that person benefiting you in a positive way?

Make today count!

Day 158

If I were to ask those closest to me to draw a sketch of me in my "typical" attire, I believe most of them would be quick to include a pair of Ray-Ban sunglasses in their sketch. I started wearing Ray-Ban's about eight years ago. It's rare to see me without a pair of sunglasses on. I spent so much of my career hanging out by pools that they are just a part of my everyday attire now. What I particularly love about my Ray-Bans is that the lenses are polarized. What polarization does is reduces the glare. If you are fishing on the river without sunglasses, you would only be able to see the surface of the water, but if you are wearing glasses such as the ones I wear, you can see through the water because the reflection has been pushed away. This gives you the ability to see things you would be unable to see with just your naked eye.

The same way that polarized sunglasses give you the ability to see things, I believe God can give us the ability to see spiritual things to understand him on a deeper level. In Ephesians 1:18, Paul prays the following over his readers: "I pray that the eyes of your heart may be enlightened in order that you may know the hope to which he has called you, the riches of his glorious inheritance in his holy people." This is my prayer over each of you today, that God would show you the desires he has for you and that you would step into the calling he has placed on your life.

Today would you ask God to open the eyes of your heart? Ask him to show you things you have never seen before.

Make today count!

Day 159

As a child, birthdays definitely rank in the top five most exciting things that happen each year. The anticipation and excitement leading up to my birthday as a kid was almost more than I could handle. And I don't know if you're anything like me or not, but as a kid, if I was nine, I always wanted to tell people I was almost 10. The idea of being just one year older always seemed more appealing. Birthdays serve as markers. Ten is the first time you hit double digits, 13 is your entry to your teenage years. In Tennessee, at 15 you get a learner's permit, at 16 your driver's license, and so on until you hit 60 at which time, I hear you get a pretty sweet discount at McDonald's! All joking aside, now I view my birthday as a time to reflect on the past year—how I spent it and how I will spend the next year moving forward.

I know are many of you desire to make a significant impact throughout your life. Each year as our birthday comes, we simply wonder, "How did I get here, and why aren't I where I thought I would be?" I am reminded of a leadership principle my dad engrained in me, "Inspect what you expect." This principle was incredibly easy for me to apply during my time in management at the YMCA with the staff I supervised. However, it seems to be that this type of self inspection is much more difficult, but I believe it is even more important. Lamentations 3:40 says, "Let us test and examine our ways, and return to the Lord!" True and honest self evaluation is an incredibly important part of reaching the goals and dreams God has given you.

Even if today is not your birthday, I challenge you to do some self evaluation on where you are in your life. What should you start today and what should you stop?

Make today count!

Day 160

It seems to be true for most of the families I know who have kids that one is a sleeper and the other not so much. Typically, it's Abi Kate who is up and down in the middle of the night. Last night around 2:00 in the morning, I heard footsteps coming into the bedroom but to my surprise, it was Cade. He was almost in tears and shaking just a little. He told me he had had a very scary dream and wanted to lay in our bed. I scooted over, reassured him while rubbing his back, and soon he fell back to sleep. A short while later I took him back into his room to sleep the rest of the night.

I can remember having nightmares as a child. At the time, the dream seemed so real. I never could articulate exactly what I had dreamed in the middle of the night. I also remember many times waking up in the morning and telling my mom about the dream. Once I began to process the dream out loud, the fear seemed to subside. Once the fear was processed out loud, instead of keeping it internal, it almost sounded silly and irrational.

As adults, fear is still a part of our lives. Many of us internalize rather than vocalize our deepest fears. Maybe it's the fear of losing a child, the fear of being unable to provide for your family, a fear of losing your relationship with your spouse, or maybe even a fear of failure. When we continue to internalize these fears, we only feed them and make them stronger. Spending time with a counselor or someone you trust and whom God has given the gift of wisdom will help to put these fears in their rightful place. 2 Timothy 1:7 says, "For God has not given us a spirit of fear, but one of power, love, and sound judgment." Fears are founded and established in silence and in isolation. God has not called us to live in isolation but to live in community.

My challenge for you today is to stop allowing your fears to thrive in the silence of isolation in your mind. Find a trusted person to bring your fears to light and allow God's truth to penetrate each area.

Make today count!

Day 161

All of us deal with doubt on many different levels. As a young child, you may have doubted your abilities when you began to play a certain sport or tried to learn how to ride a bike. As we get older and begin to progress to more difficult subjects, at times we may doubt if we will ever comprehend the content we are being taught. Doubt and unbelief are two completely different things. Unbelief would be saying there is no way possible for me to understand this new subject, where doubt allows for a chance of understanding the material. A classic illustration of understanding doubt is from the movie *Dumb and Dumber*. Jim Carrey's character is in love with a woman who is far out of his league. He asked her what the chances were of them ever getting together and she responds by saying, "About one in 1 million." Jim Carrey's character responds by saying, "So you're saying there's a chance!"

There are times when doubt will creep in about who Jesus is in our life although many of us would never want to admit that. But when we look at John the Baptist who had the job of preparing the way of Christ, we see that even John questioned who Jesus was. Luke 7:20: "When the men came to Jesus, they said, 'John the Baptist sent us to you to ask, are you the one who is to come, or should we expect someone else?'" It's crazy to see that the person whose job it was to prepare the way of Christ had doubts.

Doubt can move us to one of two places. The first is overthinking the situation causing the doubt. This can eventually put us into a place of unbelief. The other place doubt can push us to is to clarity. We can begin to investigate and push through our doubts to lead us to a place of clear understanding.

I do not believe having doubt is inappropriate. The question is, which direction does your doubt push you? My challenge for you today is to allow your doubt to push you to a place of clarity and understanding.

Make today count!

Day 162

Cade has continued to work very hard on different aspects of swimming. The goal he is pushing towards is to jump off the diving board in the very near future. Put the boy in water under 4 feet deep and he is a mini version of Michael Phelps. He swims a loose version of freestyle including rhythmic breathing and can swim from one side of the pool to the other. Yesterday we practiced going into the water without touching the bottom then turning and swimming back to a desired location. This was the best training I could think of to simulate what it would be like to jump off the diving board. After we had done this a few times, Cade looked at me and said, "I'm doing it!" I said, "OK buddy! Go for it!" I have all the faith in the world in him and his ability to jump off the diving board. I know he can swim. He wants to conquer this fear of being in water where he cannot touch. He waited in line patiently and got all the way up to the diving board where he abruptly turned, came down to me buried, and his head in my stomach and began to cry. "Dad, I'm just so scared."

God does not give us a spirit of fear to live in. But God does give us fear to allow us to make wise decisions. Proverbs 9:10 says, "The fear of the LORD is the beginning of wisdom, and knowledge of the Holy One is understanding." I don't know about you, but it's easy for me to try to bring God down to my level. This causes me to bring an inappropriate and unhealthy understanding of who God is. If you know much about our solar system, you know that our sun is enormous and incredibly hot, however, it's nowhere near one of the biggest stars. We read in Genesis that God spoke light into being. Just allow yourself to process that for a minute. Our sun and all the other massive stars in the sky came were spoken into being by God. To get an even better understanding of this, I challenge you to watch Louis Giglio's sermon titled "Indescribable." My challenge for you today is to begin your journey of wisdom by having a healthy fear and reverence for the God of the universe. He is not like us. He stands outside of time and outside of creation. He is worthy of our worship and respect today.

Make today count!

Day 163

Last night Holly and I were on our way home from a fun date night. We stopped about halfway home so she could look for a few items she needed for her school classroom. As we pulled back onto the main road to make our way back towards the interstate, I saw a man walking with a gas can in his hand. I said to Holly, "I wonder where his car is?" About 1500 yards away, I saw his truck parked right off the interstate off ramp with the hazard lights on. Cars don't run out of gas without giving significant warning. Typically, the gas light comes on giving you a minimum of 25 miles before your tank will be completely empty. This gentleman had obviously tried to push the tank to its limits, and because of that, he ended up with what I can only assume was at least an additional 30 minutes added to his final destination. When it comes down to it, this is all about pride. It's saying we are smarter than our computer's ability to tell us how much gas is left in the car.

In life there are red flags that warn us about impending destruction to come. Many times, we believe we know better than God. Proverbs 16:18, "Pride goes before destruction, and a haughty spirit before a fall." Our pride can lead to destruction. We need to allow the red flags which the Holy Spirit sends to serve as warning signs of impending destruction to come. When we decide we have the ability to manage certain interactions or temptations, we are setting ourselves up for destruction. It's important that we keep our pride in check then walk humbly and seek the counsel of God and of other wise men and women.

Maybe today you can think of an instance where your pride has cost you. What would it look like for you to practice humility today?

Make today count!

Day 164

Our fathers have a profound way of shaping us. Some of you could have been shaped by your father's incredible work ethic and leadership of your family. For others of you, your father may not have shaped you in a profound way because he was not present. Whether his presence was physically absent or mentally absent from your life, this event had a way of shaping you.

What I have found to be true through counseling sessions with other individuals is the way they view their earthly father typically strongly shapes their view of their heavenly father. For example, if a person's father was a strong disciplinarian and task manager, then likely your view of God is that you need to check off certain boxes to receive his approval. A person like this would have a difficult time comprehending God's grace. I was fortunate enough to grow up in a home where forgiveness was given, grace was extended, and love was freely given. This has shaped the way I view God. I view God in light of his grace and mercy. I tend to have a more difficult time understanding God's wrath and discipline.

Today regardless of how your father has shaped your view of your heavenly father, know this, that the God of the universe is intimately and deeply in love with you and he desires to have a relationship with you.

Today for those of you who are fathers, I encourage you to love your children in the way God has loved you. Love them in the lens of Psalm 86:15: "But you, O Lord, are a God merciful and gracious, slow to anger and abounding in steadfast love and faithfulness."

I love you, Dad. Thank you for your influence on my life!

Make today count!

Day 165

When we bought our house a few years back, there was a thin black mark on one of the entry walls. The mark must have come from some type of scrape that happened when the previous owner moved out. Because of the type of paint on the walls, it was not going to be just a simple touch up. It would require me to paint the entire wall the mark was on, along with the adjoining walls. Although we had the same paint color, when it dried, it looked different, so I decided the small black mark was something I was just going to have to live with. I would walk by the mark day after day, and it irritated me, but I believed there was nothing that could be done about it.

A few nights ago, Holly was working on redecorating parts of our living room. For whatever reason, I decided to grab a magic eraser and use it on the mark. Sure enough, it took the mark away and the paint color blended in perfectly. This was an incredibly easy solution to something I had determined was permanent.

I'm sure none of you have ever done this, but there have been times when I have written people off because I see a "mark" on them. Prior to spending any real time interacting with a person, I can easily write them off as unable to change. This may be due to some particular circumstance, situation, or addiction they have in their life. But what we see through scripture is that God has not given up on anyone. While teaching about how people can be saved, Jesus makes this statement in Mark 10:27, "...With man this is impossible, but not with God; all things are possible with God." With God, it doesn't matter what type of mark a person comes with. With him, redemption is always possible.

What a lesson for us to learn—that regardless of the appearance and circumstances of others, they can still have a radical life change when they interact with God. My challenge for you today is to view those around you through the lens of what is possible, not what is circumstantial.

Make today count!

Day 166

I would consider myself to be a highly proficient swimmer. Because of this, when I have gone kayak fishing, I have never worn a life jacket. The majority of the water I kayak in is calm and mostly shallow. After a few conversations with my father-in-law, I decided it was time to purchase and begin to wear a life jacket. This morning I woke up early to go fishing with my friend Brad. We got out to a very calm and what I'm assuming was a relatively deep spot on the river and began to fish. After just a few minutes in, I was fishing with a large crank bait lure. I cast out underneath an overhanging tree and felt a bite. I set the hook and begin to reel the fish up to my kayak. Once the fish was all the way up to my kayak, I hollered over to my buddy Brad to show him the fish I had just caught. When I reached my left hand down to grab the fish by the mouth to remove the lure, the fish tossed the lure causing it to go through my thumb.

This is the second most painful thing I have experienced, the first being tearing ligaments in my ankle. I yelled for Brad to come over to assist me. The pain and shock began to set in. I began to feel incredibly dizzy, nauseous, and lightheaded. Brad said I was sweating profusely and white as a ghost. At any point I could have passed out. Thankfully, Brad acted quickly and tied our boats together and paddled us to the shore where I was able to get some medical attention.

After the hook was successfully removed from my hand and all the excitement had subsided, Brad and I had a chance to debrief the situation. Both of us agreed almost simultaneously that had I not been wearing a life jacket and fallen in, the story could have ended quite differently. I was basing my need for a life jacket on my perceived swimming abilities. The need for a life jacket comes when outside circumstances come into play which are out of our control.

I believe many of us have this view of God. We think we can handle life on our own and we don't need anything from him. Here's a fact of life friends: Life is going to throw unexpected things at you that you cannot handle on your own. It seems to me that King David must have had a life-jacket moment. Psalm 40:17: "As for me, since I am poor and needy, let the Lord keep me in his thoughts. You are my helper and my savior. O my God, do not delay." I believe in life we will either choose to "put on our life jacket" or we will have a circumstance where we wish we had one.

My challenge for you today is that you not allow your pride to keep you from calling out to the one who can rescue you. Don't wait until a crisis moment. Allow him to be a part of your daily life so that when those life-jacket moments come, you will be prepared and he will be there to rescue you.

Make today count!

Day 167

I began my first job when I was 14 years old at Chick-fil-A. The delicious chicken and the incredible work atmosphere have forever stamped Chick-fil-A on my heart. I'm an absolute advocate for the company, for what they stand for, and for how delicious it is! Our local Chick-fil-A hosts a princess ball each year. Last night was the second time Abi Kate and I have attended together. It's a fun opportunity for the girls to dress up like a princess and to be treated as such. The event is filled with popcorn, food, dancing, singing, nail painting, and more. It is an incredible father/daughter time. A tradition we started last year, and one I will continue to do for years to come, is for me to go to the front door and pick up Abi Kate for our date with fresh-cut flowers. This probably seems a little odd considering I live in the same house she does, but I see it as an important part of my role as her father. As I was checking out at Kroger with the flowers, the young man checking me out said, "Sir, I know she is going to love them!" And I said, "I bet you're right. They are for my four-year-old daughter. I'm taking her on a date." If I don't show Abi Kate how she is supposed to be treated by a boy now, she won't have a clue. But if I set the standard through the roof, I'll never have to worry about the boys she dates.

So much of parenting is understanding your child's natural gifts and talents and helping them use those to glorify God. Another huge part of parenting is setting a standard, an expectation, of what marriage should look like and how to treat your spouse. As children, we watch our parents. As adults, we replay what we saw. Proverbs 22:6 says, "Start children off on the way they should go, and even when they are old, they will not turn from it." As we as parents continue to impart knowledge and wisdom on our children, through God's grace they will retain it. I'm sure many of you, like myself, at times feel that what we say goes in one ear and out the other. But remember this: "More is caught than taught."

My challenge for those of you who are parents is this: Be aware of the things you want them to catch. Be intentional about pouring into them through your actions, not just your words.

Make today count!

Day 168

I am currently involved in a kickball league that is played on Wednesday evenings at our church. It is a co-ed league with 10 people on the field at a time. The kickballs we play with are incredibly difficult to kick, catch, and throw. You might be remembering your grade school kickball games where Tammy could kick it to the tree a mile away. The difference is the ball we play with is an official kickball. It is much larger in diameter which makes it more difficult to use all the way around. One of the most strategic plays that can be done is if a team has a runner on first or second base and chooses to have one of their players bunt the ball. The majority of the time when a player lays down a bunt, the other runner will advance to the next base, but the player who lays the bunt down will be thrown out. This is the case in kickball and baseball and is called a "sacrifice."

The player laying down the sacrifice knows the outcome they are walking into. The other thing they know is that their sacrifice is for the greater good. They are advancing the runner's potential by setting them up to score.

As we look at the New Testament, it's easy to see that Jesus made the ultimate sacrifice for us. He sacrificed his life so we could advance into right standing before our Heavenly Father. John 3:16-17: "For God so loved the world, that he gave his only Son, that whoever believes in him should not perish but have eternal life. For God did not send his Son into the world to condemn the world, but in order that the world might be saved through him." Today each of us has an opportunity to advance from death to life.

My challenge for you today is to pause and thank God for the sacrifice he has made on your behalf. He has advanced us to new life that we could never obtain on our own. There is no greater sacrifice than this!

Make today count!

Day 169

I love fishing. Part of my love for fishing is all the gear that goes with it. You have tackle bags, tackle boxes, all the different bait and lures that go into the tackle box which then goes into the tackle bag. You have fishing poles, different types of lines, hooks, pliers, and the list goes on. This morning I'm on my way to take the kids fishing off the side of the river. When the kids come with me, that means we have to pack extra snacks and drinks. Going fishing is not something that just happens—it's something that requires some thought so you have all the things you need.

I think it's so cool that Jesus' disciples were primarily a group of fishermen. They knew what it took to catch fish as this was their primary form of making a living. In Matthew 4:19, Jesus is speaking to the disciples and he says, "Come, follow me…and I will send you out to fish for people." These men had spent their entire lives learning how to fish for fish. This is not an immediate process. This is one that requires some learning. For one, we know we are called to be "fishers of men." Have you ever thought about the preparation? In my mind, it works like this: How do you transition a conversation from the topical into the spiritual? Are you praying and asking God for opportunities to be a fisher of men?

My challenge for you today is to ask God to put conversations in your path for you to "fish for men."

Make today count!

Day 170

I took the kids fishing yesterday morning. We had a fun time fishing off the riverbank. This was the typical fishing setting that you can imagine with a dad and two kids—trying to make sure their lines didn't get hung in a tree, hung in each other, and that no one decided to release all the worms. Cade has just begun to cast his own pole and is doing a good job watching the bobber so he knows when to set the hook. He caught three bluegills back to back. After the third fish was released back into the water, he looked up at me and said, "Dad, I am a fishing master!" About 45 seconds after he had donned himself "fishing master," he cast out into the river with a hook with no bait on it. I said, "Cade, you will definitely have to be a fishing master to get a fish to bite a hook with no bait!"

There have been many times in my life I have told God that I am a "fishing master." What I mean by this is there have been times when I have told God I have things figured out. We all have seasons in our life when things seem to go exceedingly well. I think in these times, it is the most difficult to remember that God is God. We can begin to struggle with pride and over estimating our own abilities all the while forgetting Who gave us those abilities in the first place. Psalms 147:5 reminds us, "Great is our Lord and abundant in strength; His understanding is infinite." God's wisdom is infinite. We can trust him to be reliable in all circumstances.

When we find ourselves in the valley of life, it's easy to look up because there's nowhere else to look. My question for you today is where do you look when you find yourself on the mountaintop? Remember and acknowledge the True Master.

Make today count!

Day 171

I spent all day yesterday with our men's group from church. It was our annual river rafting trip down the Ocoee. For those of you who have never been down the Ocoee, it is considerably large white water. To give you some perspective, the kayaking portion of the 1996 Olympic Games was held on this river. Raft teams are typically made up of six people and a guide. Each team has one common goal—to get the raft from the top of the put in all the way down to the take out 10 miles away with everyone intact. There is no question that the group of guys I was rafting with had the same goal as I did. The problem came because we struggled significantly with synchronizing paddling strokes. It is absolutely crucial that everyone paddle in the same direction at the same time to successfully navigate the rocks and large waves down the river. There were several occasions where our guide became frustrated with our ability to stay together. Individually we all had the same goal in mind, but separately each of us found ourselves trying to achieve it on our own. Eventually we were able to work through our paddling troubles and navigated the rest of the river successfully without having anyone take a swim.

I love the picture Paul paints of the body of Christ. We are one body with multiple parts. We are moving in one direction. Each of us are contributing in a different way to the greater whole. Romans 12:5 says, "So we, though many, are one body in Christ, and individually members one of another." Although we are different parts and bring different skills and abilities to the table, we should all be working towards the same goal and moving in the same direction. We are moving to pursue holiness and to draw others to the affection of Christ.

The key to a safe and successful rafting trip is being in sync with your fellow rafters. Today for us to maintain harmony within the church, the key is for us to be in sync with fellow believers and not to allow our own agenda to override the larger goal. My challenge for you today is to make sure your actions are working towards the larger goal instead of towards your gain.

Make today count!

Day 172

There's just something about Animal Planet. Some of the footage they are able to capture is absolutely unbelievable. I find myself quite mesmerized anytime the show features a lion on the hunt. The absolute power, speed, and strength of the lion makes it one of the most feared animals in all of Africa.

When I'm watching an episode and I see a group of kudus crossing a large open area together, there is usually one that stays in the back, alone, walking just a little slower than the others. I know this one is about to get eaten. Out of nowhere, the lion gives what is typically a short chase and dinner is served.

Lions are not only incredibly powerful, they are incredibly smart. They know not to try to attack in the middle of a herd. Lions also know not to attack the strongest. They intentionally attack the isolated and the weak.

1 Peter 1:5 warns, "Be alert and of sober mind. Your enemy the devil prowls around like a lion looking for someone to devour." It should come as no surprise that Satan and his tactics cause him to be compared to a lion. He's looking to attack you when you are vulnerable, when you are isolated, and when you are weak. Each of us have different temptations that draw us away from the affections of God. Satan is crafty and deceitful. He will place these temptations in front of us when we are at our weakest or when we are isolated.

The greatest chance for us to successfully navigate the temptations Satan throws at us is for us to be in community with other believers, for us to be open and vulnerable about our personal temptations and struggles, and for us to avoid times of isolation.

Today do you find yourself with a community around you to support you and keep you encouraged and from isolation? My challenge for you today, if your answer was no, is to begin to ask God to bring these people into your life.

Make today count!

Day 173

Without question, relationships of all kinds can be incredibly difficult. When two people journey together for any amount of time, chances are that at some point in the relationship there will be some frustrations. Frustrations can arise over a multitude of topics, but the solution can most likely be found in one root cause. In my experiences with others as well as in my own life, it seems the root of relationship issues is in communication or lack thereof.

When communicating with another person, there are a few things I have found to be incredibly helpful and important. For example, let's say Holly said to me, "Next Thursday I am going to have coffee with some of my girlfriends." At no point during the conversation do I repeat for clarification or understanding. Then the day comes for Holly to go have coffee with her girlfriends, and I get frustrated with her because she "did not tell me." The reality is that I most likely was occupied doing something else and was not fully attentive to what she was saying. This is one example of how communication can create issues.

James 1:9 says, "Know this, my beloved brothers: let every person be quick to hear, slow to speak, slow to anger." Listening is one of the biggest keys to successful communication. Listening is an active process. Here are a few simple suggestions to help with communication in your relationships. First of all, after someone has told you something, it is important to repeat what you heard. This is an important step because it helps clarify what you heard. Sometimes what we hear someone say is not what they intended at all. The second step in the process is for the speaker to clarify that what the listener heard was correct. This guarantees that everyone is on the same page regarding the subject matter. Once the subject matter has been clearly articulated, it is the job of the speaker to share whatever it is they need to share from their point of view. This is not a time to point a finger. It is a time to speak about their personal feelings. The process then continues with repeating for clarification and now the listener has an opportunity to speak with the speaker, clarifying for understanding. During the course of a conversation clarifying the information in a manner that is genuinely seeking for understanding will only strengthen the relationship between you and the other party.

A challenge for us today is that we would be quick to listen and that we would be active in the listening process. Our goal should always be to strive for clarity in our communication.

Make today count!

Day 174

I wonder if this has ever happened to you: You are in a conversation with someone when they are telling you about a problem they are having. Suddenly within minutes after you begin to give them a solution to the problem, you find yourself in some type of disagreement with the person and you are confused as to what happened. Or maybe you have been sharing an issue with someone and you find them trying to give you a solution and you end up being frustrated. This is what Holly and I call "listening problems" versus "solution problems."

There have been many times when Holly has shared something she is going through and I find myself immediately giving her a solution to the problem. This only seemed to frustrate her but I never could understand why. Then one day I realized that sometimes she just wants to tell me about something she's dealing with but she doesn't necessarily want me to fix it. A tool we have put into our communication tool box is when we share a problem with the other person, we clarify if this is a problem we want them to solve or listen to. Sometimes we just need a trusted ear to vent to. At other times, we need a trusted companion to give us guidance during a difficult situation.

Proverbs 16:21 says, "The wise of heart is called discerning, and sweetness of speech increases persuasiveness." My challenge for you today is to use this verse to guide your listening and your solving.

Make today count!

Day 175

A question I wrestled with for a significant portion of my life was "What is my purpose?" While I was in college, I tried to find the perfect subject matter to master to move me closer to my purpose. Once I graduated, I began to search for my purpose to be fulfilled through my work. It seemed to always be an elusive one promotion away. I would get the next promotion and then try to determine if this was my purpose. Typically, very quickly I would realize that this was not it either. Frustrated with trying to find my purpose through my vocational work, I decided to read *The Purpose-Driven Life* by Pastor Rick Warren. A part of me thought there was going to be some super deep thought that would rattle me into my purpose. The answer was in front of me the whole time.

Each of us has the same purpose in life. It does not matter what your vocational position is. You could be a doctor, lawyer, garbage man, janitor, plumber, teacher, or any other job you want to fill in that blank with—your purpose is still the same. In Matthew 28:19 Jesus said, "Therefore go and make disciples of all nations, baptizing them in the name of the Father and of the Son and of the Holy Spirit." This is it, this is your purpose. You are here to make disciples wherever the Lord has placed you. Your particular job, neighborhood, and circle of influence is the place where he has placed you to make disciples. We should honor God through our work, but know that our work is not our ultimate purpose. We were placed where we are to draw people closer to Christ.

I hope today this has given you clarity on why you exist. Know that wherever you are, you have been placed there specifically to make disciples.

Make today count!

Day 176

I got to hang out and watch the kids at their last day of swim lessons today. It's been really awesome to see their progress. As Holly and I were talking about all they had learned in the lessons, Holly pointed out how Abi Kate had finally begun to understand that if she stopped fighting the water, she would naturally float. Since our bodies are made up of approximately 60% water, the body's natural tendency is to float. It's when we find ourselves fighting and struggling against the water that we will struggle to maintain our ability to float.

The spiritual correlation is a pretty easy one to see. When we fight against the natural order and rules God has put into place, we will sink. We can fight and thrash against him as much as we desire but it will never lead to a place where we have a prosperous life. When we submit to the things God has called us to, we will find that life seems to go much easier. While teaching the disciples how to pray in Matthew 6:9-10, Jesus said, "Pray, then, in this way: 'Our Father who is in heaven, hallowed be Your name. Your kingdom come. Your will be done, on earth as it is in heaven.'"

Jesus is encouraging us to pray for God's will to happen here on earth the same way it does in heaven. Jesus understood that submission to God's will can create a much easier "float."

My challenge for you today is to simply submit to rather than thrash against the will of God.

Make today count!

Day 177

Yesterday was a monumental day in our house. Holly and I met many years ago as lifeguards at our local city pool. Both of us have a deep love for the water and always hoped that our children would share in that love. To this day, my absolute favorite thing about the pool is the diving board. Now I'm not quite as apt to do a crazy dive like I used to, but I will still pull out a one and a half now and again. After the completion of the kids' swim lessons yesterday, they asked to go swim at the local pool where Holly and I met. Without hardly any hesitation, Cade went straight to the diving board line and made his first successful jump off the diving board. He was hooked. After watching big brother for a little while, Abi Kate said, "I want to do it." Keep in mind that Abi Kate just turned four. I was hesitant for a few minutes but decided to give her the opportunity since there was clearly no fear involved. She walked to the end of the board and jumped right off and swam to the ladder with no problem. Only weeks before both of the kids had cried because of their fear of the diving board. Today they almost cried because we had to go home. Pushing through their fear led them to a place of confidence.

When it comes to dealing with fear, I believe the best thing we can do is push through. That could look different depending on the circumstances. Perhaps the worst-case scenario fears fill your mind. I would encourage you to push through that fear by processing it out loud with another person. Maybe you have a fear of sharing story about how God has changed your life. Satan would love to keep you fearful because he knows your story has the potential to impact many lives for eternity. I would encourage you to push through this fear and find your confidence in God. Jeremiah 17:7 says, "But blessed is the one who trusts in the LORD, whose confidence is in him." When our confidence is found in the Lord instead of being centered around our own abilities, we will find ourselves able to do things we never would have thought feasible.

Today, what are the fears you need to push through? What are the fears that could be holding you back from the confidence the Lord has for you?

Make today count!

Day 178

My good friend Nathan Thomas really inspires me. Nathan is incredibly talented musically and uses his gifts to glorify God. Two years ago, he and his wife Jamie went through a difficult valley in their life. They lost their newborn son Jedediah. During the time of processing their grief, Nathan and Jamie used their God-given musical abilities to create some incredible songs. He released his CD this past week. The title of the CD is called "Battle Cry." This whole CD serves as a reminder that when we walk through deep valleys, we can always cry out to God. I have been so encouraged and challenged by their response to a difficult situation to turn and glorify God through it.

In our lives, each of us will experience mountains and valleys and all that lie in between. When we find ourselves in a valley, we know there's nowhere we can go except up. Psalms 121:1-2 says, "I lift up my eyes to the mountains—where does my help come from? My help comes from the Lord, the Maker of heaven and earth." When you find yourself in one of life's valleys, I want to remind you that you have nowhere else to look but up. God your helper is there and ready in your time of need. The question is, how can you glorify God in your present valley?

If you find yourself in a deep valley today, my challenge for you is to look up. God is ready, able, and willing to help you.

Make today count!

Day 179

Small kids are super funny. I love how they will be sure to tell you all about even their smallest scratch. Oftentimes when my kids have a new "boo-boo," the first thing they will tell someone they haven't seen in a while is all about their boo-boo. I'm sure all of you have seen some variation of a child limping or holding their arm where there is a very small cut or scrape. This small hurt is what gives them the green light for this behavior. Obviously, we as adults understand that there's no need for a child to be limping because of a small scratch on their knee, but in a child's mind, this is justified. The hurt calls for the behavior.

What I find so interesting about this is that as adults, we have our own version of this. Although we're not hopping around on one foot because of a small scrape, we do make excuses for poor choices and inappropriate behavior based on emotional wounds. It's easy for us to write ourselves a pass to explain away behavior that is not representative of Christ. We do this by pointing back to the time and place where someone emotionally wounded us thus explaining away, or hoping to explain away, our inappropriate responses or behaviors. Ephesians 4:13 says, "Let all bitterness and wrath and anger and clamor and slander be put away from you, along with all malice." It's important as Christians that we let go and forgive just as we have been forgiven. Instead of pointing to our wounds and allowing them to justify our behavior, we should use our wounds to point to the Savior.

Each of us have wounds. The question for you today is where or to whom will these wounds point people to?

Make today count!

Day 180

This summer has been the summer of Cade overcoming several different fears. One of the things he has been working on is riding his bike. I know some of you may be judging me thinking, "Why in the world can't your seven-year-old ride his bike by now? To be honest, we are not really bike people. The kids typically want to go fish, swim, or play baseball over riding their bikes. I have been excited to see Cade decide on his own that he wants to learn. The other day we were riding on the road and I had one hand on the handle bar and the other hand on the back of the bike seat. He was peddling and I was reminding him to find the point he wanted to drive towards and stare at it. I took one hand off the handle then slowly took one hand off the back of the bike. He peddled a few more feet perfectly straight before he realized I had let go. When he realized I let go, he took his attention off of the place he was going and looked down which caused him to lose his balance. I caught him before he hit the ground. When his eyes were focused, his balance was steady. When he directed his eyes to see what was around him, trouble arose.

This reminds me of when Peter saw Jesus walking on the water in Matthew 14:28-31: "Lord, if it's you," Peter replied, "tell me to come to you on the water." "Come," he said. Then Peter got down out of the boat, walked on the water and came toward Jesus. But when he saw the wind, he was afraid and, beginning to sink, cried out, "Lord, save me!" Immediately Jesus reached out his hand and caught him. "You of little faith," he said, "why did you doubt?"" When Peter's focus shifted from Christ to the waves crashing around him, he began to sink.

The same can be said about us. When we take our focus off Christ, we will begin to struggle. It's easy for us to get distracted by the crashing waves, the wind, and the feeling of a lack of balance. We must maintain our focus on Christ to keep ourselves in position. What are the winds and waves that are keeping your attention off Christ today? What steps do you need to take to redirect your focus?

Make today count!

Day 181

Happy 4th of July friends! July 4th is one of those days that serves as a fun memory for me throughout my childhood. There's nothing better than blowing up small action figures with firecrackers, eating hamburgers and hotdogs, swimming, and being with friends and family. I'm so thankful to live in a country that offers me the freedoms we experience here in the United States. Our independence was dependent on the bravery and sacrifice of many.

The same is true of the freedoms we have in Christ. The freedoms we have are dependent on the sacrifice Christ made on our behalf. We do have freedom in Christ, but we should be careful how we use this freedom. Paul writes in the book of Galatians 5:13-14: "You, my brothers and sisters, were called to be free. But do not use your freedom to indulge the flesh; rather, serve one another humbly in love. For the entire law is fulfilled in keeping this one command: "Love your neighbor as yourself." Although we have been given freedom in Christ, we should be careful not to indulge in our fleshly desires. We should use our freedoms to draw others closer to the affections of Christ.

Today how are you using your freedom in Christ? Are you glorifying him through your words and actions?

Make today count!

Day 182

To celebrate the 4th of July, we had a few friends and their families over. The plan was that we would cook out then shoot off a few small fireworks before going to watch the city's fireworks display. The kids, of course, enjoyed the small firecrackers we shot off prior to the big show. Due to time restraints, we were unable to shoot off two of the larger fireworks I had purchased. Now what you need to understand is that when I say "large," I mean very small. To give you some perspective, this fountain firework cost $2.50. You know what I'm talking about—one of those you light and it sprays different colors in the air for about 30 seconds. Yeah, that was our great finale. After we got back from the city's fireworks display, we decided we would do our grand finale — the small fountain. Just as I got our fountain lit, my neighbor just a few houses over unleashed what I'm assuming was the rest of the city's fireworks display. It was absolutely impossible to keep our focus on our small little fountain with this show that most likely inspired the Star-Spangled Banner happening behind us.

It would be easy for me in this instance to feel a sense of jealousy. No one wanted to watch my small fountain because of this guy's awesome fireworks. But once I admitted the fact that this guy had some pretty awesome fireworks, I realized I was able to enjoy the show as well. So, we just sat and watched the rest of his amazing display.

It's easy for us at times to feel insecure about ourselves when we are around someone we feel has greater gifts and talents than we do. The important thing to remember is that each of us can contribute to the body in a specific way. Your perception may be that some people have a more glamorous role than you do. The truth of the matter is that the ways you contribute matter significantly. This morning as I was leaving for work, Cade came in talking about how awesome the fountain was. In my mind, there's no way anyone would have watched the fountain over what was happening behind us, but that just was not the case.

The awesome thing about being surrounded by people who are doing awesome things for God is that we get to have a front row seat. So rather than being jealous, I would encourage you to be mesmerized by the presence of God through that person and celebrate with them. Romans 12:15 encourages us, "Rejoice with those who rejoice, weep with those who weep."

Make today count!

Day 183

I spent much of my young adult life addicted to pornography. Through God's grace, accountability with other Godly men, an amazing wife, and a strategic plan, I have been on the other side of victory for quite some time now. I feel it is part of my calling and mission to walk with men who are struggling with this addiction. It has become clear with all of the scientific research that has come out that pornography harms our brains. It is also been proven that is as addictive as taking a hard-core drug. I say these two things for those of you who have never been affected by pornography. I have a group of guys I do daily and weekly check-in's with. With the help of accountability, they are striving for purity. I was meeting with one of these men last night and he said something I thought was incredibly profound. He heard this on an online message from a pastor whose name I cannot recall. He said "every change requires a crisis and a process. When we fail in the process we must return to the crisis." We are all in process.

Regardless of whether you're actively struggling with any type of addiction or not, we are all in process. We are all striving to become more like Christ. Each day we are trying to become more like him, knowing we will never reach perfection. I love the way David talks about holiness in Psalms 51:10-12: "Create in me a clean heart, O God, and renew a right spirit within me. Cast me not away from your presence, and take not your Holy Spirit from me. Restore to me the joy of your salvation, and uphold me with a willing spirit." No matter where you find yourself today in your process, this verse applies.

My challenge for you today is to ask God to create a clean heart within you. Ask God to make his desire your desires. Then continue to strive in your process!

Make today count!

Day 184

Since Cade was very small, I have tried to create an awareness with him and Abi Kate about saving money. Each of them has a bank, and when they add money into their piggybank, we make a big deal about it. When the piggybanks are filled, I like to sit with the kids and sort the money out, explaining how each coin has a different worth. Then we roll the coins, separate the cash, and put it into their savings account. Yesterday after completing this task with both kids, they were each eager to earn some money so I decided to take them outside and let them pick up all the random firework sticks and miscellaneous items leftover between mine and my neighbor's house. I had $.12 in my pocket. I gave Cade the dime and I gave Abi Kate two pennies. Almost instinctively before taking the time to think about what each coin was worth, Cade said, "That's not fair. She got two." And then he asked Abi Kate if she wanted to trade with him. Abi Kate said, "No way!" I started laughing and told Abi Kate she would immediately be returning five times her initial investment. Of course, this didn't make any sense to her. She was quite satisfied with her two pennies.

When you understand the value of all the different coins, it's easy to see that Abi Kate did not understand. She was offered something worth far more than what she had. There's not a financial advisor out there who wouldn't suggest making a trade when you can immediately make five times your money. The thing is, we do this with God. John reminds us that God offers us new life, and life to the full, but we think what we are holding onto is worth more than what he has for us. We hold onto our pennies and tell God, "No thanks, I am good." Just like Abi Kate, we don't understand the value of the trade we are being offered until we make it. 1 John 2:2: "He is the atoning sacrifice for our sins, and not only for ours but also for the sins of the whole world." He traded his life for our sin debt. He traded his life so we can have eternity with God.

Are you holding onto your pennies today? Have you found that you have obtained satisfaction in life, or have you realized something seems to be missing? Today Christ wants to make a trade with you that is beyond comprehension, beyond understanding, and 100% in your benefit. The question today is will you give up your pennies?

Make today count!

Day 185

I met Brad Ewing prior to joining the staff at New Vision. At the time, Brad was serving as the men's pastor, and it had been suggested by our senior pastor that the two of us meet to talk about an idea I had for the men's group. From the first time I met him, I knew I liked him. From that first breakfast meeting, we made plans to hang out outside of the church setting. I'm not sure exactly what we had planned, but I can almost guarantee it involved shooting something. Brad is now someone I would consider to be one of my very best friends. Many of the church staff just call us "the Brad's." What I love about my friendship with Brad is the authenticity of it. Both of us are 100% free to share our true feelings with each other, as well as the frustrations we might be dealing with. Our friendship also works very well because we complement each other. For example, we both might have an idea about going on an overnight fishing trip. Brad would get in the truck and immediately start driving because he is so excited, but I will remind him that we need to plan: we need to decide all the things we need to bring, we should probably check the weather, and most importantly, we probably need to clear the plan with our wives. Brad is also about 10 years further down the road than I am, so he's always there to pass down his wisdom from things learned. One of the things I admire most about my friend is his relationship with his boys. He is the epitome of a great father. I look at the relationship he has with his son Jackson who is 15 and hope that my relationship with Cade looks similar when he is that age. Brad is passionate. He is not only passionate about big things, but the little things, and the every-day thing as well. Hanging out with Brad makes life fun. But what I appreciate about him the most is how he loves God and is unashamed and unapologetic about it.

True friendship is a gift from God. Finding a friend you can be 100% vulnerable with and know they are not going to judge you is rare. I'm grateful for the relationship I have with my friend.

I would say most people picture God in the clouds with a giant lightning bolt. They think he's not only there to watch creation but also to judge it. But we know as Christians that Jesus has offered us friendship.

This is an incredible thought--that we can have a friendship with the God of creation. John 15:15 says, "No longer do I call you servants, for the servant does not know what his master is doing; but I have called you friends, for all that I have heard from my Father I have made known to you." He is the friend who sticks closer than a brother.

This friendship is offered to each of us. You have an opportunity to be known by the God of the universe, and to be called his friend. The challenge for you today is to reach out to that best friend in your life and tell them just how much they mean to you.

Make today count!

Day 186

In preparation for our small group coming over last night, Holly decided she wanted to make some banana nut bread. She did not look to see if all the needed ingredients were already in the pantry prior to starting this process. When it came time to add the baking soda, she realized we didn't have any. She asked me to send a text message to our neighbors to see if someone had some they would be willing to share. I sent the text out and our next-door neighbor responded. I met my neighbor at the back fence who had what must have been the world's largest tub of baking soda. It was the standard brand of Arm and Hammer. I took the small amount I needed, thanked her, then headed back to the house. Holly finished getting all the ingredients mixed together when my phone rang. It was my neighbor's husband who is a former military guy. I answered the phone, "Hello?" The response on the other end went something like this, "Abort, abort, abort!" He then proceeded to tell me how his wife had given us Arm and Hammer laundry detergent instead of baking soda. The side of the box said Arm and Hammer, and it said baking soda. The only problem was it said "WITH baking soda." So this little bit of laundry detergent was mixed into this delicious banana bread batter, made even better by the presence of dark chocolate chips. Here's the point: poison in any form is still poison.

There were so many delicious flavors mixed into that bowl, but the presence of that small amount of laundry detergent was enough to keep us from eating it. If we knew there was poison inside of food, we would never eat it, but the crazy thing is that I believe we let different forms of poison into our mind and before our eyes because of the way they are presented. Jesus said in Matthew 6:22-23, "The eye is the lamp of the body. So, if your eye is healthy, your whole body will be full of light, but if your eye is bad, your whole body will be full of darkness. If then the light in you is darkness, how great is the darkness!" It is easy for us to justify images we see and movies we watch because of the wrapping or because "everyone has seen it." I believe we've been called to a different standard of guarding our eyes. Proverbs 4:23: "Above all else, guard your heart, for everything you do flows from it." Poison in any form is still poison.

Are you guarding your eyes, your heart, and your mind? Or are you allowing yourself a little bit of poison here and there because of the way they are presented? My challenge for you today is to treat your mind and eyes the same way you would treat your mouth.

Make today count!

Day 187

Anyone who has been around children between the ages of three and seven realizes the number of questions they can ask. Their minds are so inquisitive at this age. It seems that the majority of my children's talk tends to be filled with questions. Holly and I do our best to answer every question thrown at us, but truthfully, at times it can be absolutely draining. I heard that the average four-year-old asks 195 questions in a day. To give you some perspective of my days with Cade, our 7-year old, I timed him for 15 minutes. In that time span, he asked 22 questions. If he had continued at that same rate for 8 hours, he would have asked 704 questions. Children grow by asking questions. There are times a question is asked of me that helps me grow.

When you think about God, most likely you think about questions you have brought to him. Logically it makes the most sense to bring our questions to the one who has all the answers, but what I have found to be true in my own life is that sometimes God will ask me questions to help me grow. When God called Moses to lead the children of Israel out of captivity, Moses began to tell God all the reasons why he was not capable to lead. I love how God responded with a question. Exodus 4:10: "Moses said to the LORD, 'Pardon your servant, Lord. I have never been eloquent, neither in the past nor since you have spoken to your servant. I am slow of speech and tongue.'" God does not ask us questions because he needs help with the answer. God asks questions to help us find the answer.

You have the awesome ability to ask questions of the God of the universe and he is more than capable to answer your questions. My challenge for you today is to meditate on the questions he might be asking you. How can he be shaping your heart and mind through these questions?

Make today count!

Day 188

I wonder if you have ever begun a conversation with someone about your faith in God but before you could get one more word in, they threw something like this at you: "The church is full of a bunch of hypocrites" This is something I have heard often. It is absolutely true that the church is full of broken people. At a fundamental and foundational level, I don't believe people are opposed to Jesus or to his teachings. I believe their opposition comes from a specific group within the church, a group of individuals whose mouths claim the gospel yet their lives are lived contrary to what they claim. I don't believe anyone becomes frustrated by Christians who are earnestly striving to look more like Jesus each day yet mess up. I believe the rub is when people's lives are contrary to the gospel of Jesus every day except for Sunday.

1 John 1:5 says, "This is the message we have heard from him and declare to you: God is light; in him there is no darkness at all. If we claim to have fellowship with him and yet walk in the darkness, we lie and do not live out the truth." Walking in the light means we are aligning our life with God's commands. It doesn't mean we're going to do it perfectly. What it means is that when we mess up, we agree with God, confess where we have come short, then continue walking on his path. My question for you today is this: what gospel is your life preaching? Is your life preaching the true gospel, pushing people towards Christ, or is your life preaching your own gospel, the gospel of self pride?

I challenge you today to examine your life to see where you are pointing people.

Make today count!

Day 189

Over the past year I have been diligent about saving money to purchase a new vehicle for Holly. Her car is still in good working condition, it is just an older vehicle with high mileage. We bought the car right before Cade was born and to be honest, it will be nice to have something a little larger so the kids can have more space. I have spent every night looking at all of the different online sites trying to find some great options. After two weeks of searching, I narrowed my search down to two vehicles to look at. Through very odd and unforeseen circumstances, both of the vehicles were ruled out as options the day I was scheduled to look at them. One of the ladies was very apologetic about the circumstances that prevented me from seeing her vehicle. I told her it was no problem. Actually, something within me was telling me I was forcing the issue and it was not the right time just now.

It's easy for us to believe God does not care about the small details of our life. I mean he's busy running the whole universe, so why would he care about the little things happening with me? I don't think this could be further from the truth. I believe God cares about every major and minute detail of our lives. Matthew 10:29 says, "Are not two sparrows sold for a penny? And not one of them will fall to the ground apart from your Father."

To know God takes notice of the sparrows is assurance that he will take care and cares for us. I believe God wants to be in the little details of your life. There's nothing too big or too small for you to bring to him.

What are the little things you have neglected to bring to God because you honestly believe he does not care? My challenge for you today is to spend time in prayer with him giving up the little details weighing you down.

Make today count!

Day 190

As many of you know, I have dyslexia, but I have not allowed it to stop me from being an avid reader. I might not read books in the traditional sense, but I acquire knowledge by using an audio book app. I typically rotate the types of books I read. The two types of books I go back and forth between are Christian books written by pastors I respect and books on business written by men and women who have made their mark in a particular field. I'm currently finishing Simon Sinek's book. *Start with Why*. This is an excellent book. To summarize, he says companies should always have their "why" in mind when making decisions. The majority of companies tell you what they do, but companies like Apple tell you why they do them. When we have a clear understanding of why someone is doing something, we tend to gravitate more heavily to these companies and people. One illustration he gives in the book is about Dr. Martin Luther King. He said that on the day Dr. King gave his "I have a dream" speech, people were not there for Dr. King. These people were there for themselves. They believed in what he believed. In other words, their "why" was aligned.

Although this book was written in a secular context to help business people better understand their "why" behind their business, I found this book to be incredibly relevant for myself as not only a pastor but as a believer. I began to think through the various programs I extend to people in the ministries I am involved with. I looked at each of them and asked myself if they line up with my "why." If you are doing something that does not line up with your overarching purpose, I would say it is doing nothing but providing confusion as to what your main purpose actually is.

Starting with why creates clarity not only for yourself but for those you are leading and interacting with. My "why" is to draw people to the affection and love of Christ. This influences things I do and how I do them. If I were to write another book and the subject matter did not point people back to Christ, this would create a fuzzy sense for you and for me as to exactly what my "why" is. It is when we see consistency with people that we begin to get a full understanding of just what they are about.

Matthew 5:16 says, "In the same way, let your light shine before others, so that they may see your good works and give glory to your Father who is in heaven." Our whys should ultimately push people towards Christ.

So, what about you? What is your why? What is pushing you, motivating you, and challenging you? My challenge for you today is to process your "why." Is it consistently lining up throughout the different areas of your life?

Make today count!

Day 191

There are many leadership talks, podcasts, and books that focus on the subject of mentorship. It is easy to see the value of having a mentor to guide you in your path. Mentorship sharpens and helps to keep you accountable. It also helps you see blind spots you would otherwise miss. I have written several times about the importance of having a mentor in your life, but today is a little different. I believe it is equally as important that we mentor someone else. I see mentorship as a trickle-down effect. When I am poured into, I then turn and pour into someone else.

One of those individuals for me over the past few years has been Jeremy Fuller. I met Jeremy when he interviewed to be my assistant. He came highly recommended from several other staff members, and it was clear to see that he would be a great fit. Over the past few years, I have gotten to know Jeremy on a very deep spiritual and personal level. There have been times when our conversations have been difficult as he has listened to me speak truth he didn't necessarily want to hear. What I love about Jeremy is that he is teachable. He has a desire to be better. Today I'm honored to have the opportunity to officiate at Jeremy's wedding. I consider it a great joy to join him and Derby, his beautiful bride-to-be, in marriage.

Proverbs 9:9: "Give instruction to a wise man, and he will be still wiser; teach a righteous man, and he will increase in learning." Mentorship helps us grow. Who are you pouring into? If you don't currently have someone, who do you see tremendous potential in? God has gifted you in certain ways, and he has brought you through certain circumstances not only to grow you but for you to use to sharpen another person.

Make today count!

Day 192

Each week I look forward to spending time with the guys in my small group. It's an awesome group of young guys in leadership positions who desire to honor God in their actions, both within their work and within their private life. We are currently doing a study through the book of Colossians. Colossians 1:15-18 says, "The Son is the image of the invisible God, the firstborn over all creation. For in him all things were created: things in heaven and on earth, visible and invisible, whether thrones or powers or rulers or authorities; all things have been created through him and for him. He is before all things, and in him all things hold together." This is the supremacy of God, that in him everything is held together. It takes me back to the song from my childhood, "He's got the whole world in his hands." This understanding can create questions for us such as "what am I here for and does my life matter?"

After going around to each guy addressing these questions, there seemed to be a universal consensus. We all know our purpose is to strive to be like Christ and to make disciples. Each of us wants to believe our life is making a difference in the lives of others, but all struggle to come up with clear and consistent evidence for it. I felt the prompting to affirm each of the guys individually about the character traits and qualities I see within them. Affirmation is something we all need but most of us struggle to receive. I liken receiving affirmation to being hugged from behind. It's kind of uncomfortable, but it feels really good! Each of us need to know there is significance in our life.

Here is your daily affirmation. You are capable. You were thought out and woven together in your mother's womb. You were designed by God who loves you. The same God who loves you willingly gave himself up for you. He has a plan and a purpose for your life. He knows the number of hairs on your head. You are his workmanship.

Make today count!

Day 192

Today I'm going to share with you the secret to being blessed and being wise. We begin to understand cause and effect at a very young age. If you stick your finger in a light socket, you will get shocked. This type of cause and effect is grasped easily by a child. It is emotional cause and effect that takes longer to develop. The golden rule tells us to treat others as we want to be treated. We are trying to create a cause and effect. The assumption here is that if we treat people well, they in turn will treat us well, which we all know is not always true.

Scripture is full of verses that show cause and effect. If we do one thing, something else will happen. Scripture says if we ask for wisdom, it will be given to us.

Psalm 1:1-2 says, "Blessed is the one who does not walk in step with the wicked or stand in the way that sinners take or sit in the company of mockers, but whose delight is in the law of the Lord, and who meditates on his law day and night." If we follow God's laws we will be blessed. Cause and effect. God keeps something a mystery from us and other things he makes as clear as day. If you are lacking wisdom today, ask for it. If you are not walking in God's blessings, start by walking in his decrees.

You have been shaped by cause and effect in many different ways in your life. I challenge you today to look at the Bible to see the promises God has made to you. His cause will yield the greatest effect.

Make today count!

Day 193

Have you ever had someone hover over you while you sleep, and for some reason it ends up waking you up? If you have kids, you're probably laughing right now. My kids do this to me regularly. They will come into our room without announcing themselves and just stand right next to the bed right next to my face. It takes a few minutes and then I'll hear "Dad, Dad, Daaad." My response is typically some type of groan. Then 9 times out of 10 they respond with some sort of question. This exact situation happened this morning. Before I was even able to respond to the question, they gave up on waiting for my answer and walked out of the room.

I know I have done this with God before. I have asked him a question or voiced a concern but have not been patient enough to wait for the response. What we need to be reminded of is that our timing is not God's timing. I think of the story of Lazarus in the New Testament. Jesus showed up after Lazarus died. We see Martha's response to his timing in John 11:21. "Lord," Martha said to Jesus, "if you had been here, my brother would not have died." Martha did not wait on Jesus' response. We know how the story ends. Jesus raised Lazarus from the dead.

His timing is not our timing. No matter what situation you are walking through today--a potential divorce, job loss, or a health issues--know he hears your prayers. His timing is perfect timing. My challenge for you is to pray and tell God you trust him with the timing of your situation. Turn it over to him and wait.

Make today count!

Day 194

Critical conversations are never easy, but they are inevitably a part of life. Some people shy away from conflict rather than face necessary conversations. During these conversations, it's easy for us to find ourselves allowing our emotions to speak rather than our logic. Instead of focusing on the resolution of the issue, we turn the focus on trying to inflict as much damage as possible on the person we are having the conversation with.

Yesterday I had to have a very difficult conversation with someone. The source of the misunderstanding had happened a few days prior. Emotionally I wanted to have this conversation right away, but I knew this would not breed a healthy dialogue. In my flesh, my quick wit and sarcasm can get me into a lot of trouble so I prayed for peace to come over my heart. Once it had, I was ready to have the conversation. Ephesians 4:15 was my guide. "Instead, speaking the truth in love, we will grow to become in every respect the mature body of him who is the head, that is, Christ." Even when speaking the truth in love, conversations can be very difficult. Using this as a guide can keep your emotions out of it. I ended up having an excellent dialogue with this individual yesterday and we came to a clear understanding and agreement.

If you need to have a critical conversation with someone, my challenge to you today is to give yourself enough emotional space that you can speak the truth in love.

Make today count!

Day 195

The kids and I spent the last few days with my parents in Kentucky. We were able to surprise my mom Tuesday night. She had no idea we were coming and said it was probably the biggest surprise of her life. My dad, of course, knew we were coming and made plans for us to swim at one of his church member's pools. This was an awesome pool that included a diving board, slide, and a 9 1/2-foot-deep end. The kids love to retrieve small diving toys off the bottom of the pool. Abi Kate kept progressing deeper and deeper until eventually she wanted to try to retrieve an item from the deepest end. This would require her to hold her breath a little longer than she probably can. Determined to do it, I decided to help her by pushing her to the bottom. With a little extra push from me, she was able to retrieve the diving toy from the center of the pool.

This is what being discipled is all about. It's sitting with someone who is further along in their Christian walk than you are and having them push you just a little bit deeper than you could get on your own. In Matthew 28:19 Jesus said, "Therefore go and make disciples of all nations, baptizing them in the name of the Father and of the Son and of the Holy Spirit." Our job on earth is to make disciples and to push people deeper than they could go on their own.

Who are you are pushing deeper?

Make today count!

Day 196

Some days things just don't go as planned. Yesterday the kids and I planned to go to Lexington with my mom and dad. We planned to stop to see my grandparents for a little bit then head to a hotel where the kids could swim followed by dinner. I planned to get the kids to bed early so we could wake up early this morning to head back to Tennessee. However, our day did not go according to plans. It began with the kids having a meltdown prior to leaving my parents' house. Once we got to my grandparents' home, we realized they had a gas leak. Resolving the problem occupied the majority of the time we planned to visit with them. Then what should have been a 20-minute trip to the hotel ended up taking almost 2 hours because of severe storms in the area. Once we arrived at the hotel, we realized the power was out and they were unsure if they would regain power at all that evening. We headed to the mall because we knew there was a Chick-fil-A there where the kids could have dinner. The Chick-fil-A was closed. We ended up having to change hotels because of the power outage. We checked into the new hotel only to be told the swimming pool was closed. It was a hard day!

I recognize that all of these things are 100% first-world problems, but the combination of them made for a very frustrating day. It reminded me of John 16:33: "I have told you these things so that in me you may have peace. In this world you will have trouble. But take heart! I have overcome the world." The world we live in is a broken world. We are guaranteed to have days that are filled with frustrations. Jesus reminds us he has come to give peace. The frustrations we experienced yesterday are temporary and fleeting. Today is a new day and I am filled with his peace.

This peace is extended to you. It is an unshakable joy that cannot waver due to circumstantial situations. Where is your source of joy today?

Make today count!

Day 197

When I hit college, a lightbulb seem to come on for me that I had never experienced before. My newfound independence gave me a great desire to stay ahead of the work that was before me. Starting during my freshman year, I kept my planner at least one week ahead of the actual date. In some cases, I would go as far as one month ahead. This required me to have papers written and tests studied for a minimum one week before they were actually due. I remember the end of my freshman year during the last week of school I was trying to find someone to play disc golf with me because all of my work was already completed. I finally found someone to play with me, but it's not because his work was completed. It was because he didn't really care about his classes. This process of early preparation has continued into my life today. Even this morning I found myself preparing breakfast burritos for this week's breakfasts.

Preparation requires long-term vision and planning. Preparation involves thinking about things that may or may not come into play. Preparation is setting aside a little bit of money each paycheck in case an unexpected financial expense pops up. Preparation is being trained in CPR before you ever need to use it. The Bible speaks about preparation quite a bit. King David said: "I have hidden your word in my heart that I might not sin against you." (Psalms 119:9) Hiding God's word in our heart is a form of preparation. When temptation or trouble comes, if you have hidden God's word in your heart, it will be there to guide and comfort you.

Where do you need to be in the process of preparation today? Is it in your personal finances or maybe in your personal health plan? Maybe today it all starts with hiding God's word in your heart.

Make today count!

Day 198

Yesterday afternoon Holly came home with a small worn out children's play dresser. It was in pretty rough shape. I asked her what she was planning to do with it, and she asked me if I would be willing to redo it. I spent about an hour and a half this morning sanding it down and putting on a few fresh coats of paint. I completed the process by cleaning off the mirror to improve the reflection. Without undergoing this revitalization, this piece of furniture would have really been best suited for the trash. Restoration has given it new life.

Restoration brings a newness. The same is true for us spiritually. The Bible says God's mercies are new each day. This is a fresh start each day, a fresh coat of paint. Some of you have been beaten down by difficult situations you are currently dealing with. Maybe today is your chance to ask God for a fresh coat of paint. Psalms 98:1 says, "Sing to the LORD a new song, for he has done marvelous things; his right hand and his holy arm have worked salvation for him."

Christ came to make you new. You have an opportunity to take in his new mercies given to you today. "Therefore, if anyone is in Christ, the new creation has come: The old has gone, the new is here!" (2 Corinthians 5:17)

Make today count!

Day 199

It has begun. The fall grind has officially hit the White House. Today was Cade and Abi Kate's first day of school. Since today is Abi Kate's first day ever, she was up at 6 a.m. as excited as could be. Cade, on the other hand, going into second grade, had to be woken up multiple times and continually encouraged to get ready. Our daily routines seem to cause us to land somewhere between these two extremes. When we lose the big-picture focus, it is easy to get stuck in the frustrations of the day to day. Cade's focus was on the day at hand. Abi Kate's perspective encompassed the long-term view. She views today as the start of her entire school career. When we keep the future in mind during our daily grind, it helps us keep the bigger picture in mind.

We all know and love Jeremiah 29:11: "I know the plans I have for you declares the Lord, plans to prosper you and not harm you, plans to give you a hope and a future." I find it is easy to lose sight of this while grinding out the every day. Today let this serve as a reminder of the big picture. Today is a very small piece of a very large puzzle.

What are you going to do today that is going to push your future five, ten, and even twenty years from now?

Make today count!

Day 200

This week I am in Minnesota for a men's conference. Last night a fellow staff member and I arrived at the hotel we are staying at during the conference. The front desk attendant greeted us as soon as we walked in. During check-in she was so hospitable and mentioned several times that she wanted to make sure we had the best stay possible. After getting a workout in, I went back to the desk area to grab a bottle of water. She engaged me in conversation again and began to tell me how she wanted to know each one of her guests personally. In title, this lady was a customer service representative. Her attitude and actions, however, were those of a CEO. This lady was more than an employee. She was an owner.

When we work out of ownership, we are working as unto God. We are owners with Christ. "Now if we are children, then we are heirs--heirs of God and co-heirs with Christ, if indeed we share in his sufferings in order that we may also share in his glory." (Romans 8:17) I sense that many of us operate as workers in the church. We are children of the king, but I believe the majority of us are not living in this fullness. What would it be like for you to live as an heir of God and to take ownership of all God has for you? Be an owner, not an employee.

Make today count!

Day 201

Yesterday during one of our sessions at the men's conference, Bob, our missions pastor, talked on consistent and credible character. He defined consistency as the achievement of a performance level that fluctuates very little over time. Credibility is the quality of being trusted and believed in. Character, as defined by Bob, is who you are when others are not looking. He went on to explain that your character is revealed when you make decisions out of impulse.

Our character and credibility can be lost in a matter of just one poor decision. You are one poor financial decision, one inappropriate text, one shady business deal away from your credibility and character being called into question. Barring some massive character failure, most of us will never have our character called into question. Today I am asking you who are you when others are not looking? James 1:3 tells us, "Knowing that the testing of your faith produces endurance." A true and honest self-evaluation of our character will only help to sharpen us.

God knows who you are when no one is looking. The question for you today is who are you when no one is looking?

Make today count!

Day 202

My friend Jason and I spent the day fishing on a lake we are not familiar with. We were not smart enough to plan ahead and bring a map of the lake with us. We decided to venture out and thought it best to stay close to the place we launched from. As fishing goes, we found ourselves a little further away from our entry point than we had planned. Thankfully for us, both of us remembered certain points along our path. Working backwards to each one of these landmarks led us back to our boat launch.

We find ourselves journeying through life in a similar way. When difficult situations arise, we are often reminded of people who have gone through similar struggles. We are able to use these people and their experiences to get ourselves back on the correct path. God puts people in our life's path to encourage us when we are going through difficult situations. Oftentimes, the people who are the most encouraging are the ones who have themselves been through similar situations.

Hebrews 10:24-25 says, "And let us consider how we may spur one another on toward love and good deeds, not giving up meeting together, as some are in the habit of doing, but encouraging one another—and all the more as you see the Day approaching." God has put specific people in your path for you to lean on and go to when difficult times arise.

Maybe today you have found yourself in need of some encouragement. Who do you know who has walked through a similar situation like the one you are currently going through? Maybe today you need to do some encouraging to someone you know is struggling. God has uniquely positioned you. Use it for His glory.

Make today count!

Day 203

There is not much that has a hold on us like our money. We spend five out of seven days trying to acquire it and seven out of seven days managing it. I believe a large majority of us even take the time to budget each and every dollar to account for each cent spent. God knows we all hold onto our money dearly. Did you know money is mentioned 800 times throughout the Bible? Why does God ask us to be generous with our money? Does God need our money? The obvious answer here is "no." This is an opportunity for us to show him that he is our God and our money is not.

God clearly knew the principle of a biblical tithe of 10% would be very difficult for the majority of us. Interestingly enough, this is the only area where we have the ability to test the God of the universe. Malachi 3:10 says, "Bring the whole tithe into the storehouse, that there may be food in my house. Test me in this, says the Lord Almighty, and see if I will not throw open the floodgates of heaven and pour out so much blessing that there will not be room enough to store it."

Friends, God does not need your money. God is inviting us to join him in what he is doing. When we place our trust in him first, he will provide.

If you are not currently tithing off of your income, my challenge for you is to take a step of faith, test God, and trust Him with your money. Just a reminder—it's not your money. God owns it all.

Make today count!

Day 204

Over the last few days I have enjoyed shooting some videos for our men's ministry. A few other guys and I are fishing in a remote area of Minnesota. It is always a challenge to learn a new lake. This particular lake we are fishing has a large amount of grass growing from the bottom. Many times, you won't see it from where you are casting off the boat and often shortly after a cast, I have found myself hung up. It would be foolish to cast a similar bait around the same location. The results would not be favorable. When this happens, it is best to use a different lure or cast in another direction.

Life is a lot like this. There are things that come into our path that "hang us up." Those hang ups look different for each of us. For some of us it may be anger, for some addiction, and for others it may be pride. As believers, when these hang ups come, we are called to cast our line a different way or direction. 1 Corinthians 16:13 says, "Be on your guard; stand firm in the faith; be courageous; be strong." We should be on guard when life tries to hang us up. Let's make a change before we find ourselves stuck.

Where do you find yourself getting hung up today? What changes can you make to keep yourself "out of the weeds?"

Make today count!

Day 205

I have been fishing the same lake in Minnesota for the past few days. We have covered a good majority of the lake, and based on the map, we have hit most of the best spots. Last night we made the decision to drive to another local lake to fish today. When getting the same results, change is a must. Change is inevitable. Some change happens on its own, and other times you have to make the choice to change.

Some of us have been getting the same results in our work, in our marriage, and in our relationship with God, but we know there has to be more. What are the changes you know you need to make in these areas but you have been putting off because you know it will be difficult? Change will shape your life in some way.

No matter how much change comes at you, there is one constant—God. Hebrews 13:8 reminds us, "Jesus Christ is the same yesterday and today and forever." In the middle of our struggles, our hardships, and our changes, he is our constant.

Where is change needed in your life right now? As you process through your changes, know that God is your constant in the middle of your process.

Make today count!

Day 206

I am in Minnesota for the week fishing with a group of guys. Early in the week we caught a few fish to keep and cook. We didn't have quite enough for dinner, so last night we set out to catch a few more. The fishing was great last night. After a few hours we had caught four keepers. We pulled back into the boat slip around 9 p.m. We were all worn out from the day and no one wanted to clean the fish. We decided to leave the fish in the live well until morning. What we didn't know was the boat we were renting had a non-functioning bilge pump. This pump is used to dump water that comes into the boat. We woke up in the morning to find our boat half sunken. It was going down and going down quick. Instead of feeling sorry for ourselves, we all jumped into action clearing all of the items out of the boat then tossing water out with a bucket one scoop at a time

There are times when life hits us hard and our boat begins to sink. Trouble can come out of nowhere and begin to overtake us. The way I see it is we have two options when this happens:

1. We feel bad for ourselves and we sit back and watch our boat sink.

2. We get to work. We do everything we possibly can to better the situation including praying for God to give us guidance and direction.

Psalms 46:1: "God is our refuge and strength, a very present help in trouble." I love how David says God is very present. God is not off in heaven unaware of your sinking boat. No—he is near. Do you feel like you are sinking right now? Know that God has not left you. He is aware and he is present. Work like everything depends on you and pray like everything depends on God.

Make today count!

Day 207

My friends and I left Minnesota yesterday morning at 10:30 a.m. to make our way back to Nashville. The plan was to drive as far as we could until we were too tired to continue. We would grab a hotel, get some sleep, then continue driving in the morning. As we began our journey, so began the desire to see if we could make the trek without stopping. Three gas stops, two food stops, two restroom breaks, and 20 hours later, we made it from Minnesota back to Middle Tennessee. It was a long journey but well worth it to get home almost 15 hours earlier than expected. Keeping the end goal in mind is what kept us on track and focused.

Life, as we all know, is a journey. It is not a destination. There are times during our journey through life when we will sprint and times we will crawl. It is our end game that keeps us focused, no matter what stage of life's journey we find ourselves in. In his letter to the church at Philippi, Paul articulates what each of us as Christians are ultimately striving for. "I press on toward the goal to win the prize for which God has called me heavenward in Christ Jesus." (Philippians 3:14) I don't know about you, but at the end of my life, I hope to hear God say to me, "Well done, good and faithful servant."

What is your goal for the end of your journey? What do you want God to say of you?

Make today count!

Day 208

This morning my friend Jason and I went out and fished at Stones River. We had a great morning. We caught several small mouths. I started thinking about how these fish never planned to get caught. It's not like they woke up this morning and thought "I hope I get hooked in the mouth today and drug out of the water by a fisherman." No, what actually happened was something was tossed out in front of them that looked similar to something they would eat. They didn't realize it wasn't the real thing. They saw what they thought was a crawdad and instinct took over. This is what got them hooked.

I don't believe any of us set out to have our day and life ruined. What happens is Satan throws something out to us that looks real, but in reality, it's just something that's going to hook us. 1 Peter 5:8 warns us, "Be alert and of sober mind. Your enemy the devil prowls around like a roaring lion looking for someone to devour." We might run to something we think is going to bring us comfort in the midst of our chaos. Maybe for some of you it is alcohol, binge eating, or "retail therapy." All of these things may appear as if they will bring comfort, but the fact is, they will only lead to our demise. We need to be aware of the tactics the enemy will use against us to get us to fall.

My challenge for you today is to be aware of what is real vs. what is fake and exercise your ability to walk in what is real.

Make today count!

Day 209

Today is my beautiful wife's 31st Birthday! (And when I say beautiful, I mean inside and out.) I cannot imagine where I would be in my life without her. She has inspired me, encouraged me, and challenged me. She saw my calling to ministry on my life before I was ever willing to except it. She is a loving mother, an incredible teacher, and an amazing friend. I am truly blessed to call her mine.

Proverbs 31 describes the traits for a noble woman. She is a woman of virtue, faithfulness, reverence, strength, and endurance. She is charitable, well-dressed, the wife of a good husband, honorable, wise, and kind. She is a good mother, is praiseworthy, and she fears the Lord. "Many women have done excellently, but you surpass them all. Charm is deceitful, and beauty is vain, but a woman who fears the Lord is to be praised. Give her of the fruit of her hands, and let her works praise her in the gates." (vs. 30-31) I believe with all my heart Holly is a woman of noble character.

Ladies, this passage gives you something to aspire to. Single men, this verse gives you your blueprint for the type of woman you are looking for. I am so thankful for my beautiful bride. Happy birthday, Holly! I love you!

Make today count!

Day 210

After being gone for a little over a week, my grass was in dire need of being mowed. Let me clarify that my definition and your definition of "dire need" may differ. For some of you, dire need means that if you take your dog outside, he suddenly disappears into your grass never to be seen again. For others, dire need is when you can no longer see the multiple striping lines left by your mower. I fall into the second camp.

As I was mowing my backyard, I reversed back on my mower just a little too quickly causing me to hit my irrigation control center. When this happened, water began to shoot everywhere soaking me and my mower. I made a call and had someone come to fix the unit. I went back outside later that day to find there was a very small but steady leak. It took just a few extra twists of a knob to tighten it down so no water was able to come through. I recently saw a story online about a lady who had a small leak in her bathroom which ended up making her water bill over $1,000. A small leak left unattended could have had some costly consequences.

The same is true for us and our integrity. Integrity is defined as "the quality of being honest and having strong moral principles or moral uprightness." As with a water leak, even a small leak in our integrity can lead to devastating consequences. When we fail to maintain our integrity, we will lose the trust of those around us. Proverbs 11:3 says, "The integrity of the upright guides them, but the unfaithful are destroyed by their duplicity." If we are to be people who are trustworthy and worthy of being followed, we must be people of consistent integrity. As a small water leak can cause massive damage, a small lapse in your integrity can ruin your character.

My challenge for you today is to make sure there are no leaks within you. Be a person of consistent integrity so no one can question your motives or intent.

Make today count!

Day 211

There many times as a parent when I question my effectiveness and then there days when I see a glimmer of what I am trying to teach begin to sink in. Yesterday was one of those days.

I was stopped by one of Cade's leaders at church. Holding back her tears, she described this situation to me. Cade was sitting near a friend with special needs who was not cooperating with the teacher's wishes. Cade took it upon himself to walk over to the friend and offer him the prize he had just earned to get this child to comply. The child accepted the deal and Cade willingly gave up the prize he had just received. This was a shining glimmer of hope that what Cade is seeing and hearing is sinking in.

1 Timothy 4:12 reminds us, "Don't let anyone look down on you because you are young, but set an example for the believers in speech, in conduct, in love, in faith and in purity." Cade is seven, but yesterday he not only showed the love of Christ to the boy in his class but to the adults who were witnesses to the event. This reminded me of how I need to love people. I believe many times children can show us the purity of having faith in God and a deep and true love for him and for others.

How are you loving those around you today? Are you treating the people around you the way Christ would treat them? Are you willing to give up your prize to brighten someone else's day?

Make today count!

Day 212

Most of us will spend a significant portion of our lives at work. I did some quick math and assuming someone started to work full time around the age of 21, working 45 hours per week until age 61 with one week of vacation, they would work 91,800 hours over the course of 40 years. That is a significant amount of time and energy to invest into something. My fear is that the majority of us will spend those 91,800 hours doing something we don't enjoy or feel value in. God has gifted you in specific ways to solve specific problems.

If you're anything like me, you may allow fear to keep you from pursuing something which you really want to do deep down and instead pursue what you know is safe. Fear keeps you from pursuing that which could bring a feeling of significance and that which you would be excited to take on each day. God is, of course, more concerned with who we *are* becoming than what we are *becoming*. He has called us to be holy. In our work, "Whatever you do, do it from the heart, as something done for the Lord and not for people, knowing that you will receive the reward of an inheritance from the Lord. You serve the Lord Christ." (Colossians 3:23-24) I have found myself on both sides of this fence. I have spent days feeling like I was making no impact. I did not feel challenged, and I needed something more. Today I can tell you that I look forward to the interactions I have with people and with opportunities to spur people further along in their walk. Each of us wants to live a life of significance, and we draw much of that from how we spend the majority of our hours.

My challenge for you today is to work as unto the Lord. Has God put something on your heart, perhaps a problem for you to solve? If so, begin to pray and ask for wisdom as you open and investigate the doors before you.

Make today count!

Day 213

Abi Kate is now in her first year of preschool at Providence Christian Academy. It's fun to talk to her after school every day to hear about the new songs, Bible verses, and ideas she is learning. Apparently, they have been talking about basic anatomy. I have heard her singing "head, shoulders, knees, and toes" several times this week. This morning I was sitting next to our dog, Mowgli. Abi Kate said, "Dad, where is Mowgli's heart?" She knows exactly where *her* heart is, but it was confusing to know where the dog's heart is since he is on all fours. I stood him up on his hind legs and pointed to where his heart was located. Once I pointed to the location she said "Yep, that's it!" as if she was quizzing me the whole time.

I think her question is a good one. Where is your heart? I'm not talking about the physical location of your heart but rather the spiritual location of your heart. We grow up hearing songs like, "listen to your heart." It's a catchy song but is actually terrible theological advice. Jeremiah 17:9 warns us: "The heart is deceitful above all things, and desperately wicked: who can know it?" Our heart will deceive us when left to itself. This should remind us of the importance of surrendering our heart to the Lord. If our heart is with him and we look to him first, we are less likely to be deceived than if we are trusting our heart to ourselves.

My question for you today is this: Where is your heart? Are you trusting yourself with it or have you given your heart to the God of the universe?

Make today count!

Day 214

John Maxwell is arguably one of the greatest leadership educators of our time. He has written numerous leadership books that have encouraged and inspired leaders across the globe. One of his most famous quotes is probably, "Everything rises and falls on leadership." I'm currently reading a devotional he wrote on leadership. I read a quote by Helen Keller in one of these devotions that greatly inspired me. As you probably know, Helen Keller was a highly-educated social activist who was deaf and blind. Despite her disabilities, she was seen as a leader of her time. She said, "The only thing worse than being blind is having sight but no vision." Vision inspires, creates purpose, and drives teams in the same direction towards a common goal.

Clear vision creates purpose, builds synergy, fosters creativity, and creates an environment where each person's gifts and abilities are able to thrive. With clear vision each member of the team knows their role and is not intimidated or concerned with the other parts of the puzzle another person may be building. The team is collectively more concerned that the puzzle is built. Many times, when we begin talking about vision, we automatically think of corporate settings. The reality is that you should have a vision for your life 20 years from now, for your children, and your family unit as a whole. Vision is about the big picture. Philippians 2:3-4 says, "Do nothing out of selfish ambition or vain conceit. Rather, in humility value others above yourselves, not looking to your own interests but each of you to the interests of the others." Operating within vision is about operating as a team. It is easy to get wrapped up in what we are bringing to the table all the while losing sight of the vision.

Where are you going? Have you defined a clear vision and direction for those underneath you?

Make today count!

Day 215

This morning I took a friend fishing on the Stones River. He had not fished much on the Stones River and was relying on my experience to help him navigate the river and hopefully catch a few fish. While we fished today, I pointed out different spots in the river that are deep, spots where I have caught a lot of fish, and spots where I constantly see snakes. I by no means am an expert fishing guide. I have navigated part of the river several times, and my experience led to a safe and successful morning of fishing. Together we caught 10 smallmouth bass.

Life is a lot like your first time fishing in the river. It sure helps to have someone who has walked through it before you. Having someone who has experience walking the path you are currently navigating will only better your chances of success. They are familiar with the highs, lows, pitfalls, and snares you are facing. Most of us allow our pride to keep us from asking for guidance. The friend I fished with this morning sought me out and asked me to take him fishing. We must be owners in our own growth and development.

Hebrews 4:16 encourages, "Therefore let us draw near with confidence to the throne of grace, so that we may receive mercy and find grace to help in time of need." We have a God who is ready, willing, and able to help us when we need it. My challenge for you today is to ask for the help you desperately need. Find someone who has walked the path you are navigating and cry out to the God of the universe.

Make today count!

Day 216

I spent my morning as an assistant coach for Providence Academy's flag football league. Of the 10 kids I was assigned to help with, only three of them had any previous football experience. This league focuses on teaching the kids different routes they can run. For those of you who are not familiar with routes for football, it's simply the direction in which the person trying to catch the ball runs. One of the most important things we tried to reiterate to the kids was to catch the ball in stride. The goal is to progress down the field prior to receiving the ball. Each kid was eager for their chance to be to receiver. This is a hard lesson to teach second graders. It is also a difficult lesson for us to learn as adults.

In life we are progressing in many different areas, such as professionally and personally. There are times when the attention is on our work and leadership. There are other times when the focus is on someone else. It's important for us to understand that when the focus is not on what we are doing, that we are continuing to progress as a spouse, as a parent, and as an employee. If we continue to be faithful running our routes, there will be times when life will throw you the ball. When we run our routes well, we will catch the ball in stride. Being faithful even when no one is looking is what matters the most. Like 16:10: "One who is faithful in very little is also faithful in much, and one who is dishonest in very little is also dishonest in much." Be faithful to consistently run your route. Your day to receive the ball will come.

Make today count!

Day 217

We are back into the fall grind 100% at my house. We have developed our new normal with both kids now heading off to school with their mom in the morning. After they are ready in the morning, I have started reading Louie Giglio's devotional, *Indescribable*, with them. It is incredibly engaging and age appropriate for kids.) Most mornings we are pushing it to the absolute last second to get everyone ready and the devotion completed. Occasionally we may have a little excess time which I like to utilize to share some form of a life lesson with the kids.

Last week we had enough time for one of these lessons. The lesson was "you get to choose what type of day you have." Sure, life may throw some things at you, but ultimately your attitude will determine the outcome of your day. As my dad likes to say, "Attitude determines altitude." Craig Groeschel, one of my favorite pastors, gives this illustration: Each morning a buzzard wakes up and finds things that are dead. Each morning a hummingbird wakes up and finds something sweet. Both of these are birds, but the difference is in what they search for. Proverbs 17:22: "A joyful heart is good medicine, but a broken spirit dries up the bones." You get to choose how this day goes.

If you are being honest with yourself, there are mornings when you wake up like the buzzard. My challenge for you today is to wake up like the hummingbird. Search for something sweet. Your attitude determines your altitude!

Make today count!

Day 218

My men's Sunday evening small group is currently studying the book of Colossians. This is a study by Louie Giglio. Each week God has revealed so many amazing things through this study.

Colossians 3:9-10 says, "Do not lie to each other, since you have taken off your old self with its practices and have put on the new self, which is being renewed in knowledge in the image of its Creator." In an Instagram world, this is hard for us to live out. I love what he said specifically about Instagram. "Instagram is my best life on my best day with the best filter." This is the way we love to portray our lives.

When we lead with truth and vulnerability, we open our lives up so others can see Christ in us despite our weaknesses. Our Instagram culture creates a picture that our lives are absent of struggle. As we all know, this is not reality. When we lead with our weakness, we show others we are accessible. Our transparency makes us easier to relate to. I can't relate to someone who is always on vacation, but I can relate to someone who is having a hard time with their 4-year old. Authenticity creates trust, and trust can create change.

My challenge for you today is to use your social media platform to lead with weakness and to point people to Christ.

Make today count!

Day 219

Have you ever had a time when your mind was flooded with 1,000 reasons why you were not qualified or good enough to do whatever it is God has called you to? Being totally honest, today is one of those days for me. This morning my mind has been filled with all the reasons why I'm not qualified to be in the role I am in, to write something that will truly benefit someone, or to speak boldly and confidently enough to draw people to God. Today's truth might be for you also, but it is 100% for me.

We can look throughout scripture to see all the different characters God used to see that God does not call the qualified, he equips those he calls. Moses had a speech impediment, David was just a boy, King Manasseh was just 12 years old when he took the throne, and the list goes on. Our calling has nothing to do with our abilities or what we bring to the table. Our calling is 100% about our willingness to be a part of what God is doing. When lies fill your mind, you must remind yourself of the truths in God's word. Hebrews 13:20-21: "Now may the God of peace, who through the blood of the eternal covenant brought back from the dead our Lord Jesus, that great Shepherd of the sheep, equip you with everything good for doing his will, and may he work in us what is pleasing to him, through Jesus Christ, to whom be glory for ever and ever. Amen." Our equipping comes from God. There's nothing we need to bring to the table other than a willingness to participate.

Today I'm reminding myself of this verse and I am going to walk in the truth of it.

Make today count!

Day 220

Cade loves baked potatoes. It has been awhile since we had them for dinner, so I decided to make them for him last night since he's been asking for them. After baking them for over an hour in a 400° oven, it was time to take them out. I clearly was a bit distracted as I reach my hand into the oven with a partial oven mitt to grab the tray the potatoes were on. I came in contact with one of the burners on the top of my exposed hand. It's been quite a while since I've had a good burn. I forgot how much it hurts. If you had seen my hand, you would have seen a clear mark where it was obvious that something had made an impact.

A mark creates evidence there has been an impact. We who are in Christ have also been marked. Ephesians 1:13 says, "You also were included in Christ when you heard the message of truth, the gospel of your salvation. When you believed, you were marked in him with a seal, the promised Holy Spirit." His mark on our lives shows that we have intertwined our life in his. He gives us life.

If someone were to look at my hand, I would assume their next question would be, "What happened?" Today my question for you is this: When people see your life, do they see Christ in you and ask, "What happened?" Is your mark pointing people back towards Christ?

Make today count!

Day 221

The theme for our small group at church this year is "Don't do life alone." I spent several years of my life with a private struggle that I continued to fight alone. I had small periods of success but then I would find myself right back where I started. It was not until I was willing to get into a group and spend my time with other men that I really began to experience victory. I am like most men in the fact that I hate to admit it if I am unable to figure something out. The reality is that God has made us so we don't have all the answers. We need to rely on him and on others so we can live our lives to the fullest.

There are several verses in the Bible that speak to this idea of community. Proverbs 27:17, "As iron sharpens iron, so one man sharpens another." Ecclesiastes 4:12, "Though one may be overpowered, two can defend themselves. A cord of three strands is not quickly broken."

What's interesting about both of these verses is they give imagery of a process happening--iron being forged and chords being braided. Being in community is work, but it will strengthen you. Those of you who have been stuck and in need of a breakthrough, I can tell you that your breakthrough is on the other side of entering into a biblical community.

If you are not involved in a small group, my challenge for you today is to contact your local church and find out how you can get involved. On the other side of uncomfortable is a breakthrough. Don't do life alone!

Make today count!

Day 222

One of the great things about the school my kids attend is that they are required to wear uniforms. What I like about the uniform is the fact that it makes getting dressed each morning quite easy. You know what's required and you know what your options are. This morning Abi Kate pulled out a different pair of socks that are not within the uniform guidelines. I reminded her that she had to wear the uniform, that it was not an option, and that all of her friends would be wearing the exact same thing. She looked at me and said, "But I want to be different." If a child were to come to school wearing tie-dyed socks in a school filled with children who are in uniform, they would certainly stand out because what they are wearing goes against what everyone else is doing.

In our culture, certain things are accepted as normal—the use of a certain language, the majority of movies, and sexual relationships outside of marriage, just to name a few. Blending in with culture is aligning yourself with what everyone else agrees is normal. As believers, we see from scripture that we are called to live our lives in a way that is countercultural and should look so different that it makes people ask and wonder what gives.

Galatians 5:22-23: "But the fruit of the Spirit is love, joy, peace, forbearance, kindness, goodness, faithfulness, gentleness and self-control. Against such things there is no law." If Christ is within us, then these descriptors will be evident in our lives. Having peace in the midst of chaos makes you different. Having self-control when you feel you cannot restrain yourself makes you different.

My question for you today is this: Is there something about your life that makes people wonder why you are different?

Make today count!

Day 223

Last night Holly and I decided to have a family date night. It is not often that we go out for an activity and dinner with just our family. We thought this would be a great way to surprise and reward the kids for a great start to the school year. We decided to go see a movie at the new theater in town and prior to the movie, we would go out for dinner. We had a great time at dinner then made our way to the movie theater. We saw *Christopher Robin*. This is the story of the grown-up Christopher Robin from the Winnie the Pooh series. In the story, Christopher became focused on his business as his number one priority and forgot his family. Pooh Bear shows back up to remind him about the things in life that are most important. At the end of the movie, Christopher Robin and Pooh Bear are sitting on a log and Pooh bear asks this question: "What day is it?" Christopher Robin, who has previously been caught up with his future and all the things that need to be completed, responds and says, "Today is today."

This quote really focuses on the mental shift that occurred for Christopher Robin. He realized that today is all he has. The same is true for each of us. This moment right now is all you are guaranteed. I'm not saying we don't need to plan to prepare for the future, but I do believe it's important for us to cherish today. As an unknown author said, "Today is called the present because it is a gift."

Matthew 6:34 reminds us, "So do not worry about tomorrow; for tomorrow will care for itself. Each day has enough trouble of its own." Find joy in your family and those you love today. Make the most of today because you will not get it again.

Make today count!

Day 224

Yesterday evening Holly and I went to watch a Tennessee Titans game along with some friends. I am a people watcher. I love to watch people and how they interact with each other and their surroundings. At a professional football game, you will see several different types of people. The first type is those who are decked out in gear for the home team. The second group is those who wear gear for the opposing team. The third group are those who wear team gear from a team not represented at that day's competition. The last group are those who wear normal, everyday clothes. However, this last group is broken into two categories: those who wear normal everyday clothing that matches the team colors and those who do not. You can tell a lot about people just by looking at them at a football game. I know that the guy who has his entire body painted in team colors cares far more about the game than the guy who comes in with wearing a golf polo and khaki shorts. It's easy to know that the guy with the painted chest is a super fan, but it is much more difficult to identify which team the guy in everyday clothes is cheering for.

Regardless of whether we are Christians or not, we each represent a side. We have the home team of Christ followers and we the away team, those who know the gospel and have clearly refused it. Then there are those who try to look like the home team but haven't bought into what the home team is about, but they are there checking it out. These people are looking for a team to belong to, on the fringe to coming to faith.

Just as we can identify true sports fans, we as Christians can be identified by our fruits. In John 13:34-35, Jesus says, "A new commandment I give to you, that you love one another, even as I have loved you, that you also love one another. By this all men will know that you are My disciples, if you have love for one another." This love will point those on the fringe of faith towards Christ. But it is not enough for them to see our actions. We must be able to use our words to share what Christ has done for us.

My challenge for you today is to use your love for others as a team jersey. Use it as a way to let people know who you are for!

Make today count!

Day 225

AS part of the routine to prepare for school each morning, Holly and I have clearly defined our morning roles. She gets up and irons the kids' clothes and then wakes everyone up. Once I'm up, I typically iron her clothes for her after taking the dog out, then begin to make the kids some breakfast.

After the first few weeks of noticing that the kids still seemed very hungry later in the day, I decided to start making them a much larger breakfast. This morning I made omelets with a side of oatmeal. Cade was thankful and ate his breakfast well. Abi Kate, on the other hand, complained about the amount of oatmeal she had received. She wanted cereal and her omelet was not cut just the way she liked it. As the one attempting to make a nice breakfast for her, I found this to be quite frustrating. My goal is to feed her a nutritious breakfast to give her a great start for the day. She wanted to argue over petty issues.

I started thinking about how this relates to the church world. We have all heard of churches separating over various issues. The majority of the time the issues which separate the church are preference issues rather than spiritual issues. I realize there are times when problems arise in the church due to a true sin issue. This is not what I'm talking about. I'm talking about churches that split over the specific type of music, the decor in the worship center, and other personal preferences. The church does not exist as a place to meet your personal and preferential needs. 1 Corinthians 1:10 reminds us, "I appeal to you, brothers, by the name of our Lord Jesus Christ, that all of you agree, and that there be no divisions among you, but that you be united in the same mind and the same judgment." The church exists to edify Christ and to point others to him. We are called to be the hands and feet of Jesus. When we allow our preferences to interfere with what God is doing, it affects more than just the church. The outside world takes note.

Have you allowed your personal preferences to interfere with the movement of God? What can you do today to unite and encourage your local church body?

Make today count!

Day 226

This morning Holly was making the lunches for the kids and she asked me if I would peel and slice an apple to add to their lunch. I grabbed an apple I had bought some time last week. Nothing felt odd about this apple. It did not look bad from the outside. I washed it off and began to peel it. Once it was peeled, I used an apple wedge cutter to cut it into eight equal slices. I pushed firmly down to insert the blades into the apple then without much pressure at all, I was able to cut all the way through the apple. I have used this tool dozens of times and it has never been quite this easy. When the apple slices fell, upon further investigation I saw that the slices were all dark brown. Starting at the core of the apple, it was completely rotten all the way out to the outer parts of the apple but the remaining quarter-inch was perfectly white and crisp. From the outside, this apple appeared to be fresh, but from the inside, it was only fit for the trashcan.

This got me thinking about the many times in the New Testament where Jesus spoke to the religious leaders of the day. Several times throughout the gospels Jesus reminded them that it is the inward man that matters, not the outer man. If the inside is rotting away, fruit is not worth consuming. Matthew 23:28 says, "So you, too, outwardly appear righteous to men, but inwardly you are full of hypocrisy and lawlessness." This serves as a warning for us as well. It's easy for us to want to appear to have it all together, but on the inside, we are wasting away.

My challenge for us today is to do an inward examination of our heart to ensure that the fruits that are being produced are worthy of consumption.

Make today count!

Day 227

Demos' is a family-owned restaurant chain in Middle Tennessee with quite possibly the best soup I have ever had. Their signature soup is a chicken and rice soup which they serve with some amazing bread. They have a great lunch combination where you get all-you-can eat soup and salad for $7.95. I went there yesterday with two of my buddies and the soup and salad combo was the obvious choice. There's something about all you can eat that will push you beyond your normal limits. The way the math works in my mind is the more I eat, the better the value. The problem is that this type of splurging causes problems.

I believe there are many Christians who live with an all-you-can-sin mentality. We have an understanding that we are saved by grace and that once we are in a relationship with Christ, there is nothing that will change this. Our relationship with Christ should not be used as a license to sin. The apostle Paul explains this well in Romans 6:1-2: "What shall we say, then? Shall we go on sinning so that grace may increase? By no means! We are those who have died to sin; how can we live in it any longer?" If we continue to live in our sin once we have been freed from it, we are like someone who has been kept in captivity and then released yet chooses to stay in the jail cell. True freedom is found in living out our relationship with Christ daily.

Have you made the grace of God a cheap grace? Have you used it as an excuse to live a life that is contrary to what he is calling you to? My challenge for you today is to meditate on the cost of this grace that was freely given to each one of us.

Make today count!

Day 228

I am not a light sleeper. Typically, I'm not easily awakened in the middle of the night. The majority of the time it takes Holly nudging me a little bit to wake me up if there's an issue with one of the kids or she has heard a strange noise. Last night was an exception. I found myself waking up almost every hour on the hour. After this happened for about the fifth time, the thought crossed my mind that maybe God was trying to get my attention. I said a quick simple prayer asking God if he was trying to tell me something. A few seconds later today's entire devotion was given to me.

The book of 1 Samuel details the story of a young boy named Samuel who lived with the prophet Eli. During the middle of the night, a voice called to Samuel three separate times. Each time he went to Eli thinking he had called him. After the third time, Eli realized it was God trying to get Samuel's attention. We read in 1 Samuel 3:8-10: "Then Eli realized that the Lord was calling the boy. So Eli told Samuel, 'Go and lie down, and if he calls you, say, Speak, Lord, for your servant is listening.' So, Samuel went and lay down in his place. The Lord came and stood there, calling as at the other times, 'Samuel! Samuel!' Then Samuel said, 'Speak, for your servant is listening.'"

We live a life that is fast paced, busy, and noisy. The reality is we leave little margin to hear from God. Throughout Scripture God tends to speak through a still small voice. I don't know about you, but one of the only times I am truly still and quiet is when I am sleeping. My guess is that many of you have some restless nights. Maybe, just maybe, God is trying to get your attention. The next time you find yourself stirred in the middle of the night, my challenge for you is to tell God you are here and you are listening and then wait to hear what he might have to say.

Make today count!

Day 229

I think we would all agree that it's easy to find yourself among people who are pessimistic. You can be on social media for less than 45 seconds and encounter a barrage of negative comments. Optimism is contagious. My friend Brad is one of the most optimistic people I know. Prior to ever leaving for a fishing trip, he makes me feel as if we are the disciples when Jesus told them to cast their nets on the other side of the boat. This was probably the most epic amount of fish ever caught in his day and time. Optimism is contagious and encouraging. It's also highly encouraging when someone lets you know they are praying for you. It's so impactful to know someone is taking the time to lift you up to the God of the universe.

We have so many reasons to be optimistic. As believers, our eternity is secure. My favorite reason for being optimistic is found in Romans 8:34: "Who then is the one who condemns? No one. Christ Jesus who died--more than that, who was raised to life--is at the right hand of God and is also interceding for us." I think we all can agree that to have a friend or family member tell you they are praying for you is a great feeling, but today I want to remind you that Jesus Christ, God in human form, stands before the father and intercedes on your behalf. I can't think of anyone I would rather have making my requests known to God than Jesus Christ himself.

Maybe today you find yourself discouraged, down, and maybe even a little pessimistic. I want to remind you that you have the greatest reason of all to be optimistic because Jesus is interceding on your behalf.

Make today count!

Day 230

The weather yesterday was absolutely amazing. After both kids were home from school, we spent most of the rest of the day outside. The kids love to ride the go cart, so we decided to take it out for a little while. After taking Abi Kate on a long ride, it was Cade's turn. I turned the go cart off while they were switching places then turned it back on once Cade was settled in. The plan was for us to go very slowly following Abi Kate in a power wheel she is learning to drive. I turned the go cart on and hit the gas. The go cart jumped forward but then would not move. It was making a very strange sound. I went behind it and looked at all the wires. Everything seemed to be in place. I took the cover off to make sure the belt was still in place, which it was. Then something prompted to look at the opposite side of the go cart. Sure enough, Cade's seatbelt had become wrapped underneath the cart prohibiting it from moving forward. The problem wasn't the engine or the belt. The problem was us.

Each of us strive to make progress in our lives. Most of us strive for progress in our business, in personal relationships, and in our relationship with God. I know that in each of these areas there have been times when I have felt completely stuck. At times, it felt as if no matter what I tried to do I could not move forward. The truth is that 75% of the time when I am failing to make progress in any of these areas, it's not due to an outside circumstance or another person. It tends to be about me.

I don't know about you, but my tendency is to look at other people first. Lamentations 3:40 says, "Let us examine and probe our ways, and let us return to the LORD." This makes it clear that we should first examine ourselves then we should look to the Lord. If you are not finding progress where you desire, my challenge for you today is to begin your search within your own heart and mind.

Make today count!

Day 231

I have been promising Cade for some time that once he developed proficiency with his swimming abilities, I would take him kayak fishing down the river. It worked out that we were able to go with a group of my friends last night. Cade was super excited. The back of my kayak has an area large enough where we were able to put a small foam cushion for Cade to sit on. This allowed him to lean against the back of my seat so his view down the river was quite different than mine. It typically takes us about 2 1/2 hours to get to our fishing spot from our entry point. However, last night we were taking out from a spot I was unfamiliar with. My friend told me it was near our normal location, so I just assumed it was one of the houses that was right before our normal takeout.

Two of my buddies were ahead of me quite a distance and the other two were quite a bit behind me which left me and Cade somewhere in-between them. As we got to the location of the normal takeout, I called my friend and asked how much further it was. He told me it was around a half mile more. The problem was it was beginning to get dark at this point. What I found so interesting was that although I was unsure of exactly where we were going and I could see what was in front of me, Cade could not. He could not have been more sure of one thing—me. He had 100% confidence in the fact that his dad was going to get him safely back home.

There are times in life when you feel like you are floating down a river facing the other direction. You don't know what's coming next. In these times, it is of extreme importance that you know who you are trusting in. By the time we made it to the takeout, it was completely dark, but in the darkness and going backwards, Cade never doubted his father. Proverbs 28:26 says, "Those who trust in themselves are fools, but those who walk in wisdom are kept safe." Who is wiser than God? The obvious answer here is "no one."

My question for you today is when life gets bumpy, dark, and off schedule, who are you trusting in?

Make today count!

Day 232

Throughout the course of my life, I have had several different coaches and mentors. Each of them has been crucial in different seasons of my growth and development. Some of them worked with me academically, some physically, and some spiritually. There is one who has been the most consistent and has been with me in every season of my life. The person I'm describing is, of course, my dad. My dad has walked with me through my best and worst days. He has walked with me through the tragic accident of a friend, through a deep valley of panic attacks, and through heartbreak. On the other side of these times, he has been there to celebrate with me through marriage, the birth of two children, and seeing me finally fulfill God's vocational calling on my life. Ultimately in all things, he pointed me back to God and to his word. He is a constant source of inspiration, truth telling, and wisdom.

Our job description as fathers is one that includes an overwhelming amount of duties, a few we feel qualified and comfortable to perform, but in many others, we have to rely on the support of other men as well as wisdom from God. The most important thing we can do as fathers is to instill God's truth into our children's lives. Deuteronomy 6:6-9 encourages: "These commandments that I give you today are to be on your hearts. Impress them on your children. Talk about them when you sit at home and when you walk along the road, when you lie down and when you get up. Tie them as symbols on your hands and bind them on your foreheads. Write them on the doorframes of your houses and on your gates." This passage provides a visual illustration of what it looks like to live this out. It is bringing God into all areas of your conversation as you teach your children. As a father, there's nothing more important you can do than to point your kids back to Christ.

Maybe for some of you your experience with your father does not come near my sentiments above. Today you have an opportunity to be the catalyst for change in your family. You can start a new tradition of what an earthly father looks like.

Make today Count!

Day 233

For four years now, I have driven the exact same direction to work every day, and during my drive, I noticed a particular piece of property which has been for sale for an extensive period of time. What's interesting about this piece of property is that four years ago it was a mowed field. However, through the years, the field has been completely unmanaged and untouched. Because of this neglect, what was a short grass field has now become filled with small trees, large bushes, and a breeding ground for different types of weeds. This property as it stands currently would not be good for much.

Things will grow in our hearts and minds the same way if they are unmanaged. Anger unmanaged can turn to resentment, rage, and ultimately to hate. Desire turns into lustful thoughts and ultimately turns into lustful actions. Our minds and hearts left unmanaged will only breed something that is not useful. Romans 8:6: "The mind governed by the flesh is death, but the mind governed by the Spirit is life and peace." We must allow the Holy Spirit to guide and manage us in these areas so this negative growth will not occur.

This is all easier said than done. Each of us have our defaults where we are most likely to let these patterns of unwanted growth get out of hand. My challenge for you today is to pray and ask God to show you these areas and ask him to take over the management.

Make today count!

Day 234

It was during my fifth grade year that it became evident that there was a cause for my struggle to read/learn. My parents decided the best option was to homeschool me for one year. During my sixth-grade year, I met weekly with an intensive reading specialist. My parents were promised that if they followed the plan that was outlined for us, I would begin to read better and establish a learning process that would work for me. Week after week for the entire school year, I met with this lady. My mom and I would review and practice the content I was taught that week and though my learning style is different than many others, the promise was fulfilled and I was able to adapt and find success throughout my education. This promise required a process.

In the Old Testament Abraham was promised he would become the father of many nations. However, within this promise there was a process that required him to move away from everything he knew. God promised the children of Israel that he would lead them to the Promised Land, but again we see that there was a process they had to go through before they entered the Promised Land. They spent 40 years wandering in the desert learning how to properly worship God.

We all want the promise, but we don't want the process. We have no problem believing and receiving Jeremiah 29:11 which says, "For I know the plans I have for you declares the Lord, plans to prosper you and not harm you, plans to give you a hope and a future." I don't know about you, but I am not as prone to get excited about Isaiah 48:10: "See I have been testing you for myself like silver, I have put you through the fire of trouble." We will not see the promise unless we walk through the process.

What are the things God has promised you today? What are the dreams and goals you know he has called you to? When you find yourself deep in the process, remember the promises are on the other side.

Make today count!

Day 235

The men's ministry at my church is currently working through a six-week series entitled, "Stay Positive." Last night we looked at encouragement. The three main points of the message were: Encourage others daily, encourage others spiritually, and encourage yourself in the Lord. I believe practicing any of these three with some consistency and regularity will cause you to be a blessing to others and in return will bless you. Upon deeper conversation with my small group, it was mentioned that without encouraging yourself in the Lord, it would be much more difficult and potentially impossible to do the other two. It really goes back to the old adage of "you can't give away what you don't have." If you have not first been encouraged by the Lord, it will be much more difficult for you to in turn encourage others.

I believe the Holy Spirit prompts each of us at random times to be an encourager to another person. Have you ever found yourself driving and had a random person pop into your mind? I believe this is the Holy Spirit putting this person on your heart. You never know what's on the other side of your willingness to be an encourager. My friend Brad tells the story about when he was stepping into a difficult situation and was literally seconds away from knocking on the door of his biological father who he has little to no relationship with. He hesitated and was almost to the point where he was just going to go home when his phone rang and it was it encouraging text message from a friend. That encouraging text message is what pushed him to knock on the door. The person who sent the text message probably thought it was seemingly insignificant, but it mattered a great deal to Brad, and it mattered for eternity as Brad was able to have a salvation conversation with his father.

1 Thessalonians 5:11 says: "Therefore encourage one another and build each other up, just as in fact you are doing." My challenge for you today is to first encourage yourself in the Lord through prayer and reading scripture. Secondly, encourage another person. Pray and ask God to put someone on your heart and step out of your comfort zone. You never know what is on the other side of your encouraging words.

Make today count!

Day 236

In the past few weeks, suicide has come up multiple times through social media, the news, and through a coworker who is grieving due to the suicide of someone close to them. Having walked through a very difficult season of severe panic attacks, I know firsthand that anxiety and depression are incredibly difficult to experience. During my late elementary/early middle school years, I remember my dad went through a deep depression. As a child, it is very difficult to understand just what is going on. All you know is that you would do anything in the world to make what that person is experiencing go away.

We will experience difficulty. We will experience hardships and trouble. Jesus tells us in John 16:33, "I have told you these things, so that in me you may have peace. In this world you will have trouble. But take heart! I have overcome the world." Not one of us wants to experience pain. In my own life, it was when I experienced the most pain that I experienced the most growth. Each of us will have times when we feel like we have come to the end of ourselves. Suicide is a very permanent solution to very temporary problems. Even in the midst of the darkest forest on the darkest night, the sun will rise in the morning.

No matter how dark your situation may seem right now, know the God of the universe is madly in love with you. He wants nothing more than to have a personal relationship with you. John 3:16 tells us the great extent he went to to show us his love: "For God so loved the world that he gave his one and only Son, that whoever believes in him shall not perish but have eternal life." If you need an ear, I am here for you! You matter, your story matters.

Make today count!

Day 237

Today is one of my favorite days of the year. Today is the opening day of dove hunting season. I enjoy duck hunting because it is a very social event. Typically, a duck hunt begins with a big group meal. It's a lot of fun be in the field with friends talking and creating great memories. I've always enjoyed duck hunting but in the past two years, it has gotten even better since Cade is now old enough to come with me. As men, we love to pass down knowledge of our hobbies to our children. I find myself looking for opportunities to teach Cade about hunting before we go as well as while we are there. As we drive down the road if I see a group of birds, I quiz him on whether they are adults or not. I teach him as we are going along.

I believe most men would agree that it's easy for us to tell our kids about our favorite hobbies, sports teams, and other passions. We feel knowledgeable, excited, and equipped to share with them about these things. I believe the majority of us find it much more difficult to talk to our kids about our faith in God. We're unsure we have the right words to say, and we have a fear that we will be unable to answer their questions. Deuteronomy 6:5-9 says, "Love the Lord your God with all your heart, with all your soul, and with all your strength. Take to heart these words that I give you today. Repeat them to your children. Talk about them when you're at home or away, when you lie down or get up. Write them down, and tie them around your wrist, and wear them as headbands as a reminder. Write them on the doorframes of your houses and on your gates." To live this out doesn't mean you have to hold a seminary degree. It means you are telling your children how you love God practically and how God meets your needs every day.

My challenge for you today is to share your story. Share your faith with your kids as you go. Don't trust in your own abilities or your own words. Trust in God and he will give you the right words and will lead you as you lead your children.

Make today count!

Day 238

One very important process for young minds to develop as they are growing and learning is memorization. I'm sure you can remember memorizing sequences of numbers, rhymes, and ways to remember all the states or presidents in your early childhood days. Memorization makes our mind sharper. I love that my kids' school not only works on helping the kids memorize those important facts, but they also work on memorizing God's Word. Each week Cade is required to recite a new scripture and to write the scripture out. By the time the school year is over, he will have memorized more than 35 passages of scripture.

There are multiple verses in scripture that talk about the importance of keeping God's word in our hearts and minds. Colossians 3:16 says, "Let the word of Christ richly dwell within you, with all wisdom teaching and admonishing one another with psalms and hymns and spiritual songs, singing with thankfulness in your hearts to God." As you dedicate yourself to memorizing scripture, it's amazing how scriptures will pop up in your mind at just the right time.

My challenge for you today is to memorize Romans 6:23. You will have to do a little work and look it up, but what you'll see is that this verse encompasses the entire gospel. It is a wonderful verse to explain just how much God is in love with you.

Make today count!

Day 239

"Rejoice always, pray without ceasing, in everything give thanks; for this is the will of God in Christ Jesus for you." (1 Thessalonians 5:16-18) I make a sincere effort to be in prayer throughout my day. Am I saying I am constantly praying? No. Do I ever forget to pray before a meal? Yes. This is an area that I am growing in. One of the things I try my best to do is immediately stop and pray about a need the moment I am aware of it. Guys often come to me and say, "Hey, will you pray for...?" I try my absolute best to stop and pray with them right then. I don't do this 100% of the time, but I sure try. I believe to pray without ceasing means to make your request known to God in the moment that it's known to you.

1 Peter 5:7 says, "Cast your cares on him, because he cares for you." I don't see any stipulations in this verse that requires your prayer request to carry a certain burden. It says if it is your care, then you can cast it on him. There are times I pray for things that other people would think are seemingly meaningless. Here's an example: Just last night I was trying to fix something in Holly's car and I knew I had it connected correctly but it just would not work. I was getting frustrated, so I prayed and asked God to help me out. Five seconds later, it was working. If it is a burden to you, and it is creating anxiety, fear, or frustration, it is worthy to bring to God.

My challenge for you today is to make your requests known to God regardless of how insignificant they might seem to you. They matter to you and you matter to him.

Make today count!

Day 240

Cade and I had the opportunity to go on two dove hunts this weekend and it was an awesome experience. His excitement level both days was unmatched. He absolutely loves every second of it. You would assume that having a seven-year-old with you would be incredibly stressful and difficult to manage. The truth is, it is actually very helpful to have him with me. He loves to be the one to get the birds that have fallen. With his small stature, it's easier for him to get under and over the top of fences where the birds may have landed. Without his assistance, we probably would have lost birds that fell in places difficult to access. It's easy to dismiss small children or others we feel for whatever reason will be an inconvenience to us.

In Luke chapter 18, we see a similar narrative play out. A group of small children began to gather around Jesus, and the disciples decided these children did not need to interrupt Jesus. But look what we discover from Jesus in verse 16: "But Jesus called the children to him and said, 'Let the little children come to me, and do not hinder them, for the kingdom of God belongs to such as these.'" I think this story represents a broader scope than just Jesus welcoming the children. Jesus was constantly welcoming those others considered "unwanted." What we see is that these people, like the woman at the well, spark change and create impact.

Who are the people you have dismissed? My challenge for you today is to change your mindset about them and see what God has in store. Chances are these individuals will teach you more than you could ever teach them.

Make today count!

Day 241

In our social-media-driven culture, it's easy to believe everyone is doing great. Privately many of us wonder why we are experiencing hardships while Sally is on her fourth vacation of the month posting pictures of her toes in the sand. We wonder if we can ever catch a break. Hardship and difficulty are all around us. Here are a few situations I am currently aware of. I have a friend who is fighting to save his marriage. I have another friend who just lost a family member due to a tragic accident. Another is finalizing a divorce, and yet another is struggling with addiction. I have friends who are living in fear and one wondering if they will make it this month financially. These trials can feel overwhelming.

The first thing I do each morning is open the Bible app and read the verse of the day. It's amazing how just one verse can be such an encouragement. Today's scripture of the day is the reason for this devotional thought. It is found in 2 Corinthians 4:18 and says, "So we fix our eyes not on what is seen, but on what is unseen, since what is seen is temporary, but what is unseen is eternal." When we are in the midst of tragedy or trial, it's easy to stay focused on our situation. What this verse articulates so clearly is that these situations are fleeting and that we should have an eternal focus. By no means am I saying there aren't times we should spend grieving and processing hurt. What I am suggesting is that we filter our grief through an eternal lens.

Today know that you are not alone in your trials. I'm here to remind you to keep an eternal perspective on your situation.

Make today count!

Day 242

From my elementary years through high school, I woke up each morning to a delicious smell coming from the kitchen. Each day when I arrived in the kitchen, there on the table was breakfast made for me. It might have been a delicious western omelet, a breakfast burrito, or maybe even an egg sandwich with a perfectly runny egg yolk in the middle. This was my reality each and every day—until the day I woke up in that wonderful place called college. When I woke up in my dorm room, I realized this breakfast that I came to expect every day was no longer there waiting for me. My expectations had been met day after day, and this caused me to have a lack of gratitude for what I was blessed with. It's like the great theologian Randy Houser says, "You don't know what you got till it's gone."

In the Gospel of Luke chapter 17, the story details the time when Jesus healed 10 men who had leprosy. Leprosy is a terrible skin disease that is highly contagious. These men had to live in exile from the rest of the community. They cried out and asked Jesus to heal them, which he did. Only one of the 10 returned to give thanks. Gratitude is something we have to choose each and every day. We have to recognize that all the blessings we have are gifts given by God. Our default is to want to give ourselves praise for working hard or storing our money well. The fact of the matter is that God has given us our abilities to work, think, and to live. I love what Craig Groeschel says about gratitude: "We should not let what we want rob us what we have." Ecclesiastes 6:9 encourages, "Enjoy what you have rather than desiring what you don't have. Just dreaming about nice things is meaningless—like chasing the wind." As Americans, we have so much to be grateful for. If you're reading this, I feel confident in saying you have air conditioning, clothes, a bed, clean water, and the ability to get to and from your job.

My challenge for you today is to choose gratitude. When we choose gratitude, what we have, and more importantly, whose we are, will be enough!

Make today count!

Day 243

Have you ever found yourself in the woods or on a path late at night? When I was in college, I worked at a camp in the middle of Indiana. We were nowhere near any large towns, so when it was dark, it was really dark. My mode of transportation to get to and from the camp was a bicycle. At night it required me to wear a headlamp so I could see where I was going. If you ever found yourself using a headlamp when it is very dark, you know that the headlamp provides just enough light for your next two steps. You can't see what's way out in front of you. You can only see approximately 5 to 10 feet ahead. But the thing is, if you continue to trust the light and follow the path, it will lead you to your destination.

Psalms 119:109 says, "Your word is a lamp for my feet, a light on my path." This verse really takes on a whole new meaning when you've experienced walking with a small light in a very dark place. The way I understand this verse is that God's word will give us just enough direction and guidance for each day. We might not be able to see the whole picture, but we will be able to see enough to get us to our destination. Without a flashlight in the middle of the night, it would be nearly impossible to find your way to your destination. Most people would hesitate to begin making a journey without any type of light to guide them. I believe the same is true for us as Christians. We should allow God's word to be our light to guide us before we make moves forward.

Today are you allowing yourself to be guided by God's word? If not, my challenge is for you to start today!

Make today count!

Day 244

I love to cook. My mom started teaching me how to cook when I was in the sixth grade. It has become something I thoroughly enjoy and consider myself to be relatively good at. One of the best things about living in Tennessee is that grilling season is quite a bit longer than in other states. Chicken and steak fajitas are my favorite things to grill. The trick to making these taste amazing is all in the marinade. The day prior to cooking the fajitas, I marinate the chicken in half a cup of Italian dressing and half a cup of soy sauce. The steak is marinated in half a cup of soy sauce and a teaspoon of garlic salt. The smell of these as they are grilling is incredible, and the taste is unmatched.

The trick to great fajitas is the seasoning used. The trick to great and healthy conversations is that they be seasoned with grace. Colossians 4:6 says, "Let your speech always be seasoned with grace, as though seasoned with salt, so that you will know how you should respond to each person." What I believe this verse is pointing us to us is preparation. Preparation keeps us from responding too quickly in conversations if we allow them to be seasoned with salt. To season something takes time. The idea is that we should take time to allow grace and kindness to come into our response to others.

Do you ever find yourself responding too quickly in tough conversations? My challenge for you today is that you would season your conversations and allow grace to flow over them!

Make today count!

Day 245

Today is a monumental day in Cade's spiritual journey and in our family. This morning I had the privilege of baptizing my son. He has an incredible understanding of just what Christ did on his behalf on the cross. I would love to tell you that when Cade came to us and told us he had prayed to receive Christ that we shared a beautiful moment together. The truth is, I allowed my intellectual knowledge to get in the way of his spiritual transformation. I began to question him about what it really meant to be a believer. It was after several conversations that I realized I was making the gospel much more difficult than it really is. Jesus called for the little children to come to him understanding their great faith. Scripture reminds us if we have faith as small as a mustard seed, we too can experience great things. I think most of us would agree that it is much easier for children to have mustard-seed faith than adults, thus Jesus' encouragement to let the children come.

I know God has incredible plans for my son, despite me. My hope is that he will live out Hebrews 12:1-3. "Therefore, since we are surrounded by so great a cloud of witnesses, let us also lay aside every weight, and sin which clings so closely, and let us run with endurance the race that is set before us, looking to Jesus, the founder and perfecter of our faith, who for the joy that was set before him endured the cross, despising the shame, and is seated at the right hand of the throne of God." God has given Cade certain gifts, abilities, and talents. These things have been given to him so he can in turn bring glory to God. He has a race set out in front of him that has been marked and created just for him. The same is true of you. God has a race marked out for you. My question for you today is will you run it?

Make today count!

Day 246

The right set of keys matters. A friend of mine let me borrow his boat for the week. My senior pastor towed the boat to the location where we would be putting it in. Prior to getting in the water, I ran all the pre-check items, the last step, of course, being to put the key in the ignition and turn the boat on. For the life of me, I could not get it to turn on. It felt like the key just wasn't the right fit. When my friend gave me the boat, I remembered the keys were on a yellow floating key ring. After unsuccessfully trying for a few minutes, I finally gave up and called my friend and asked if there was a trick to turning the boat on. He said, "No, there's nothing special. Just make sure you're using the key that ends with the letter N." About the same time, my pastor emerged from his truck with another set of keys with a yellow floating key ring. Unbeknownst to him, I had been trying to use his boat keys to start my friend's boat. We switched the keys out and what do you know? Just like that, the boat started right up. The right keys made all the difference!

There are things all around us in life that look like the real deal. There are counterfeits that look like real a Rolex, real Oakley's, and genuine Jordan shoes. These things are nothing but counterfeits. Within our spiritual lives, Satan will also throw counterfeits at us, things that look like God-centered truth but are truly only traps to steal, kill, and destroy us. In 1 John 4:1 it says, "Beloved, do not believe every spirit, but test the spirits to see whether they are from God, because many false prophets have gone out into the world." If we test these things, we will be able to see how they line up against scripture. Anything that does not line up precisely with what the Bible says is not truth.

My challenge for you today is not to simply accept things you are told to be true. Question them, investigate them, and use discernment along with wisdom from God. Don't fall for the counterfeit! It leads nowhere.

Make today count!

Day 247

There aren't many people who shape our lives like our parents do. When it comes to parents, I would say that I hit the jackpot. Today just happens to be my mom's 60th birthday. When I think about my mom, I think about her relationship with the Lord. I can remember seeing her early in the morning kneeling by her bedside praying over my brother and me and many other requests. Her choice to be intentional with the first part of her day every day has marked me in a meaningful way. There's no telling how much trouble her prayers have kept my brother and me from. I often wonder who I would have become absent of her prayers. Many people in my family joke that if my mom prays for it, it will happen. She is a true blessing to me and to my family, and I am so thankful for her!

I'm sure each of you, if you received some difficult news and were in need of prayer, would know just who you would call first. What is it about these people that draws us to them? I think we could agree upon the common thread of consistency. It is their consistency in prayer that I believe has shaped the outcome of their prayers.

My challenge for us today is that we would become the type of people our friends and families know they can come to when they need prayer. Today would you pray in agreement with David? I love how he boldly approached God in Psalms 4:1: "Answer me when I call to you, my righteous God. Give me relief from my distress; have mercy on me and hear my prayer." Make your requests known to God because he cares for you.

Make today count!

Day 248

After my freshman year of college, I spent the summer working at a summer camp as a wake board and water ski instructor. It was an absolutely incredible job. Each day I got to hang out with a different group of young men and teach them the ins and outs of skiing and wake boarding. One of the most common mistakes I saw from week to week was the boys would try to do all the work of pulling themselves up rather than allow the boat to do the work for them. When they realized they needed to rely on the boat power, they found success.

Many times in my own life, I try to accomplish things on my own strength. No matter how much I try to push with my effort alone, time and time again I fail. However, when I invite God to be a part of the process and I truly rely on his strength, I find success. Isaiah 40:29 says, "He gives strength to the weary and increases the power of the weak." I don't know about you, but there are times when I feel incredibly weary and in need of his strength.

What about you? Do you find yourself pushing hard, feeling weary, with no results to show for it? Could you ask God to give you just what Isaiah 40:29 offers and see just what happens?

Make today count!

Day 249

I love water skiing. I think I was around 14-years old the first time someone took me out and I was able to experience it firsthand. While I worked at a summer camp teaching water skiing, I had the opportunity to water ski regularly. Now I really enjoy it when I have the opportunity to teach someone how to ski who has never done it before. For the past couple days, I have had that opportunity multiple times. It's fun to watch as they grow and develop in each stage of learning to ski, from watching them get up in the water, to standing, to getting the rope in the correct position, to then going from left to right of the wake. During each of these phases, there are different things that can cause them to stumble, but to watch them persevere and push through and eventually successfully ski is very rewarding. Each time there is failure, there's a clear opportunity to learn.

As Christians, there are times when trials and struggles come at us hard. We wonder why God would allow these trials to come. I believe that it is similar to the learning my friends have experienced as they learned to ski. The trials produce growth. James 1:2-4 says, "Consider it pure joy, my brothers and sisters, whenever you face trials of many kinds, because you know the testing of your faith produces perseverance. Let perseverance finish its work so that you may mature and complete, not lacking anything." Trials produce maturity.

Whatever it is that you're pushing through today, know that it is in front of you to make you better tomorrow than you are today. Thank God for the trial you're currently going through. Ask him to show you how this is going to grow and mature you on the other side of it.

Make today count!

Day 250

I hate it when my car gets dirty, but we all know how it happens. Life kicks in, things get busy, and cleaning the car goes to the bottom of the priority list. This morning I spent a solid hour cleaning every nook and cranny and getting every speck of dust I could possibly reach cleaned out. I even went as far as to clean the engine and put in a fresh car deodorizer. Maybe I'm weird, but when my car is dirty, I am ashamed for people to ride with me. When my car is clean, I feel a great sense of pride. It's as if I have nothing to hide.

To me, this correlates to unconfessed sin. There's something about unconfessed sin that creates a cloud over my heart and mind. I feel a sense of shame and judgment, whether they are true or not, but when I make sure I am in right relationship with God and others, I feel a deep sense of boldness and freedom. Proverbs 28:13 says, "You will never succeed in life if you try to hide your sins. Confess them and give them up; then God will show mercy to you." I wholeheartedly believe that if we want the favor of God, we must ask for the forgiveness of God.

What unconfessed sin do you have in your heart? Remember, it is only unconfessed—it is not hidden. God is aware of it. Today would you ask God to make your heart clean?

Make today count!

Day 251

We have been working hard with Cade on learning to ride his bike. He watches kids ride by and can see them practicing great balance. The method I have taken trying to teach him to learn is to coast down our driveway which is enough of an incline to keep him going without peddling. It is also long enough to give him enough time to practice his balance. There's also nice soft grass on both sides, should he end up falling. I don't think any of us would disagree that balance is probably the most important part of riding a bike.

I believe balance is an integral part of our lives also. Without balance, our lives will become too heavily weighted one way or the other. I, like most men, struggle to keep an appropriate balance between work and family. Like all of you, I have many different things I am working to balance. My family, work, my own growth and development, my hobbies and entertainment. Proverbs 11:1 says, "A false balance is an abomination to the LORD, but a just weight is His delight." I heard someone say it this way once: we are all juggling. We have several different balls we are juggling—work, family, finances, and more. All of the balls are rubber and if they are dropped, they bounce back off the floor. Of course, our relationship with God is number one, but there is another ball, that if dropped, shatters. That is the ball of family. It is so important that we keep our balance in all areas of our life, remembering that after our relationship with God, family is the most important.

Where do you find yourself out of balance? How can you get yourself correctly balanced back out today?

Make today count!

Day 252

It seems that regardless of what stage of life I'm in, I always feel like I am busy. I can look back when I was a newlywed with no children and feeling like I was absolutely swamped. That thought is laughable to me now that I have two small kids and an even more demanding work schedule. Many times, we align success with busyness, but I do not believe busyness always results in success. Busyness drives busyness. In our fast-paced culture, it's difficult for us to find times to be still and to truly be with God. Often the environments we find ourselves in pull us to the next season of busyness.

I was talking recently with a friend who told me he has a hard time staying focused during his quiet time each morning. As we talked more in depth about it, he told me he was spending his time with God first thing in the morning at his office. Through the course of our conversation, we both determined that the environment he had set to hear from God was affecting his ability to truly be still before God because once he gets to his office, he begins to think about all the things he needs to accomplish that day. In Psalms 46:10, God says, "Be still and know that I am God: I will be exalted among the nations, I will be exalted in the earth." I believe for us to truly be still before God, we must quiet our hearts and remove any distractions to enable us to hear from him.

Today where do you find yourself getting quiet before God? Do you find yourself distracted during these times? My challenge for you today would be to be intentional about the place where you spend time with God. Make it a place where you can truly quiet your mind and humble your heart.

Make today count!

Day 253

Punctuality is a trait I consider to be incredibly important, and one I consider myself to be very consistent with. I'm a planner, so I'm constantly thinking ahead about where I need to be considering possible roadblocks that could possibly hinder me from being on time. I do everything in my power to make sure I am where I'm supposed to be when I am supposed to be there. This morning something happened that has not happened in the history of my marriage with Holly. Holly and I overslept our alarm. Typically, this would not be a problem since we have two small kids and they tend to wake up very early in the morning, but today they also slept in. When Holly woke up and realized it was 40 minutes past her normal time to get up, she woke me up and we sprang into action. I'm happy to report that Holly and the kids made it to school on time and I made it to work.

Our minds function around time. We understand how much time it takes to get from point A to point B, how long it takes for a baby to develop in a mother's womb, and we even have an understanding of our projected life span. Where I find myself struggling with timing is when God doesn't respond to a request in my timeframe. In my mind, I truly believe I understand time better than he does and I believe I know when he should intervene. Proverbs 16:9 has a clear response to this idea: "In their hearts humans plan their course, but the LORD establishes their steps." We can have our timing planned out and set in our mind, but our plans will not come to fruition until God allows them to. I can find myself easily getting frustrated when I feel God's timing does not line up with my own. However, I believe it's important for us to remember that his timing is perfect.

Have you found yourself frustrated with God's timing? Today I hope Proverbs 16:9 will help remind you that God is sovereign over your steps.

Make today count!

Day 254

I'm sure many of you are like me in that you have been driving so long that it has become second nature. You don't put much thought into putting the car in drive and reaching your destination. To be honest, there are times when I arrive at my destination and realize I don't know how I got there. Terrible, I know.

Every car is equipped with three mirrors—two side view and one rear view. These, of course, are to give you a look at what's behind you so you can successfully navigate what's in front of you. Speaking to a crowd of people, Jesus talked about how no one is fit to plow who does it while looking back. We read in Luke 9:62: "Jesus replied, 'No one who puts a hand to the plow and looks back is fit for service in the kingdom of God.'" I couldn't agree more. There's not a single one of us who would feel comfortable knowing someone was going to try to drive from point A to point B looking behind them the entire trip. But here's what I believe to be true—we should not live in what is behind us, but we should allow it to shape our future direction. Think about the mirrors in your car. You will take a quick glance into your mirrors to make sure no one is in your path prior to changing lanes. I think the same methodology works in life. We can take a quick look back at our mistakes and use these as course adjustments to help us travel safely down our path.

What quick look at what's behind you is helping mold the direction you're going today? Give your past to God, but allow the lessons from it to shape you.

Make today count!

Day 255

A few days ago, one of the teachers at the school my kids attend asked me to speak for their lower school chapel. To be honest, my immediate thought was, "No way—I don't know how to speak to kids." My week-to-week has me speaking primarily to grown men. I found myself coming up with a thousand reasons why I was incapable. After praying about it, I felt like God was telling me, "Suck it up buttercup, you're up. It's not about you. It's about me."

After spending some time in prayer, I felt like God gave me just what he wanted me to say. He gave me a truth that was simple enough for children to remember, but deep enough that it can profoundly impact them the rest of their lives. This was my one and only point: "God's word gives us direction." I am living proof that God does not call the equipped, he equips the called. Hebrews 13:21 says, "(Jesus will) equip you with everything good for doing his will, and may he work in us what is pleasing to him, through Jesus Christ, to him be glory forever and ever. Amen." If God has called you to do something, he will equip you to complete the work.

What do you know God is calling you to today but you are afraid to step into it? Trust him and his equipping to meet you where you need it the most.

Make today count!

Day 256

There's a man by the name of Mr. Will who unofficially works at the downtown YMCA in Nashville. Mr. Will is a shoe shiner. He has a small section carved out just for him on the main hallway that comes off both the men's and women's locker rooms. Mr. Will is one of the most enthusiastic people you could ever possibly meet. He loves to sing in the hallway. He loves to give people compliments about their dress and provides suggestions about how he could make their shoes look a little bit better. His enthusiasm changes the environment around him.

There are really two types of people. The first type is the person who allows the environment to determine their enthusiasm and the second are those whose enthusiasm determines the environment.

The word enthusiasm translated from the Greek means "in God" or "filled with God." I believe it is true that enthusiasm is really a posture of our heart. When the heart is filled with enthusiasm, our outward circumstances have little to no effect on it. Philippians 4:4 says, "Rejoice always! Again I say rejoice." This verse shows the posture of our heart. It is not based around circumstances. To rejoice always means to rejoice even when times are hard and struggles are real.

Today are you living your life in such a way that people know you are filled with God? Are people being drawn to him because of your enthusiasm?

Make today count!

Day 257

This past week our men's ministry looked at the life of David, both as a kid and as a king. What we learn from the story of David is that when he was a kid and charging shoulder to shoulder with men, he was humble and always gave praise and glory back to God. As king, 2 Samuel 11:1 tells us, "In the spring, at the time when kings go off to war, David sent Joab out with the king's men and the whole Israelite army. They destroyed the Ammonites and besieged Rabbah. But David remained in Jerusalem." David seems to have lost his concern for his calling and was more concerned about his comfort. We know how the rest of the story plays out. David wandered out on his roof and saw Bathsheba which ended up costing him big time. When David was not where he was supposed to be, he saw something he should not have seen, and did something he should not have done.

I don't know about you, but this is so true with me. When I'm not where I'm supposed to be, chances are high that I'm going to see something I should not see, and do something I should not do. Each of us who has a relationship with Christ knows we have been saved from the penalty of our sin, but it's easy for us to forget just what we have been saved from. We, like David, can easily get our focus on our comfort rather than the calling God has for us.

Today if you find yourself walking around your palace concerned with your comfort, would you allow God to remind you of just what he saved you from and what he saved you for? You were bought with a price for a purpose.

Make today count!

Day 258

I recently saw a study that said millennials struggle with making important decisions. This is attributed to the many choices they have in their everyday life. An example of this would be Netflix. You turn on Netflix looking for a movie to watch but find yourself overwhelmed with choices and you end up either watching nothing or your old standby, *Friends*. I don't believe millennials are the only ones who struggle to make decisions. I think this is common for most of us.

Proverbs 15:22 says, "Without counsel plans fail, but with many advisers they succeed." I have found time and time again that when I make plans without petitioning God through prayer first, they seem to fail. When I invite God and other wise counsel to be a part of my planning processes, my plans seem to prosper. Do you currently find yourself frustrated or stuck in a situation? I encourage you to seek wise counsel.

Before you make your next big decision, my challenge for you is to spend some time in prayer asking God for his wisdom.

Make today count!

Day 259

Here's a tip for those of you who don't care a lot about your grass: September is a very important month for grass care. The things you do in September will help to produce the grass you want come Memorial Day. Between the sidewalk in front of the road at my house lies a patch of grass, or should I say a patch of weeds, that I despise. This year I decided I would completely kill off this patch of weeds in order to grow some new healthy grass for next year. The first thing I had to do was mow the weed patch very low. The second step was to apply Round Up all over the weeds to kill them. The third step in the process was getting an aerator to plug the large holes all across this patch. The final step was to apply new grass seed that will hopefully germinate inside these deep holes to produce new grass. What's interesting is that at the same time you are killing something ugly, you can be creating something beautiful. These two steps can be accomplished simultaneously.

Many of us have habits, traits, or characteristics about ourselves we would like to change but we're not sure what this process would look like. For some of you, it could be a food addiction. Maybe for you this process would involve killing the Coke and making a healthier choice with water. For some of you it could be living in the land of perpetual negativity. You might begin by intentionally finding the good in seven situations each day. The objective here is that we substitute bad habits and traits with better ones.

One of the most important habits we can put into place is killing our laziness and creating intimate time with God each morning. Psalms 5:3 says, "In the morning, O LORD, You will hear my voice; In the morning I will order my prayer to You and eagerly watch." Killing bad habits and creating new healthy ones is a way to bring God honor and glory through your life.

Make today count!

Day 260

In marriage, it is not a question of IF you will fight. It is a question of *how* you will fight. Healthy couples fight for resolution. They keep their focus on the issue at hand, where an unhealthy couple could allow the focus to shift onto the other person. Craig Groeschel, pastor of Life Church, advises that couples follow these guidelines when fighting to keep the fight "fair."

Don't get historical. (Things in the past should stay there.)

Don't use never or always (These statements are rarely true.)

Don't call names. (It's not nice.)

Don't raise your voice.

I would add one additional guideline: Don't use the word "you." (You put people on the defense, whereas "I" statements speak from your place of feeling.)

Ephesians 4:26 says, "In your anger do not sin. Do not let the sun go down while you are still angry." Where is the line between anger and sin? I believe we cross from anger to sin when we change our focus from the situation to a person. It is okay to be angry about a situation, but it becomes unhealthy when that anger is redirected to another person. Pastor Craig says that when we go to bed still angry, we create a foothold for Satan to come into our marriage. He says that all large issues are issues that started small but were not dealt with when they were manageable.

What steps can you take today to fight fair with your spouse?

Make today count!

Day 261

Two months ago I purchased a "new to us" vehicle for Holly. It is a 2009 model with just over 100,000 miles, so when the opportunity to purchase a warranty was presented, I thought it was a wise purchase.

When Holly and her friends returned home from a women's retreat this past weekend, we realized her AC compressor had gone completely out. If you don't know much about cars, anything related to the air conditioning is incredibly costly. I wasn't concerned though because I had purchased a warranty that specifically listed the AC compressor as one of the covered components. Long story short, what I purchased turned out to be only a parts assistance program. They find the cheapest remanufactured parts they can and offer that much towards the price of your repair. This left me with a substantial gap to cover the cost of the repair.

As I was thinking about how a true warranty should cover me 100%, this verse came to mind: Ephesians 1:13-14 which says, "And you also were included in Christ when you heard the message of truth, the gospel of your salvation. When you believed, you were marked in him with a seal, the promised Holy Spirit, who is a deposit guaranteeing our inheritance until the redemption of those who are God's possession—to the praise of his glory." This is a warranty we can take to the bank. We can trust completely that our eternity is secure because of the deposit of the Holy Spirit when we accept Christ.

What guarantee are you trusting in for your eternity? Is it because you have been a "good" person? My question back to you is this, based off whose moral scale have you been good? I believe that compared to a holy and perfect God, we don't stand a chance without a deposit of the Holy Spirit. That is a guarantee you can take to the grave.

Make today count!

Day 262

Craig Groeschel has an incredible leadership podcast that I would encourage you to listen to. I listened to one of the episodes recently and he was talking about being a second-level leader. He says first-level leaders are responsive to problems as they come to the surface, where secondary-level leaders solve problems before they really hit the surface. He quoted hockey player Wayne Gretzky. Gretzky says, "What makes me a great hockey player is not being where the puck is. It is being where the puck is going to be." If we as leaders can embrace this concept of forward thinking, our momentum and productivity will go off the charts.

In our leadership, we can either be reactionary, solving problems as they present themselves, or we can be proactive, looking for potential problems and solving them before they raise their head. This is an incredible principle we can apply in business and in leadership, but I believe we can also apply it to our spiritual lives. If we are proactively looking at things that could trip us up or damage our relationship with Christ, we can do what needs to be done to mitigate these potential stumbling blocks. James 1:13-14 says, "When tempted, no one should say, 'God is tempting me.' For God cannot be tempted by evil, nor does he tempt anyone; but each person is tempted when they are dragged away by their own evil desire and enticed." As we are proactive within our spiritual walk, we can identify temptations that might trip us up by discovering and developing plans to keep ourselves from these situations in the first place.

How could you use secondary-level leadership today to draw you closer to the things God has for you?

Make today count!

Day 263

As a boy I can remember loving the story of Samson in the Old Testament. When you are nine years old, there's nothing cooler than reading a story about a guy who literally fought a lion and killed it. I can remember thinking how incredible it would be to be as strong as he was. As a man, my opinion of Sampson has shifted dramatically. Samson was a guy who had everything in the world going for him, but because of his pride, he lost it all. Judges 16:1 says, "One day Samson traveled to Gaza. While there, he saw a prostitute and had sex with her." This comes across as if it was a quick decision. In reality, these two locations are significantly distant from each other, 25 miles to be exact or roughly 56,250 steps. That is 56,250 opportunities Samson had to turn and walk the other way. Each step led him closer to his destruction.

In our own lives each of us are taking steps. We are progressing towards something. We are either progressing towards the things God has for us or, like Sampson, away from them. It's a simple truth but a truth nonetheless. When you're going the wrong direction, all you need to do is turn around.

My question for you today is which way are you walking? Are you finding yourself walking closer towards the things God has called you to or further away?

Make today count!

Day 264

Today is a unique day. It's September 28, 2018. It is the only September 28, 2018 you will ever get. There's a quote I am sure you have seen that serves as a great reminder about focusing on the days we are given. It says, "Yesterday is history, tomorrow is a mystery, but today is a gift. That is why it is called the present." If we truly view each day as a gift, I believe it will push us to do everything within our power to optimize every minute of it.

Psalms 118:24 says, "This is the day the Lord has made, let us rejoice and be glad in it." What I love about this verse is that there is no clause to it. It does not say rejoice unless things aren't going well. It doesn't say rejoice only if everyone around you that you love is healthy. It simply says rejoice. Choosing to rejoice regardless of our circumstances is a posture of our heart.

My question for you today is this: Will you choose to rejoice regardless of your circumstances? My challenge is to make today the best you possibly can. Choose to rejoice!

Make today count!

Day 265

Since the age of 16, I have only had four different vehicles. My first car was a 1993 Mitsubishi Eclipse. During my college years until 2010, I drove a Ford Explorer Sport. Around the time we sold our first home, I got a vehicle I really wanted—a Nissan Frontier pickup truck. Shortly after paying the truck off, I was hit from behind which totaled the truck. I then ended up with my FJ cruiser. Of all of the vehicles I have had, the FJ has the largest blind spots. If you're not familiar with what an FJ Cruiser looks like, imagine a cross between a Jeep and a Hummer. Before switching lanes, these blind spots require me to check and doublecheck before I merge.

Blind spots are not problems secluded to vehicles. Blind spots are a part of each of our lives. A blind spot is an area of ourselves that we cannot see. Oftentimes it requires another person to point out these areas of our lives to us. Proverbs 27:17 says, "Iron sharpens iron, so one man sharpens another." All of us have things in our lives that we don't necessarily see. It is so important to have someone who can come alongside and help you navigate these blind spots. Blind spots in our lives, just like in cars, could be devastating if we do not recognize them.

What are your blind spots? What are the things in your life that others have pointed out to you that you would have failed to recognize without them? As hard as it is to hear about these areas in your life, know that these people are only pointing them out to you to sharpen you.

Make today count!

Day 266

Plans are part of our lives. Some of us are short-term planners, and others of us are more proficient long-term planners. If you had asked me five years ago what the plans for my life were, I could have given you a step-by-step accounting of how I was eventually going to become a COO of an urban 30-group YMCA. I was making steps towards the plans I set for myself when God showed up in a radical way and changed everything. I had two job offers at the same time. Either one would have helped me continue to move down the path I had set out for, but I clearly heard from God that neither one these opportunities was for me. After much prayer and consideration, I turned down both of these jobs. I then sat and waited for what seemed like an eternity. It was during the waiting that I had to trust even more that God truly had better plans for me than I did for myself. Now working full time in vocational ministry, I would not trade it for the world.

Proverbs 19:21 says, "Many are the plans in a person's heart, but it is the LORD's purpose that prevails." This verse has been so true in my life. I believe that it will be true in your life as well. What would it look like for you to stop trusting in your own plans and ask God to reveal his plans for you? There was a point in my story that I failed to mention. One day prior to these two job openings, I told God whatever he wanted, I was in. What could God do with your life if you fully surrendered it to him?

My question for us today is, "Will we trust in the plans he has for our lives?" Do we truly believe his plans are better than our own?

Make today count!

Day 267

I'm sure many of you, like myself, participated in a corporate worship experience recently. Within our culture we have identified Sundays as the day we gather with our church body to bring our praise and admiration to God. As I was thinking about this, I began to think about the other six days of the week. What is it, or who is it, that is receiving our worship? I believe we can identify our "little gods" by looking to see where our time and money is being spent.

Our American culture makes it easy for us to place our children, our money, or our hobbies into God's rightful place. Matthew 6:21 says, "For where your treasure is, there will your heart be also." The World English Bible translates the passage as: "For where your treasure is, there your heart will be also." In the previous two verses Jesus explained why one should store one's treasure in heaven rather than on earth. We are all created to worship. The question is not "*Will* you worship?" The question is *what* or *who* will you worship?

Make today count!

Day 268

Holly and I just got back from a resort in the Dominican Republic celebrating our 10-year anniversary. I believe the marriage relationship is the most significant relationship we have with another person. Through the health or dysfunction of this relationship, so many other outcomes will result—some good and some not so good. I think it's incredibly important for couples to take time away from the busyness of kids, work, and everyday life to reconnect and have fun. I believe with all my heart that besides pointing our kids to Christ, focusing on the health, stability, and longevity of our marriage is the most important thing we can do for our children. Children derive a great sense of security through their parents' marriage.

"Husbands, love your wives, just as Christ loved the church and gave himself up for her." (Ephesians 5:25) Christ gave himself up for the church because his love was so great. In the same way, husbands are to love their wives. Being intentional about taking time to be with each other is so important and it will pay dividends in the long run.

My challenge for you today is to prioritize time to have fun with your spouse. Use your marriage as a way to bring honor to God and point others to Christ!

Make today count!

Day 269

Like most men, I will do everything within my power to avoid going to the doctor. I will, however, jump on WebMD, type in my symptoms and figure out just what I'm dealing with. It doesn't seem to matter what symptoms you list on WebMD., one of the diagnosis always turns out to be cancer or Ebola Using web M.D. to diagnose yourself does nothing but create worry.

In a web M.D. world, don't let your worry win. If we allow our worries to win our thoughts, that means something loses. What I believe we lose is our joy, and ultimately, we lose. Don't allow things that are off in the distance, that are not fact, to steal your joy in the moment. The moments you spent worrying about something else are moments you will never get back. Worrying about an upcoming test is not nearly as productive as studying for it.

Luke 12:25-26 asks, "Who of you by worrying can add a single hour to your life? Since you cannot do this very little thing, why do you worry about the rest?" The challenge for you today is to focus on today. Think about things that are true, lovely, and admirable.

Make today count!

Day 270

This morning I write to you from Henry Horton State Park where we are having our men's retreat. We spend a lot of time together in community doing various activities. We have corporate worship and teaching, but the best part for me is the small group time. Generally speaking, most men don't want to open up and share their feelings, struggles, and hang-ups. What I have found during retreat each year is that men allow the walls to come down.

It's absolutely amazing how when a man shares openly about his struggles and his true self is shown, connections are made on a very deep and authentic level. It's amazing to hear the stories each year after retreat is over about friendships that have been formed and accountability partners that were established. God did not intend for you to keep your struggles to yourself. Not only is sharing profitable for you, but you never know how your story might impact another person.

My challenge for you today is to step into the fear of honest accountability, find someone you can open up to and with whom you can show your true self. You never know how it will impact them, but I guarantee it will impact you.

Make today count!

Day 271

Dr. Stephen Covey has a premise in his book *Seven Habits* where he says, "Begin with the end in mind." There's an exercise in the book where he has you imagine that you are viewing your own funeral service. The exercise is designed to allow you to get to a place where you think about the things that really matter to you. What are the things you would want people to say about you, about your life, and about your priorities?

In our fast-paced world, it is easy to get consumed with producing wealth, creating notability, and pursuing positions of power. Will these things really matter at the end of your life? Dr. John Maxwell said it well when he said, "At the end of your life will you ask to see your college degree hung in the walnut frame to hug it one more time? Will you ask to be carried out to one of your vehicles so you can sit in it? Will you be comforted by reviewing your financial statements? No, you will desire to be around those whom you love." If it will matter then, why doesn't it matter now?

Your children are not going to remember the positions you held, the amount of money you acquired, or the people who looked at your life with great envy. Your children will remember if you showed up at their ballgames, if you were there to watch their piano recital, if you laid in the floor and colored with them, and if you in a moment's notice would drop what you were doing to focus on something they wanted to tell you. Matthew 6:19-20 reminds us, "Do not store up for yourselves treasures on earth, where moths and vermin destroy, and where thieves break in and steal. But store up for yourselves treasures in heaven, where moths and vermin do not destroy, and where thieves do not break in and steal."

My challenge for you today is to begin with the end in mind. Prioritize now the things that will matter at the end of your life.

Make today count!

Day 272

There are times for all of us when insecurity creeps in. Insecurity is an inevitable part of life. We have areas where we feel insecure. The definition of insecurity is "uncertainty or anxiety about one's self or a lack of confidence." James McDonald, senior pastor of a prominent church, says insecurity is the gap between who we are and who we want to be. He suggests that we either try to overcompensate this gap or allow ourselves to be paralyzed in fear when faced with situations that make us feel insecure.

It's so interesting that God chooses to use people who are insecure to accomplish his plans and purposes. When God called Moses to lead the children of Israel into the promised land, Moses came up with many reasons why he was the wrong guy. He was trying to navigate the gap from who God needed him to be versus who he was. I love Moses' interaction with God in Exodus 3:11 when God had just called him to lead the children of Israel out of Egypt. Moses responded this way, "But Moses said to God, "I am nobody. How can I go to the king and bring the Israelites out of Egypt?" If I'm being honest, I have this feeling in my own life. I am a nobody, God. Why would you call me? God wants to use nobodies like us to complete his purpose so he gets the glory.

What are the things that God has called you to step into today, but you are allowing your insecurity to keep you from it? My challenge for you is to allow God to work through you. You might be a nobody, but HE is Somebody!

Make today count!

Day 273

A number of years ago, I believe it was even prior to Holly and I being married, Holly and I took a trip to Auburn, Alabama, to see my brother Jared. This was prior to the days of GPS. This was the Map Quest era. Do you remember that? You get on Map Quest and print out 37 pages of directions to navigate you to your destination! Anyway, on our return trip back home, I somehow got turned around. I was convinced that I was going the right direction, but Holly thought otherwise. We drove for probably 40 minutes before I realized I was indeed headed the wrong direction. If I remember correctly, we were headed towards North Carolina. No matter how sincere my intentions were, I-20 East would never have gotten me back to Tennessee. If I wanted to know where I was heading, all I really had to do was look at the path.

The same is true for our lives. If you want to see where you're going, look at the path you are on right now. Who are you surrounding yourself with? How are you prioritizing your time and money? Who are the people who are influencing the decisions you make in your life? You can look to these factors and see exactly where you're going.

I clearly needed some guidance coming home from the trip. God offers his guidance in the book of Psalms 32:8. "I will instruct you and teach you in the way you should go; I will counsel you with my eye upon you." My challenge for you today is to evaluate the path you're on to determine the direction you are heading, and if it's the wrong way, turn around.

Make today count!

Day 274

As a child I remember that anytime we were expecting company or were preparing to go somewhere, two things were always required. The first was that I made my room presentable--bed made and dirty clothes put away. The second was that I made myself look presentable. Clean shirt, clean pants, hair brushed, and teeth brushed. There was an understanding that we had to make ourselves presentable for whoever it was we were going to see.

In my line of work now, I have numerous conversations with people who are hurting and broken. I can't tell you how many times I've heard someone tell me that they just need to get their life cleaned up before they come to God. I'm not sure if this thought process has developed out of the way we have lived our lives over the past many years, or if it's something deeper within our own heart that we want to present ourselves as best we can to God.

The problem here is that we will never clean ourselves up enough for a perfect God. John 6:37 says, "Everyone whom the father gives me will come to me, and the one who comes to me I will never send away." This verse doesn't say anything about your life being "perfect" or even presentable. God loves you as you are, with your messy hair, dirty room, and unbrushed teeth.

Make today count!

Day 275

When I was working at the downtown YMCA, one job I found myself becoming quite proficient at was canceling memberships. These memberships were not cancelled because individuals had made a job change and were headed to another city. No, these cancellations were based on inappropriate behavior on their part. This helped me learn how to calmly deal with confrontation. In the beginning, I was absolutely terrible at it. Confrontation is never easy. My goal with confrontation, regardless of what I'm dealing with, is always the same. Confrontation needs to yield to clarity. Clarity doesn't necessarily mean everyone's hugging and sharing cocoa afterwards. Clarity means both parties have an understanding of what the issue was, how each party contributed to the problem, and both have a grasp on what the solution is and how they will move forward.

It's not natural for a person to enjoy confrontation. However, if you want your relationships to be at their maximum level of health and effectiveness, confrontation is required from time to time. There's a high likelihood that if you feel the chance that there's a confrontation brewing between you and another person, they know it as well. Instead of delaying the inevitable, push through in hopes of finding clarity on the other side.

Step one in dealing with confrontation is taking it to God privately in your prayer time. Matthew 18:15 says, "If your brother sins, go and show him his fault in private; if he listens to you, you have won your brother."

Step two in dealing with confrontation is to plan a time to meet with the person one on one. I would suggest that when you meet with this person that you sit down and make sure your body posture is open towards them (i.e., Don't cross your legs or arms. Turn your entire body towards the person).

If you have a pre-existing relationship with the person, this is a good time to talk about a few of the things that you really appreciate about them. Then keeping your tone of voice in mind, in as few words as possible, and as direct and clear as you can possibly make it, explain what the issue is. After you have explained your side of the issue, it's now your turn to actively listen to their side. After they have told you their understanding of the issue, it is helpful to repeat back what you have heard for clarity purposes. Remember, you are working on coming up with a solution to a problem. The person is not the problem. Stay focused on the issue at hand. Make your goal in confrontation to come out on the other side with clarity.

If there is an issue in your life that needs to be dealt with, my challenge is to push through. Whatever the issue, it is holding you back from something that God has for you.

Make today count!

Day 276

All of us understand that routine car maintenance is part of owning a vehicle. Regularly getting the oil changed, tires rotated, and making sure the car is in line are absolute essentials to making sure the car operates the way it should. Can you imagine the consequences if you failed to maintain the alignment of your vehicle? It would become nearly impossible to keep your desired course of direction. I know I feel no sense of shame telling someone I'm going to get routine maintenance for my car. Everyone understands the importance of it.

When we hear the word "counseling," many of us draw a negative connotation. I believe counseling is as vital to our life and our marriages as routine maintenance is for our vehicles. Counseling provides clear direction for us and helps to be sure our alignment is correct. Proverbs 27:17 says, "Iron sharpens iron, so one man sharpens another." God did not design us to be isolated and to deal with our problems alone. By allowing another person who has Godly wisdom to speak into your life, you're helping to ensure that you are able to pursue the correct path.

I know there are some reading this who are currently privately struggling through a situation. Humble yourself and seek Godly counsel. Don't allow the stigma of the term "counseling" to outweigh what God can do through it. You would not neglect your car maintenance. How much more important is your marriage and your life? My challenge for you today is to stop trying to fix the problems on your own and reach out to someone who can walk beside you!

Make today count!

Day 277

It doesn't matter where I am--Chuck E. Cheese's, at the park, at a swimming pool, or at the indoor playground, or Chick-fil-A--if I hear one of my kids crying, I know immediately that it's them. It doesn't matter how much other noise or how many other kids may be crying. I know the distinct cry each of my children. As a father I am so in tune to my own kids that I can distinguish the sounds of their cry versus the cry of other kids.

In the same way, God knows us so intimately that he can distinguish our cry. He hears and cares about the cries of his children. Psalms 34:17 tell us, "The righteous cry out, and the Lord hears them; he delivers them from all their troubles."

God not only hears your cries, he cares deeply about them. He wants to deliver you from your troubles today. Cry out to him.

Make today count!

Day 278

How has the year been for you? Has this been a year of massive gains? Has it been a year that's been filled with tremendous joy or tremendous sorrow? Maybe this year has been a year you would be more than willing to in essence repeat again next year, or maybe you're holding onto the hope that this coming year will be the complete opposite. A new year marks a fresh start. This is a chance for you to make a game plan, set a goal, and push until you reach it. This new year can represent a new mindset for you, a mindset that operates through the eyes of Christ. Offering forgiveness and grace when they are not deserved. A new year means a new chance.

Revelations 21:5 serves as a wonderful reminder of what God is up to. "And he who was seated on the throne said, 'Behold, I am making all things new.'" He wants to take your broken relationships and make them whole. He wants to take your fear and give you a spirit of peace. He wants to take your heart of stone and give you a heart of flesh. (Ezekiel 36:26) He wants to mend your brokenness.

Regardless of what your reality has been this past year, my challenge for you today is to submit the new year to him and what he wants to do.

Make today count!

Day 279

This morning as I made my way into work I came across a road detour. This detour took me far off my normal path. I continued to trust that the detour would get me where I need to be. Sure enough, after a few minutes I found my way back onto the road where I recognized my location.

Life is the same way. There are times in life we know where we're going and then suddenly there's a detour, change in plans, a change in direction. Don't let life's detours frustrate you. Look at them as an opportunity to learn new roads and a new path that you wouldn't have ever gone down.

What you think may be a detour maybe in fact be the new path God has for you. Psalm 23:2-3 reminds us, "He leads me beside still waters. He restores my soul. He leads me in paths of righteousness for his name's sake."

Make today count!

Day 280

AS a gift to Holly for Christmas, I decided to burn all our home videos which were stored on the computer onto DVD discs. Last night we sat with the kids and watched one of these videos. This particular video was when Abi Kate was born. The kids really enjoyed seeing themselves as babies. I woke up this morning around 6 a.m. to hear Abi Kate crying in her room. When I went to check on her to see what was wrong, she was crying and told me she wanted to be a baby again. I explained to her that it was impossible for her to become a baby again. I told her about all the exciting things that were to come for her as she matured and all of the fun things she would get to do.

Obviously, we all understand that it is physically impossible for us to go back in the past and experience something again for the second time. I do think it is easy for us to stay focused on the past. It's easy for us to do well there. Maybe you allow yourself to focus on what might have been, or what could be. Chances are there is a situation in which you wish you could have a redo. We cannot allow ourselves to live in our past and continue to move forward to what God has called us to. Luke 9:62 says, "Jesus replied, 'No one who puts a hand to the plow and looks back is fit for service in the kingdom of God.'" You can't keep your eyes on what's in front of you when you're looking in the rear-view mirror.

The future is not the same. There's uncertainty. There may be fear and there will definitely be growth of some kind. Your past experiences are not meant to define you, they are meant to help you grow. Philippians 1:6 reminds us, "Being confident of this, that he who began a good work in you will carry it on to completion until the day of Christ Jesus." The work Christ started in you will continue to progress into next year to draw you closer to what he has for you.

My challenge for you today is to stay focused on the here and now. Use your past to be a starting point for growth.

Make today count!

Day 281

Last night was another exciting evening of seven and eight-year-old coach pitch. I can't prove it, but I'm pretty sure some of the kids on the other team were about 27 years old. Cade's team had a very difficult time staying in the mix against them. These kids hit the ball much harder and much further than Cade's team. After the second inning the score was 10-2. My particular job as a helper coach yesterday was to stand in right center field and organize the right and right center fielders. Around the fourth inning the coach sent one of our better players to the outfield to allow some of the other guys a chance to play in the infield. When this kid made it out to me, his head was hung low and then he sat down on the ground. The head coach asked the young man why he was sitting. He responded by saying, "If I can't play first base, I don't want to play." My young friend was very confused. He did not realize this was a team effort and every position mattered. Instead he decided to focus on the fact that he was not receiving what he wanted then and now.

As the body of Christ, we have one mission and objective. That mission is to show and tell as many people as possible about the life-changing relationship they can have through Christ. I believe we fall short on this mission largely because we get caught up in "who is playing first." God has given each of us different gifts and abilities. He has strategically placed each of us where we can benefit the greater good. By default, our human nature can kick in and we can look at someone who is playing a role we wish we were playing and decide to take our ball and go home. Ephesians 4:16 says, "from whom the whole body, joined and held together by every joint with which it is equipped, when each part is working properly, makes the body grow so that it builds itself up in love." Each of us has a role to play. We must not get caught up in "who is playing first" but rather remain focused on the big picture.

Know that whatever your role is, it is needed and significant. It might not be the most glamorous, but we do not play for the satisfaction and applause of man. Today my challenge for you is that you focus your approval on God, the One on whom your placement comes from.

Make today count!

Day 282

In my job I have the opportunity to counsel several men each week. I recently had an opportunity to meet with a man who had a failing in his life. He was allowing the circumstance to drive the direction of his life. In essence, he was allowing his failure to define who he was as a person.

Failure itself is inevitable. All of us will have times in life where we fail in different areas. As Craig Groeschel says, "A failure is an event. It is never a person." Just because you have failed at something doesn't make you a failure. Take the isolated event that was a failure and use it to push you to a place of unparalleled success. Proverbs 26:4 says, "For though the righteous fall seven times, they rise again."

My challenge for you today is to allow God to use your failures to shape the purpose he has for you. Don't let your failures define you. You are not your failures. You are who God says you are.

Make today count!

Day 283

A couple weeks ago, Cade had a dentist appointment where they discovered he had a small cavity on one of his back teeth. Yesterday we had the appointment to get the filling. Cade generally does very well at the dentist and at the doctor's office, however, he had a lot of fear going into the dentist appointment about getting the filling. I assured him over and over that he would be fine.

It's easy for fear to take hold of us in new situations. We find ourselves making assumptions about what we are stepping into. Our mind always takes us to the worst-case scenarios. I love Philippians 4:8: "Finally, brothers and sisters, whatever is true, whatever is noble, whatever is right, whatever is pure, whatever is lovely, whatever is admirable—if anything is excellent or praiseworthy—think about such things." I think this verse is a roadmap on how we should respond when fear takes over our thoughts. If it's not true, excellent, or praiseworthy, it doesn't deserve your time.

After Cade was done with his procedure, he said "It was easy." He said, "If I had known that's all it was, I wouldn't have been scared." How often is this our response after we have gone through a situation that we had built up in our mind? My challenge for you today is not to allow fear to steal from you. Live in what you know is true and worthy of praise!

Make today count!

Day 284

I have many fond memories from childhood of driving to Kentucky to see both sets of grandparents over the holidays. We always knew we were getting close when we began to see the white fences around the beautiful horse farms in Lexington, Kentucky. These long white fences added to the beauty of the scenery, but they also served a great purpose in keeping the horses off the highway. We all understand the importance of having fences. They serve as a barrier to keep things out and as a barrier to keep things in. We can control what gets into our fences since we have access to the gate.

In the book *Every Man's Battle*, Dr. Steven Arterburn spends the last chapter discussing the importance of having "fences" set up to protect your heart and mind. See, ultimately you are in control of who gets access into your mind and heart. No one thinks anything negatively of a farmer who puts up a fence to keep coyotes away from his livestock. In the same way, we must put up barriers to protect our hearts, minds, and ultimately our families.

Proverbs 4:23 tell us, "Above all else, guard your heart, for everything you do flows from it." My challenge for you today is to know that there are real threats against your heart, mind, and family. If you haven't already done so, it's time to set up clear fences to protect these things that matter so deeply.

Make today count!

Day 285

My sweet and beautiful wife despises putting gas in her car. This morning she told me that of all the little chores of life, putting gas in the car is her absolute least favorite. Interestingly enough, ignoring this chore probably has one of the greatest consequences. Here is a little window into our conversation this morning.

Holly: "If my gas light came on when I pulled into the driveway last night, will I be able to warm up my car and make it to school this morning?"

Me: "You do realize that you can put gas in your car prior to the gas light coming on, right?"

True, this is hilarious, but I believe it also has some spiritual implications. Many times in life, we don't think about God until our life is running on empty. We wait until we receive warning signs that we are about to run dry, and then we run to God to get filled up. The same way it is true for the car, it is true for your life. Just as you can go to the gas station any time you want, you can keep your life running on full. It requires intentionality, persistence, and dedication to allow God to fill you each and every day. Psalms 91:1 says, "Whoever dwells in the shelter of the Most High will rest in the shadow of the Almighty." Some days it's harder to get out of the car and fill up because of external circumstances. My challenge for you today is to push through and fill up—make the extra effort to spend time with God each day through being in His word and in prayer.

Make today count!

Day 286

Something a lot of people find surprising about me is that I love to bargain shop. Yesterday after Abi Kate and I had gone on our traditional Friday date, we went to one of my favorite stores. I am never looking for anything in particular when I go there. I'm just looking for something that peaks my interest and is a good deal. Yesterday I found a watch that had sticky glue on the front of the face. The back panel of the watch was disconnected. It appeared that the battery was dead and it was missing the piece that holds the watch together around your wrist. The watch retails for about $50. Most people probably would have put this watch in the trash. I looked at it and saw a small project with a huge return. After a short conversation with the manager, I was able to acquire the watch for $2.30. When I got home, I changed out the battery, used a tool to snap the back onto the watch. I used some Windex and got the face looking perfect. I then took an old watch band and attached the metal piece onto the new watch band. Long story short, this watch looks like I bought it from a normal store. No one would know the difference.

I wonder if this is how God looks at us. Other people would look at our life and see something that's not worth a whole lot. When God looks at us, I believe he sees our hidden potential. He knows he's going to have to refine us. He might have to do a little hammering and a little painting. He sees a treasure underneath. I wonder what it would look like if we looked at others through the same lens that Christ looks at us? "This is my commandment, that you love one another as I have loved you." (John 15:12)

My challenge for you today is to see the best, see the potential in others. Don't look at people and see all the things that are wrong with them. Instead, see the potential of what they could be. What would it look like if you even invested a little time to make someone the best version of themselves that they can possibly be?

Make today count!

Day 287

There was a crazy amount of fog this morning. The fog made it very difficult for me to see more than a few hundred yards in front of me while driving. As I was driving, the next few hundred feet of my path was made clear, but when I looked off into the distance, I was unable to see any of the landmarks I normally rely on. Even though the visibility was very low, I continued to travel the path as it was revealed to me and it led me to my destination.

It's easy to find ourselves in a fog in life. There are times when we are unsure of the direction we are headed. All we can see is what is currently in front of us. It's so difficult to be in a place where you're not sure exactly where God is leading, but in these times, I would encourage you to be diligent to continue to travel the path that is made clear to you. Psalms 119:105 reminds us that God's word is a lamp for our feet, a light for our path.

Make today count!

Day 288

I'm sure you have seen one of the new escape rooms which seem to be popping up everywhere. If you haven't had the opportunity to participate in one of these games, you really should. It's a lot of fun. In essence you're locked into a room and given one hour to find clues that will lead to your freedom. At any point during the game, should you need to go to the restroom or take a phone call, you can simply walk out and then walk back into the "locked" room. We would consider it sheer insanity if a prisoner was able to walk out of a locked cell at any point but chose to stay locked up. My fear is that that is where many of us are today.

Forgiveness is something that most of us believe we are giving to a person who has wronged us. However, forgiveness is really for us. There's a song on the radio now that talks about forgiveness. There is a line that says, "Forgiveness—the prisoner it really frees is you." Lack of forgiveness is only negatively affecting you. Marianne Williamson said, "Unforgiveness is like drinking poison yourself and waiting for the other person to die." Your lack of forgiveness for another person is not harming them. It is harming you.

Ephesians 4:31-32 says, "Get rid of all bitterness, rage and anger, brawling and slander, along with every form of malice. Be kind and compassionate to one another, forgiving each other, just as in Christ God forgave you." My challenge for you today is to forgive because you have been forgiven. The door of the cell you are in is open, but you have to choose to walk out of it.

Make today count!

Day 289

This year for Christmas my parents decided to buy my grandmother an iPhone. My Nana is pretty text savvy. The problem has come with transferring the service from one phone to the other. I'm not sure on the exact details of the situation, but I do know that my mom and dad have been on the phone for about an hour and 45 minutes trying to get the situation rectified, and as of now, the situation still has not been resolved. We've all been in that situation with the phone company or cable company. Nothing can be more frustrating than waiting on these folks.

In life, it's easy to become frustrated with God when we feel like he is making us wait in situations where we want resolution. Lamentations 3:25-27 says, "The Lord is good to everyone who trusts in him, so it is best for us to wait in patience—to wait for him to save us—And it is best to learn this patience in our youth." Patience in the waiting can be incredibly difficult. But oftentimes, our resolution is being worked while we wait. It's also worth pointing out that as this verse mentions, it's best to learn this patience in our youth. Parents, this is for us. Teaching patience to your children is as difficult as being on hold with Comcast.

My challenge for you today, regardless of your situation, is to be patient in the waiting. Trust in God's sovereignty and timing.

Make today count!

Day 290

In flag football, teams must plan for the defense to come after their quarterback. When the quarterback comes under pressure, they have to have a plan in place to protect him or give the ball to one of the other receivers. In the same way, in our lives we must come up with a plan when we face pressure. When we face temptation, we need to have a plan in place not to fall into it. James 1:13 says, "When tempted, no one should say, 'God is tempting me.' For God cannot be tempted by evil, nor does he tempt anyone; but each person is tempted when they are dragged away by their own evil desire and enticed."

It's not a matter *if* temptation is going to come. It's a matter of what we do when the temptation arises. What's your game plan?

Make today count!

Day 291

Without fail nine out of ten mornings, my three-year-old daughter Abi Kate wakes up prior to the alarm going off. She will come into my room and inform me that the sun is not up. We tell her it's still nighttime, and that the sun will be out in a little while and that it's time to go back to sleep.

She has an expectation in her three-year-old mind that if she wakes up, the sun should be out. When she's ready for it to be morning, it should be morning. Of course, we all know that's not how it works.

I believe in the same way it's easy for us to be waiting on God to answer our concerns, and we keep wondering where is the Son is, all along not realizing that in our situation, it's not time for the alarm to go off. God has plans for us, but they don't always happen on our timeframe. Rest assured the alarm will go off, and the sun will come out. "Your kingdom come, your will be done on earth as it is in heaven." (Matthew 6:10)

Make today count!

Day 292

The world we live in is filled with consumer-based people. Our mindset operates out of how things can benefit us. We want the fastest, the best, and the brightest. What is scary is that we will often use this consumer-based mentality when it comes to church. Many people approach church with an attitude of "how can it benefit me?" Church is not meant for our benefit. The church is created to offer worship to God and to serve others. Each of us has been given a special gift. Our service should flow out of our gifting.

Craig Groeschel, in his book, *Divine Direction* suggests an exercise that is an easy way to identify your gifting. Say you are at dinner with a group of friends and you see one of your friends about to take a bite of his chocolate pie. The problem is that the pie is close to the edge of the table. As his fork sinks into the pie, the pie spills into his lap. Your immediate reaction will most likely determine your spiritual gift. Do you decide to buy him a new pie? (Giving) Do you orchestrate the cleanup effort? (Leadership) Do you suggest the proper way to position the pie prior to eating it the next time? (Teaching) Do you tell him you knew it was going to happen? (Prophecy) Are you the first one to grab a napkin and start cleaning? (Service) Do you feel a deep sense of concern for your friend? (Mercy) God has given you this gift to share with others and to glorify him.

Together let's be reminded not to approach God with the consumer mentality. Today, are you using your gifts to build *your* kingdom or to build *his*?

Make today count!

Day 293

I started feeling a bit under the weather Saturday morning, and as the day progressed, I felt worse. By the end of the day on Sunday, I found a walk-in clinic where I was told I had the flu. It has been a while since I've been this sick, and I had honestly forgotten how terrible it is to have a high fever. It's interesting how even something as small as getting the flu can help me better understand just how much I have to be grateful for.

Since Sunday I found myself sitting underneath a warm shower a minimum of three times a day. I've always been grateful for the fact that I had a shower, but with this being the only thing that's giving me any relief, my sense of gratitude has grown. Isn't it odd how when you are sick you can't taste food? I'm grateful that God gave us taste buds to enjoy different types of food. The old saying, "You don't know what you've got until it's gone" has proven to be true.

My challenge for you today is to stop and assess, and I mean really assess, all that you have to be grateful for! 1 Thessalonians 5:18 encourages us to "Give thanks in all circumstances; for this is God's will for you in Christ Jesus."

Make today count!

Day 294

Do you ever feel like you're living in the movie *Groundhog Day*? I know I do. My morning routine during the work week looks very similar. It's easy to find ourselves feeling stuck—stuck doing the same tasks, stuck living similar day after similar day. How do we break out of this cycle? How do we find meaning and significance in each day?

I believe significance comes from giving purpose to the minuscule. What if we approach our daily tasks with the mindset that these tasks are ways to bring glory and honor to God? Ecclesiastes 9:10 says, "Whatever your hand finds to do, do it with all your might, for in the realm of the dead, where you are going, there is neither working nor planning nor knowledge nor wisdom."

My challenge for you today is to approach not only your vocational work but your daily tasks with an attitude of gratefulness for the ability and opportunity to do them. My dad always says, "Today's work is an interview for tomorrow's job."

Make today count!

Day 295

Lately, my oldest son Cade has been experiencing growth pains. Over the past seven months he has grown significantly. He loves to measure himself against the growth chart we have in the house to see his progress. He loves to come up to me and show me how much "higher" he has gotten. He loves to tell me how close he is to being as tall as I am. Side note, as you probably know, that's really not much of an accomplishment. As much as he loves getting taller, he hates the growth pains that come with it. He doesn't understand what's taking place in his body and why it does not feel good. I explained to him that these pains are part of the growing process.

We will experience growth pains as we grow in our relationship with God as well. Although they might not be physical pains, they still hurt. As we move closer to Christ, he wants to refine things in our lives that are keeping us from the fullness of a relationship with him. Today don't focus on the pain of the things that are being changed in your life. Go stand next to the growth chart and thank God that he's moving you closer to him.

"But grow in the grace and knowledge of our Lord and Savior Jesus Christ. To him be glory both now and forever! Amen. (2 Peter 3:18)

Make today count!

Day 296

Have you ever been asked a question that you were not prepared to answer? Well, it happened to me this morning. My three-year-old Abi Kate asked me, "Daddy, how do babies get in mommies' bellies?" Just for the record, Holly is not pregnant. Her question took me off guard to say the least. I had not processed how I would respond to this question ahead of time. My response: "Go ask your mom." I completely copped out of coming up with an age-appropriate answer for this question. I pawned it off 100% on Holly, who I know handled it with grace and elegance.

This got me thinking about questions we have for God. It's not possible for us to catch him off guard. He's ready for our questions. It doesn't matter how difficult they are. When diagnosis comes, when job loss comes, when divorce happens, and even death, God is not offended or taken off guard by our questions. James 1:5 says, "If any of you lacks wisdom, you should ask God, who gives generously to all without finding fault, and it will be given to you."

The silent treatment with God just doesn't work. Don't allow your anger, fear, or frustrations to keep you up from earnestly seeking to understand the situation you are in. 1 Peter 5:7 reminds us to "Cast your cares on him, because he cares for you."

Make today count!

Day 297

I don't know about you, but as a parent, I sometimes feel like I need to hold it all together. I need to make sure the kids are well taken care of, getting smarter, learning about God, and learning how to be kind. I need to make sure there's food in the pantry, that we plan nutritious things to eat, handle the finances, juggle work schedules and meetings, take care of my own relationship with God, and then of course make time for my beautiful wife. And the list goes on. It can be incredibly overwhelming when you stop and think about all the different ways you're pulled during the day.

Those of you who know much about science know that inside of an atom, positively charged protons are held together by what scientists call "nuclear fusion." This is a pretty cool thing because without it, these protons would repeal each other as they are both positively charged. I believe what nuclear fusion shows us is intelligent design by a God who is the source of nuclear fusion. He is the One who is holding it all together.

Colossians 1:17 states this truth: "He is before all things, and in him all things hold together." God stands outside of time. He is before it, in it, and in front of it. My challenge for you today is that in the chaos you call your life, know that he is holding it all together. You don't have to hold it any longer—HE has it all held together!

Make today count!

Day 298

This morning as I was sitting on the bathroom counter getting ready for work, Cade was in the bathroom with me. I asked him to grab my toiletry bag from underneath the cabinet so I could get a few things out of it. He promptly grabbed the bag, opened it and set out lotion, beard oil, and cologne. Then he said "I watch you all the time. That's how I knew what to get out!" I had no idea that he was watching me in the mornings as we get ready. He was watching me in such detail that he knew exactly what I needed as part of my morning routine.

That served as a reminder to me today that someone is watching me and you. There are people who are watching the way you live your life, the way you conduct yourself, and the way you respond to the situations that come to you. For those of you who are Christians, the way you're living your life is either drawing people closer to the affections of Christ or pushing them away. For those of you who are not Christians, the way you're living your life is impacting the proximity to which people want to gather around you.

My challenge today is to be a person worth watching. Be someone who drives people to the affections of Christ. "Be imitators of me, just as I also am of Christ." (1 Corinthians 11:1)

Make today count!

Day 299

Those of you who know me well know I love my grass. I have realized the great benefit of aerating the yard. Aeration is a process where small plugs of dirt and grass are pulled from the yard. This creates several small but deep holes. The small holes allow air, water, and nutrients to penetrate the deep roots. This process creates a much thicker and healthier lawn come springtime.

Are you aerating your soul? Each morning by spending time in God's word, this is just what is happening. Hiding God's word deep in your soul will result in healthier responses, attitudes, and behaviors. His words are nutrients to the roots of our souls.

My yard would not look nearly as healthy in the springtime if I do not go through the process of aerating. In the same way, our attitudes, behaviors, and actions will not be as healthy without the process of hiding God's word into our heart each morning. "I have hidden your word in my heart, that I may not sin against you." (Psalms 119:11)

Make today count!

Day 300

Earlier in the week Cade came home with a spelling test he had taken earlier that day. His spelling test had a note on it from his teacher letting us know that during their self-grading time, Cade had edited a few of his words to make them correct. I pulled him aside and had a conversation with him about honesty and integrity. His response was, "Dad, it doesn't really matter. It's just a spelling test."

As adults, we face many "just spelling tests." What I mean by this is that we are often presented with opportunities where we can compromise our integrity for our own personal gain. There are many things in life that once lost can be found or regained again (money, keys, even a job). However, the problem with integrity is that once you have lost it publicly, it is incredibly difficult to regain and very difficult for people to ever trust you again. Proverbs 28:6: "Better the poor who is blameless than the rich whose walk is perverse." Quite simply, it is better for us to have few possessions and have our integrity intact than to have all the riches one could possibly acquire without a thread of integrity.

My challenge for you today is to be aware that your integrity is worth more than you could possibly profit by "rewriting your spelling words." Choose today to value your integrity over any position that you have or could acquire.

Make today count!

Day 301

During my freshman year of college, I landed a job as a swim team coach at the Pennington Swim Club in Indiana. The swim team consisted of children as young as five and went all the way up to seniors in high school. I was the swim team coach for the five and six-year-olds. We spent a significant amount of time working on improving each of the basic strokes. Our major focus for their swim meet was to keep their attention on the lane they were in. We needed them to understand that they only needed to pay attention to their race. It was so tempting for them to watch other people in other lanes, making it impossible for them to swim their best race.

As adults, I believe most of us struggle to run our own race. Paul tells us in Hebrews 12:1-2, "Therefore, since we are surrounded by such a great cloud of witnesses, let us throw off everything that hinders and the sin that so easily entangles. And let us run with perseverance the race marked out for us, fixing our eyes on Jesus, the pioneer and perfecter of faith. For the joy set before him he endured the cross, scorning its shame, and sat down at the right hand of the throne of God." It's important that we understand "the race that has been marked out before us." God has put each of us on a specific journey. Our specific skill set and talents are what makes this journey ours. It's so easy for us to get distracted with what others are doing that we forget to run our own race.

My challenge for you today is to understand how God has wired you and run the race he has set before you with perseverance. Run the race to win, and run keeping your eyes on him.

Make today count!

Day 302

We have a small Yorkie named Mowgli (Mow for short). Inevitably, at some point during the morning while the kids are eating breakfast, Mow will go and sit by the door indicating that he needs to go outside. When he comes back into the house, he will spin around on his back paws. This is an indication that he believes he has done something worthy of earning a treat. The kids love to give him the treat. The past few mornings Abi Kate has given him his treat. This morning Cade asked if today could be his turn since his sister had been giving the treat for the past week since he has been sick. I said sure and gave him the treat to give to the dog. Abi Kate lost her mind.

When this happened, it got me thinking about jealousy. She has given at least the past seven treats to the dog and Cade hasn't given him any. Yet when Cade was given the opportunity, she deemed it unfair in her three-year-old mind.

I think at times we can all be susceptible to having a 3-year-old mentality. We see other people getting opportunities, possessions, or recognition, and instead of rejoicing with them, we go into our corner and pout.

Sometimes life is not fair. There are going to be people who get recognition, possessions, and opportunities when you feel like you deserve them. Romans 12:15 says, "Rejoice with those who rejoice; mourn with those who mourn." My challenge for you today is to get out of your pity corner and truly rejoice with those around you who are finding success right now.

Make today count!

Day 303

Happy Halloween! I trust that the excitement level in your house is similar to mine. Abi Kate will don the roll of "Moana" and Cade "Kylo Ren." Cade is more than excited about his costume and the mask that goes with it. All this is quite hilarious to Holly and me because Cade has never seen Star Wars. I always enjoy seeing the complexity of some of the costumes out there and just how realistic they look.

The crazy thing is that tomorrow on November 1, there will still be plenty of people wearing a mask. I don't mean a physical mask. I mean a mask of a false self. This is one of the things that absolutely drives me crazy about social media. People can make you believe their life is picture perfect based on their pictures and posts. Here is the truth—none of us have it all together. We are all broken people searching for significance. One of my favorite values that we hold as a church at New Vision is "relating authentically." As a church, we want to represent our true self, our broken selves, so people can see the power of God to transform our lives.

The problem with wearing a mask is that it does not allow anyone to truly know you. It puts a shield up preventing people from seeing your true self. Luke 12:2 reminds us, "You can't keep your true self hidden forever; before long you'll be exposed. You can't hide behind a religious mask forever; sooner or later the mask will slip and your true face will be known." Allowing people to know you intimately and deeply—that is where the deepest freedoms are found. My challenge for you today is to take off the mask you are wearing and give people the opportunity to really know who you are.

Make today count!

Day 304

Did you ever have one of "those" mornings?" I had one today. I just finished making my coffee and was about to head out the door when I heard Cade walk into the living room. He caught me right as I was leaving, and he asked if I could get him some orange juice and cereal. I said, "Sure." I started to help him get out everything we needed to make this happen. He got out a small cup and a big bottle of orange juice. He walked over and started to pour it himself. Instead of stopping him, I decided to let this play out which resulted in a small mess. Once I had that cleaned up and was once again on my way out the door, Abi Kate said "Good morning!" She then asked for a bowl of Cheerios and some milk. Once I had her cereal ready, I handed it to her. She dropped it within a matter of three seconds causing Cheerios to go all over the floor.

As all parents will agree, situations such as these can be incredibly frustrating. As I was cleaning up all of the Cheerios, my mind flashed back to a conversation I recently had with a couple in my office at church. In the past year and a half, this couple has dealt with what I would consider to be one of the most tragic life events anyone could endure. They tragically lost their oldest son who I believe was around 11 years old. It's been unbelievable the way that the conversation with this couple has shaped my days since. I will gladly clean up Cheerios, spilled milk, and any other mess of the sort and do so with a joyful heart. If you have children who are healthy, loud, messy, and frustrating at times, you have one million reasons to be thankful.

1 Thessalonians 5:18 says, "Give thanks in all circumstances; for this is the will of God in Christ Jesus for you." The word "all" is a universal term. It's all encompassing. It means we don't have the ability to pick and choose what to be thankful for. When we look at the big picture, we can always find a reason to give thanks. My challenge for you today is to take five minutes and see how many things you can write down which you have to be thankful for. I'm confident your list will be lengthy.

Make today count!

Day 305

After many weeks of patiently waiting, yesterday we arranged to take the kids to see Santa at Bass Pro Shop. We arrived there around 4 o'clock only to find out that all of the Santa passes for the day had already been given out. Long story short, the kids were not going to get to see Santa. You can imagine their disappointment, as well as mine and Holly's.

I decided my best possible course of action was to seek out a manager and see if we could get the situation rectified. I'm not even going to pretend to you that I was happy. I was ticked. I didn't let my emotions get the best of me. I stayed very composed and kind. I first approached a staff person to see if they could be of any help. No luck. They said, "Come back tomorrow." I sought out the assistant manager. His news was more of the same. Finally, I found a third manager. I explained the situation to him and asked if there was anything he could do to help. He was able to get the kids a pass to see Santa. This was a huge dad win.

Moral of the story, let Colossians 4:6 be your guide when you find yourself in frustrating situations. "Let your speech always be gracious, seasoned with salt, so that you may know how you ought to answer each person." My challenge for you today is to remember you catch more flies with honey than you do with vinegar!

Make today count!

Day 306

I don't know about you, but sometimes I find myself sitting at a stop sign or a traffic light wishing I could just go. We all understand why we have stop signs and traffic lights. It might seem fun to live in a world where you could just go whenever you wanted. It probably would be for a little while at least. It's clear to see what the results of that would be--chaos and injury.

In the same way, God has given us laws to guide our lives. Many times, we find ourselves choosing not to obey them, and then the result is chaos, hurt, and injury. Oftentimes we then go to God asking why he allowed us to experience hurt and pain, all the while not understanding that we, with our own selfish decisions, brought it upon ourselves.

God's laws are not put in place to take your fun away but to protect you in the same way the traffic lights are not there to take your fun away but to keep you safe. Stop trying to fight against what you know God is calling you to. True freedom comes in your surrender.

Deuteronomy 30:16 say, "For I command you today to love the LORD your God, to walk in obedience to him, and to keep his commands, decrees and laws; then you will live and increase, and the LORD your God will bless you in the land you are entering to possess."

Make today count!

Day 307

In John 11 we see the story of the death of Lazarus. Lazarus was a close friend of Jesus'. When Jesus arrived on the scene, Lazarus had been dead for four days. Many of Jesus' followers were frustrated with him because he did not arrive sooner. They believed that if he would have come before Lazarus died, he could have healed Lazarus. Little did they realize what Jesus was capable of. Now, could Jesus have healed Lazarus prior to him dying? Absolutely! We see many other stories of miraculous healings prior to this situation. How much greater faith do you think Jesus produced in his followers by raising Lazarus from the dead?

Jesus called Lazarus specifically by name out of the grave and Lazarus comes out, still wrapped in his grave clothes. Many who were there believed because of what they had seen. I don't know about you, but I think it would be incredibly easy to believe someone was the Son of God if I had just witnessed them raise someone from the dead right in front of me.

Lazarus' story is an important one for us. See, no matter where he was after this happened, when people saw him, they immediately thought about what Jesus has done for him. No one could look at him without immediately thinking of how Jesus had saved his life. See, Lazarus' life was a living, breathing testimony to the saving grace of Christ.

What or who do people associate your life with? When people see you, do they see a person who was dead in their hurts, habits, and hang ups? Do they see someone whose life has been radically changed to find an authentic encounter with the God of the universe? My challenge for you today is to use your life to point to the One who saved it.

Make today count!

Day 308

I think we all face times in life where we are faced with a task that seems impossible. This task could take many different shapes and forms. It could be physical, spiritual, or emotional. Let me provide a few examples for clarity. Someone might have a physical goal of wanting to lose 100 pounds. Someone might have a spiritual goal of wanting to see their child come to faith in Christ. And someone might have an emotional goal of wanting to mend a broken relationship with a family member

Any of these tasks seem pretty huge. Telling someone they need to lose 100 pounds is an overwhelming thing for them to hear. It's a huge goal that's far off in the distance. What I have found that brings the most success when faced with large goals is to take it little by little. As my mom would say, "Life by the inch is a cinch. Life by the yard is hard." If someone was trying to break the habit of smoking and I told them, "Don't ever smoke again," this would be a very difficult task for them to accept. On the other hand, if I said to this person, "Don't smoke for the next five minutes," chances are they would be successful.

Whatever it is that you are working towards today, be reminded of the words from Colossians 3:23: "Whatever you do, work heartily, as for the Lord and not for men." What are the small steps that you need to take today towards your big goal? Remember, Rome was not built in a day. Continue to pursue your goal little by little working as unto the Lord and you will have success!

Make today count!

Day 309

As a child, in 1994 one of the major highlights of this time of year was receiving the Sears Christmas catalog. There was nothing better than getting lost inside the catalog for hours on end circling potential items for the upcoming Christmas holiday. In my prime, I was easily capable of circling well over $2,000 in goods. A pool table always made the list.

As youngsters, it's easy to believe that ultimate Christmas fulfillment can be found in a catalog. In our culture, we are programmed to believe that we are only one purchase away from happiness. There's absolutely nothing wrong with having nice things. There is a huge difference, however, in nice things having you. Remember, the Christmas season is one that was established on the greatest gift ever given. I believe that society as a whole has changed Christmas to make it about acquiring for ourselves.

1 John 3:17 reminds us, "But if anyone has the world's goods and sees his brother in need, yet closes his heart against him, how does God's love abide in him?" My challenge for you throughout this holiday season is not live with a Sears catalog mindset, but one that's looking for opportunities to meet the needs around you.

Make today count!

Day 310

Last night I was awakened at about 2:30 a.m. to a very peculiar sound followed by a very familiar sound. The first sound was Cade making some type of odd noise, followed by him throwing up. For the next 4 1/2 hours, Holly and I did a routine that was similar to wash, rinse, dry, repeat. Working in the aquatics industry for a number of years, I definitely saw my fair share of emergencies--everything from small cuts to a brain aneurysm. I never had any problem responding to these types of situations. In fact, in most cases, I was the go-to person if anything ever happened. However, for whatever reason, the site of my own child's throw up freezes me in my tracks, and I lose all cognitive ability. Luckily, I have Holly by my side to keep me task and away from cleaning throw up.

The past couple months have been tough ones for us. We just cannot seem to keep everyone well. I was reminded this morning of James 1:2-3 which says, "Consider it pure joy, my brothers and sisters, whenever you face trials of many kinds, because you know that the testing of your faith produces perseverance." When you're on a three-month stent of sickness, it's verses like this that are super encouraging. Has it been an enjoyable experience? No. But it has pushed us to serve each other in love and to be so appreciative of the days when everyone is well.

My challenge for you today is whatever your situation is, find the joy in it. You have the ability to choose to . . .

Make today count!

Day 311

I have been very fortunate within my professional career to seem to have always had someone to take me under their wing and mentor me. I think back to the first real business trip I ever went on with the YMCA. My mentor at the time, Gary Cobbs, pulled me aside and asked me if I had a nice winter overcoat. On this particular trip, I was heading to Chicago with our COO. What Gary knew was that this man valued the appearance of his employees. Now, this does not even scratch the surface at the beginning of the wisdom I learned from Gary, but it still serves as a valuable tool today.

As I made the transition out of the business world and into the church world, my desire and need for mentorship has only grown. Through a lot of prayer and God's direct interaction, I now meet weekly with another older and much wiser man. This man is there to help give me sound wisdom and advice in all aspects of my life. He leaves no rock unturned. Our conversations are not always easy, but they are needed for my growth.

In the biblical narrative, we can look at the life Moses and see that he specifically invested in and mentored Joshua (Numbers 27:12-23). Joshua does not reciprocate the process which leads to Israel's destruction. You cannot put a price tag on mentorship. Without mentorship, future leadership is in jeopardy.

What about you? Do you have someone who is pouring into you each week? Do you have someone who knows all of the areas you are struggling with and trying to grow in? I understand that this is a tough place to push into, but I can promise you the results on the other end are well worth it.

Make today count!

Day 312

I don't know about you, but there are times when it's hard for me to be benevolent with my money. There is something about controlling money that is so ingrained into the nature of humans. Oftentimes we tend to trust our money more than we trust the One who gave us the ability to generate an income. Have you ever felt compelled to give a gift over and above your tithe but chose not to do it out of fear?

Two weeks ago, I was approached by a church member who felt God had put it on his heart to pay for 14 men to attend the men's retreat in November. The total cost for this was $1,400. He was stepping out in faith because he did not actually have the money to pay for it. He believed God would provide. I received a phone call from him two days ago telling me he had unexpectedly received just over SEVEN TIMES the amount that he felt prompted to give!

God uses money to test us. He does not need our money—he already owns it all. He wants us to trust him. Malachi 3:10 challenges us to, "Bring the whole tithe into the storehouse, that there may be food in my house. Test me in this,' says the LORD Almighty, 'and see if I will not throw open the floodgates of heaven and pour out so much blessing that there will not be room enough to store it.'" By withholding the gifts God has given you, you are missing an amazing blessing on the other end. These blessings don't always come in the form of a monetary gift, but I can promise you they are always worth the amazing stories that will follow!

Where is God calling you to give? Don't allow money to be your master. Step into a place of faith and see what God will do!

Make today count!

Day 313

The moon was still out this morning at 6:30. It was a beautiful, incredibly bright, full moon. I've always been fascinated by the moon. As crazy as it might sound, going to the moon is one of my life goals. There's something about it that is just so captivating.

What's interesting about the moon, as you know, is that the moon is essentially a bunch of rock and dirt combined together. The moon itself has no light source. It reflects the light of the sun which we interpret as "moonlight." The moon by itself has no ability to produce light of any kind, yet it makes an incredible reflection of the sun's light.

Here is the special parallel. We are the moon. We have no light source of our own to give to anyone. However, we can reflect the light from the Son. We have nothing that we can give to anyone other than that which is being given by God. In the book of Matthew, Jesus reminds us to let our light shine before men. Matthew 5:16 says, "In the same way, let your light shine before others, that they may see your good deeds and glorify your Father in heaven." My challenge for you today is to realize that you are nothing but rock and dirt, but you have the ability to reflect the light of the Son.

Make today count!

Day 314

For the past three mornings, I have gone into Cade's bathroom and found that he has thrown his toothpaste away. He is at that the place with the toothpaste that we've all experienced when we have to work a little harder to get anything to come out of the tube. He keeps assuring me that it's empty. I'll bend it and am able to produce enough toothpaste to take care of his needs for the day.

Do you ever find yourself in that place in your life? A place where you feel like you just don't have anything else to give. You couldn't possibly produce or provide what it takes to care for what's needed for today. Philippians 4:13 says "I can do all things through Christ who gives me strength." With God by your side, all things are possible!

My challenge for you today is to know that you are like that tube of toothpaste. There's more in you. You have more to give. It might require a little more push, but you WILL overcome!

Make today count!

Day 315

One of my favorite pastimes is kayak fishing. I've been doing it for several years now and I find it to be incredibly enjoyable and relaxing. It's like a mini vacation in the middle of the week. I recently came across an incredible deal on a high-end kayak. I was able to get my old kayak sold and made the purchase. This kayak is absolutely remarkable. It has one huge advantage over my old one—I have the ability to stand up in it. Nothing has changed with my ability to cast or to reel. What has changed is my perspective over the water. With the ability to stand up, I can see structures in the water such as stumps and logs that otherwise I would be unable to see from a seated position. This perspective change gives me the ability to see natural fish habitat which allows me to catch more fish.

There are times in life when a change in perspective is needed. In my previous kayak, I couldn't necessarily see if I was casting at anything in particular. I was simply casting and hoping for the best. Changing my perspective allows me the ability to see the larger picture. Colossians 3:2 reminds us to "Set your mind on the things above, not on the things that are on earth." When we change our perspective and allow ourselves to focus on the eternal, it can bring clarity to what could otherwise be confusing situations. We may find ourselves "casting blindly," but when we change our perspective to the eternal, it can create a clear understanding of how God is moving and working in our situation.

Maybe today you need a change in perspective. Your situation may seem confusing and unclear. I challenge you to set your mind towards the eternal perspective in the situation and I believe clarity will follow.

Make today count!

Day 316

By now I'm sure you realize I am very much into working in my yard. This past weekend I had to remove a tree that had grown up too high and was coming in contact with the side of my house. I replanted something a bit smaller that will not outgrow the side of the house. I also had to trim the tree in the front yard that has begun to grow excessively. For optimal growth to occur, plants require pruning.

In the same way, for us to reach our optimal growth potential, we require pruning. Obvious I'm not talking about removal of any limbs. I'm talking about spiritual pruning. This is a process where God removes parts of us that are actually making us weak. Oftentimes the pruning process is not a pleasant one, but on the other side of it, we look more like Christ. Each of us have areas in our lives that are in the pruning process. We will continue to go through this pruning process until the day we stand face to face with God. Pruning puts us closer to perfection.

What are the areas in your life where God is pruning you? Don't resent the process. If you will go through it, you will be better for it.

Make today count!

Day 317

Recently Holly and I watched a documentary about people who are trying to summit the mountain K2. If you're like me, you probably don't know a whole lot about this mountain. K2 is one of the most dangerous climbs someone can make. Of everyone who attempts to summit this mountain, 25% do not make it. The thing that was the most interesting about this documentary to me was that everyone who goes into this climb goes with the understanding that they will not have any help. It's too dangerous for another person to try to help. It's every man for themselves.

There are times in life when God gives us the opportunity to climb a mountain. Of course, I'm not talking about a physical mountain. I'm talking about a huge task to be performed. I have just been given a mountain to climb. I will be in charge of orchestrating all aspects for our new Thursday night service at church beginning January 4. See, the big problem I have is similar to the one that the climbers face on K2. I tend to look at my mountains as if I'm going to have to do it all alone. In the next month, I need to find 20 people who are willing to serve in our new Thursday service. I have to humble myself and realize I cannot do this alone. I know without a shadow of a doubt that I need help.

What is the mountain God has you climbing right now? Are you trying to do it on your own? Galatians 6:2 encourages us, "Carry each other's burdens, and in this way you will fulfill the law of Christ." My challenge for you today is first of all to ask for help with your personal mountain, and secondly, help someone else climb the mountain God has called them to climb.

Make today count!

Day 318

When Michael Jordan was a sophomore in high school, he was cut from his high school basketball team. The story goes that he went home, locked himself in his room, and cried. He did not let this failure define him. He used it to push him to become one of the greatest basketball players in history.

All of us have failed at some point in our life. We cannot let our failures define who we are. Allowing your failure to define you is like driving your car forward while looking in the rearview mirror. If you're looking in the review mirror at all the destruction behind you, all you are going to do is create destruction in front of you. You can't change the past, but you can control your future.

Choose today to propel your future to the places and direction you know you are being called to. 2 Corinthians 5:17 says, "Therefore if anyone is in Christ, he is a new creature; the old things passed away; behold, new things have come."

Make today count!

Day 319

It's been 7 1/2 weeks now since I injured my ankle playing flag football. Throughout this process, I have had two sets of x-rays, both of which came back clear, and I've had multiple physical therapy sessions (shout out to Mollie Wright Carver who is great!). This past Saturday I had an MRI since I am still having pain on both sides of my ankle. This is my first experience having an MRI. It was neat to see how it was able to pick up everything that was happening inside my ankle. For those of you who have never seen an MRI image, it essentially shows every ligament and bone. My results came back, and I have a partially torn main ligament, two bone bruises, and some fluid and swelling. This seems odd considering the fact that my foot doesn't look much different than what you would expect a foot to look like. They had to look deep inside to see the true picture.

Scripture speaks to something similar of our hearts. Jeremiah 17:9: "The heart is deceitful above all things, and desperately sick; who can understand it?" As humans, our nature is to be self-centered and to allow our heart to deceive us. I wonder what my results would look like if I could have a spiritual MRI of my heart. I believe this is why God calls us to be in community with other believers. Having someone else in your life who you trust and who can speak the truth to you about what they really see inside of you is valuable. When I experience physical pain, I tend to dismiss it or pass it off as something else. I think it's easy to do the same thing spiritually. Having another person who can speak to us in love about something they see can give us clarity on how to begin the healing process.

My challenge for you today is to spend some time alone reflecting on the true nature of your heart. How/where is your heart pulling you away from the things God has called you to? I know I say it all the time, but if you're not in community with at least one other person on an intimate level, begin praying that God will bring an "MRI technician" into your life.

Make today count!

Day 320

No matter where Holly and I have a lived, we have always seemed to hit the "neighbor jackpot." We have been super fortunate in our nine years of marriage to have had nothing but amazing neighbors.

In the book of Mark, we find Jesus speaking to a group of religious leaders. They asked him which commandments were the most important. Jesus' response is recorded in Mark 12:30-31: "Love the Lord your God with all your heart and with all your soul and with all your mind and with all your strength. The second is this: 'Love your neighbor as yourself.' There is no commandment greater than these." The call here is pretty clear—love others as you love yourself. I am by no means perfect at this, but I try my best to live my life in a way that shows others the love of God regardless of their race, education, or background.

God is love. Love is a verb. Put love into action today.

Make today count!

Day 321

I really enjoy cooking. Recently I came across a video of Gordon Ramsay teaching the "correct way to cook scrambled eggs." After watching this video, and considering my way versus his way, I realized our methods were completely different. I have always prepared eggs in a bowl then put them in a pan on medium heat until they were done. On this video, he showed that it is ideal to keep them on medium heat for 25 to 45 seconds then let them cool for the same amount of time. Repeat this process until the eggs are done. The difference is that the eggs turn out much creamier. My method for making scrambled eggs was not necessarily wrong, but this technique is much better (and my kids would agree).

Some years ago, I had a similar experience when reading the Bible. It's easy to miss some really important things in scripture if you don't have someone to provide insight. Allow me to give one example. John 1:1-3 says, "In the beginning was the Word, and the Word was with God, and the Word was God. He was with God in the beginning. Through him all things were made; without him nothing was made that has been made."

Now, read this passage again substituting the words "the word," "he," &, "him" with "Jesus." It reads as follows: "In the beginning was Jesus, and Jesus was with God, and Jesus was God. Jesus was with God in the beginning. Through Jesus all things were made; without Jesus nothing was made that has been made." Talk about making your eggs better! It's life-changing to have a true understanding of what this verse is saying. It would be easy to scroll right through this and miss this incredible truth.

My challenge for you today is to think outside the box for things that you can improve that might not necessarily be broken.

Make today count!

Day 322

Psalms 149:13 says, "For you created my inmost being; you knit me together in my mother's womb." I love the visual David paints for us in this verse. When I think of someone knitting, I think of someone carefully, slowly, and purposefully bringing together individual threads to create beautiful and unique designs and patterns. Not only is there a design in a pattern when someone knits, there is also a unique purpose for their creation, whether it is a blanket or a sweater.

Many of us as believers have chosen to stay silent over the issue of abortion. There is fear of stirring up a hornet's nest of opposition. I have found myself in this majority until just recently. I've come to believe that whatever persecution might come to me, it's far less severe than the consequences of sitting idly by in silence.

Many who are pro-abortion lead with the argument that the fetus is not recognized as a life since it is dependent on the mother to survive. I would counter this argument by saying my four-year-old daughter is dependent on her mother to survive also. Left on her own, there's no way she would be able to take care of herself. This would also apply for some senior citizens and those in the hospital on breathing machines and feeding tubes. I simply will not accept this as a rational argument. Having two children of my own, I have been able to experience the joy of watching their progression inside the womb, of hearing the heartbeat, and watching them move. I heard a pastor list off some of the worst possible scenarios that one could imagine where abortion would seem like a likely option. With each one of the circumstances, whether disease, poverty, or rape, he listed individuals who fell in one of those categories but were born rather than aborted and have been beyond influential in our world.

I believe with all my heart that if you or your significant other have had an abortion, God in heaven loves you and has plans for your life. The emotional baggage that comes with an abortion is not too much for God to redeem. My challenge for those of you who share my pro-life stance is not to place shame or guilt on anyone, it's not to act out in violence, but rather to show the love of Christ.

Make today count!

Day 323

Over the past few weeks, it has been interesting to see how my body has compensated for the pain in my ankle after spraining it playing flag football. I have found myself putting more weight on my left side than I normally do when I walk. This is nothing I do intentionally, it just happens as a result of the pain on my right side. The better option instead of putting more weight on the left side, has been to put my weight onto a crutch on the right side. When physical pain comes, we will compensate as needed to get a sense of relief.

When emotional pain comes, I believe we compensate as well. For some people it might be substances, avoidance, or various other ways. The problem with options that are inside of ourselves is that it is similar to me putting weight on the opposite side of my body. What that ended up doing was causing pain in other places. I believe the solution to compensating for pain is outside of ourselves. Psalms 147:3 says, "He heals the brokenhearted and binds up their wounds." My challenge for you today is to allow God to be the source outside of yourself to compensate for your pain.

Make today count!

Day 324

I am a big fan of the Facebook memory feature. Today I had a memory from four years ago pop up. This particular memory was a video of my six-year-old, Cade, who at the time was two. This was a video Holly posted while I was in South Africa for two weeks with the YMCA. In the video Cade is playing with a cup and spoon and Holly was asking him questions. He responded then Holly interpreted what he was saying. I'm sure years ago I would have understood his baby language, but watching it today, I was grateful for Holly's interpretation.

Do you ever have times when you find it almost impossible to bring yourself to pray? Perhaps it's due to the lack of having the right words and not knowing what to say or being in such a deep anguish that you don't even know where to begin. The video of Cade reminded me how God's word tells us that the Holy Spirit will intercede for us when we don't know what to pray. "In the same way, the Spirit helps us in our weakness. We do not know what we ought to pray for, but the Spirit himself intercedes for us through wordless groans." (Romans 8:26) How amazing is it that we have an interpreter—someone who stands between us and God and clearly communicates our needs and the desires of our heart?

No matter where you find yourself today on the spectrum of need or the spectrum of ability to communicate that need, you have One who intercedes on your behalf. Make your requests known to God. Philippians 4:6 encourages us, "Do not be anxious about anything, but in every situation, by prayer and petition, with thanksgiving, present your requests to God."

Make today count!

Day 325

This year I volunteered to be an assistant coach for Cade's five and six-year old boys basketball team. As many of you know, if you indicate that you're interested in helping in any way, this means that you have just signed up to be the head coach. Long story short, I'm the head coach of the five- and six-year old Rockets for the city. Having played competitive basketball for much of my life, I understood that there are a lot of things for these little guys to know. This is their first taste of organized basketball. Before the first practice, I spent about 20 minutes writing out a detailed practice schedule in increments of five-minute drills. You might think this seems a bit excessive, and maybe it is. As I was watching the practices that were happening before practice, I noticed a common theme. Most of the other coaches had not prepared. One coach had his team attempting to scrimmage when these little guys don't even understand how to dribble. Having spent time to prepare has made this experience less like herding cats and more like a foundations of basketball class.

Preparation is the key to success. Can you imagine if a professional sports team decided not to practice and then tried to compete? They would undoubtedly end up being defeated. The same is true in our lives. Our preparation and planning is what will help lead us to success. Ecclesiastes 9:10 tells us, "Whatever your hand finds to do, do it with all of your might." Mapping out your day and your week will give you a clear picture of where you're going, and I believe that it honors God because you're putting your absolute best into everything you do.

My challenge for you today is to be a person who prepares. Use your preparation as an act of worship to God.

Make today count!

Day 326

It It was an absolute privilege yesterday to be a part of the wedding celebration of my sister-in-law Sara Perkins and her new husband Chris Hardman. The setting was absolutely beautiful. It was an outdoor venue with white chairs in the countryside. My favorite part about a wedding is watching the groom as the bride is revealed, and comes down the aisle. Chris's face was filled with joy, happiness, and I'm pretty sure I saw the thought run across his mind "Dang girl."

Our wedding day serves as a beautiful representation of the feeling of love. I think most people would agree that your wedding day is probably one of your easiest days in marriage. Marriage is a challenging journey meant for our holiness. Dr. Stephen Covey had this to say about love: "Love is a verb. Love, the feeling, is the fruit of love the verb or are loving actions." What Dr. Covey is reminding us is love is not a feeling. Love is a choice.

My challenge today for the beautiful newlyweds, and for those of you who are married, is this: Choose to love your spouse today. If they don't deserve it, sacrifice, listen, appreciate, and affirm them.

When all else fails, love through the lens of 1 Corinthians 13:4-8: "Love is patient, love is kind. It does not envy, it does not boast, it is not proud. It does not dishonor others, it is not self-seeking, it is not easily angered, it keeps no record of wrongs. Love does not delight in evil but rejoices with the truth. It always protects, always trusts, always hopes, always perseveres. Love never fails."

Make today count!

Day 327

I had an incredibly busy day at the office this week. I had several meetings and there were a lot of people in and out of my office. I kept getting a whiff of a less than "fresh" smell. I didn't really take any time to figure out where the smell was coming from. Honestly, I was assuming it was from one of the many people who had been in the office that day, or perhaps some trash or food that was hidden somewhere on the other side of the office.

I was alone yesterday morning in my office when the foul odor hit my nose again. All of a sudden, the thought came to my head, "Oh my gosh, it's coming from you." After short investigation I realize that my shoes must have gotten wet somehow. They absolutely stunk. I'm talking, make you gag type of stink. See, as Dr. Stephen Covey would say, my "problem was the way I was viewing the problem." Internally I had already decided the smell was an external problem. I didn't want to believe or did not allow myself to believe internally that the smell could possibly be coming from me.

In Mathew 7:3, Jesus says, "Why do you look at the speck of sawdust in your brother's eye and pay no attention to the plank in your own eye?" I believe it's human nature that when we "smell" something that's bad, we automatically start looking for external sources to blame. My challenge for you today is to stop and smell your own shoes. I apologize to Kevin and David for having to sit through an hour discipleship meeting with me and my stinky feet!

Make today count!

Day 328

Today is the final day for our church flag football league. The league will come to a conclusion today when the final two teams play to determine the champion. The winners, beyond receiving, glory, fame, and crazy amounts of press (sarcasm) will receive a really nice long-sleeve dry fit shirt. The word "Proven" is written on the shirt. When people see the shirt, they will know that this person has done something to deserve this shirt.

If your life could be made into a shirt with a single word on it, what would the word be? The amazing thing about being in a relationship with Christ is that our shirt would never have to say "proven" on it. There's absolutely nothing we can do to earn this relationship. Our standing will never be good enough and our deeds never worthy enough. You can never clean your life up enough to bring it as a worthy offering to God.

Ephesians 2:8 says, "For it is by grace you have been saved, through faith--and this is not from yourselves, it is the gift of God." You don't have to prove yourself before God. All you have to do is receive what he is offering. Instead of trying to earn a shirt that says "proven," my challenge is to accept a shirt that says "forgiven."

Make today count!

Day 329

I don't know about you, but sleeping on the couch is never something I do intentionally. Last night I slept on the couch. No, Holly and I did not have a fight. She has a terrible virus that's going around. Although our bed is a much more comfortable option, I thought it wise to sleep on the couch in the living room. There is no guarantee I would end up with a virus if I slept in the bed, but I did not want to take the chance.

Why is it that when it comes to our physical health, we are super aware of pending dangers, but then when it comes to our spiritual health, we tend to be far less cautious. We will toe the line in situations that could lead to our detriment. Maybe in your finances you find yourself flirting with more debt. Maybe you have taken one step closer to a relationship with someone who is not your spouse. James 1:13-15 says, "When tempted, no one should say, 'God is tempting me.' For God cannot be tempted by evil, nor does he tempt anyone; but each person is tempted when they are dragged away by their own evil desire and enticed. Then, after desire has conceived, it gives birth to sin; and sin, when it is full-grown, gives birth to death." Maybe it's time to go sleep on the couch. My challenge today for you is to be as aware of your spiritual proximity to danger as you are to your physical.

Make today count!

Day 330

Anyone who has traveled with me knows how much I love my pillow. It would be a rare occasion for me to travel without it. Up until recently, I had an amazing goose down pillow. This pillow became a sore spot between Holly and me as she believed it was time to replace it. I, on the other hand, would have kept this pillow far longer than I really should have. Knowing that she was right, I set out to find the perfect replacement. I ended up at a sleep store where the salesman allowed me to lay on multiple pillows. I ended up choosing a down alternative pillow simply due to the fact that it felt okay in the store and the fact that it had a 30-day guarantee. After just one night of sleeping on this pillow, I knew this pillow was not right for me.

It ended up being a week before I was able to exchange the pillow. When I went back to the store, I upgraded to a similar pillow, like my original pillow which I got rid of. This was a true goose down pillow, or as I like to put it, "laying your head on a cloud." The quality of rest I am getting because of this pillow is great.

What is it that you are resting in? There are things in your life that are good, but they may not be meant for you to completely rest in. In Psalms 23:2-3, King David paints a beautiful picture of what it looks like to completely rest in God. “He makes me lie down in green pastures; He leads me beside quiet waters. He restores my soul; He guides me in the paths of righteousness For His name's sake.”

It’s easy to allow the troubles of today to keep us from a place of rest. God has invited us into a place where we can fully rest in him. We can give him all of our troubles, worries and fears.

My challenge for you today is to allow yourself to rest in God. Give him the things that are hindering and holding you down. Allow him to lead you to quiet water where he can restore your soul.

Make today count!

Day 331

We live in a non-stop, fast-paced world. Most of operate on Go, and we stay there until the end of our day when we sleep. This is not how God designed us to operate. When God created the world, he did it in 6 days and he rested on the 7th. Was God tired? I don't think so. I believe he rested to set the example for us.

When is the last time you had a "retreat to attack?" When was the last time you renewed your mind, allowing Christ's words to fill you? I want to challenge you to strategically plan a time to get away and get in God's word!

Romans 12:2 says, "Do not conform to the pattern of this world, but be transformed by the *renewing of your mind.* Then you will be able to test and approve what God's will is--his good, pleasing and perfect will."

Make today count!

Day 332

Have you ever found yourself in the middle of a task and found that you just did not seem to have the right tools for the job? A few months back I was helping a friend put some stone up in his bathroom. I had my miter saw with me to make the needed cuts. The normal saw blade was still on. I needed to change it out for a masonry blade. Once I got the cover off, I realized I did not have the tool I needed to change the blade. I tried for almost 30 minutes to get the blade changed using other tools that were not designed for the job, all to no avail. After reaching a point of sheer frustration, I drove to a nearby friend's house. He was able to change the blade in a matter of seconds. He had the right tool for the job.

There are times in life when we have situations that come to us and cause us worry, frustration, and questions. Many times in my own life, I try to remedy the situations with the wrong "tools." I might seek the opinion of others, I might research solutions on my own, or I might just allow worry to consume me. Some of these things are not necessarily negative, but I don't believe they are the best tool for the job.

No matter what situation you find yourself in, God's word has wisdom and encouragement to help you through. 2 Timothy 3:16 says, "Scripture is God-breathed and is useful for teaching, rebuking, correcting and training in righteousness, so that the servant of God may be thoroughly equipped for every good work." Praying you will use the tool God has provided for us.

Make today count!

Day 333

My wife is hands-down one of the most thoughtful people on earth. I am leaving to go to men's retreat this afternoon. As I woke up this morning and made my way into the kitchen, I found a goodie bag and a note card with my name on it. The goodie bag contained some of my favorite snacks and a very kind and encouraging note. Holly goes above and beyond when it comes to being thoughtful.

That's the cool thing about gifts. You don't do anything to deserve or earn them. They are simply given out of love. Romans 6:23 says, "For the wages of sin is death, but the gift of God is eternal life through Christ Jesus." God gave us a gift through what Jesus did on the cross to pay the penalty for our sins. Just like any gift, we must choose to receive it.

If you are not a Christian, my challenge is to wrestle with this question: Why did Jesus die on the cross? There's plenty of historical evidence to prove Jesus lived and was crucified. Don't take my word for. Do some research on your own. If you are Christian, my challenge for you is to share your story of what God has done in your life!

Make today count!

Day 334

This morning as I was watering my grass. I noticed a small section of Bermuda grass growing in the yard. I made it a point to get some grass killer to take care of it. I could have pulled the grass right then to see some immediate effect. However, I most likely would not have gotten to the root. Over a short period of time, I would have seen the grass pop up again.

Many times in our own lives, we look to temporary solutions to take away our hurt and pain. These temporary solutions are just like me pulling the grass. It might seem effective in the moment, but in reality, the root, the hurt, is still there. Jesus says in Matthew 11:28, "Come to me, all who are weary and are heavy laden, and I will give you rest."

The challenge for us today is to cast your cares on him, because he cares for you (1 Peter 5:7).

Make today count!

Day 335

In the summer of 2006, Holly Perkins and I were sitting at the end of my parents' driveway on Turfland Drive in Murfreesboro, Tennessee. We were having a pretty deep discussion about life, future hopes, and dreams. I will never forget it. In a moment that seemed to come completely from left field, Holly said, "I think you're going to be a pastor." Now, this notion made me laugh. I had a front row seat of what ministry life looked like since my dad is a pastor and I am a "PK."

As the story goes, Holly Perkins became Holly White on December 13, 2008. As I progressed in my work at the YMCA, I had two different opportunities to move out of state for two great job opportunities. During the process of determining which of the two would be best for our family, Holly once again pointed out God's call on my life to ministry. This stopped me dead in my tracks. This time I listened to her. And as God's plan has unfolded, I am now going on year three at New Vision where I am blessed to serve as the men's and recreation pastor.

Holly Perkins saw something in me that I did not see in myself. She continued to believe this to be true until six years later when I was able to see it as well. Holly is a gift to me. To this day, she can discern things and see things that I do not. Proverbs 31:10-12: "A good woman is hard to find, and worth far more than diamonds. Her husband trusts her without reserve, and never has reason to regret it. Never spiteful, she treats him generously all her life long."

My challenge for those of you who are not married is to find someone who sees your greatest potential, even if you don't. For those of you who are married, my challenge for you is to continue to recognize the potential God has given to your spouse and continue to praise and encourage them as they progress in it.

Make today count!

Day 336

This morning Abi Kate came out of her room frantically crying. She was incredibly upset about something to the point that she was having a hard time articulating exactly what the issue was. After a few minutes of coaxing, I was able to understand that she could not find one of her favorite stuffed animals. I asked her if she had looked for it and she told me that she could not find it. I pressed her further, "Abi Kate, have you looked for it?" She looked up at me and said that she had not. After this, it took me no more than 10 seconds to walk into her bedroom and see the stuffed animal she was looking for sitting right in the middle of her bed.

You cannot find what you are not looking for. Matthew 7:7: "Ask and it will be given to you; seek and you will find; knock and the door will be opened to you." Many of us desire to know God yet we spend no time seeking him. This verse in Matthew makes it very clear that God does not want to remain hidden from you. He desires for you to know him, but as we look at the action words in this verse, we see that it requires just that—action. We must seek and knock. I know that there are many of you who are on the fence in regard to believing in God. He, like Abi Kate's stuffed animal, is right in the open waiting for you to find him.

Make today count!

Day 337

I believe there are two different types of people in the world. There are those who keep their email inbox at zero and those who allow their inbox to linger somewhere around 5,000 unopened emails. I would assume that like me, the vast majority of the emails you receive are from businesses soliciting their products or services. Many of these emails come as a part of a purchase or an inquiry of the company. I have found myself in the habit of opening my emails in the morning and going through and deleting all these emails without reading them. Then one day thought hit me, "Al I need to do is unsubscribe." I had, by choice, opted to receive all of these emails, but quickly found them cluttering up my inbox. Instead of allowing them to fill up my inbox, I decided to take a little extra time and click into each one and unsubscribe. The result is that the content in my email is meaningful and relevant to me each day. The clutter is no longer a part.

This got me thinking about the things I subscribe to within my mind. What are the thoughts, patterns, and actions I am subscribing to but are simply nothing but clutter? It's easy to allow our minds to be filled with things that are not true, and are things that promote our kingdom here on earth. Colossians 3:2 reminds us, "Set your minds on things above, not on earthly things." The challenge for us is to subscribe to the truths God has given us through Scripture instead of allowing our minds to be filled with all of the earthly clutter that can so easily overtake us.

My question for you today is what are the thoughts, behaviors, and feelings you need to unsubscribe to? What steps can you take today to set your heart and mind on things above?

Make today count!

Day 338

Do you remember that part of your wedding vows that went something like this: "I promise to love and cherish you in sickness and in health?" I feel almost certain, and can guarantee you, that Holly White didn't imagine should would be putting my socks on me when I was 31 years old. She has embodied the Biblical description of love to me over the past few days following an ankle injury.

1 Corinthians 13:4 says, "Love is patient, love is kind. It does not envy, it does not boast, it is not proud." Although I find it very hard to allow her to serve me, she has served me with grace, patience, and love. Not once has she been judgmental of the fact that I need to receive this love and service from her.

1 John 4:8: "Whoever does not love does not know God, because God is love." This verse clearly states to us that God is love. God is patient, kind, gentle, and he never fails. God doesn't look at your weaknesses, struggles, or the fact that you need to receive his love with judgment. He freely gives his love to anyone who chooses to receive it.

My challenge today is to allow someone to love you and know that God loves you. You are worthy of receiving love!

Make today count!

Day 339

Lately it seems that we cannot go more than a week on social media or on the news without hearing about another case of sexual misconduct or some sort of sexual allegations. I understand that for some of you when these allegations are dropped, you are in disbelief and shock. Here is the sad truth—as a society we have accepted something that is far from God's sexual standard through television, movies, and online pornography. It's interesting though that when we hear about someone like Matt Lauer, we are in complete disbelief.

We wonder how someone could reach a point where they make this type of decision. Well, it starts one step at a time towards the wrong thing. I don't think anyone wakes up in the morning and says, "Today I think I will ruin my marriage and publicly shame myself and my family." It starts with one small step in the wrong direction I know that there are some of you today who are privately struggling with some form of sexual sin, whether that's pornography, adultery, or something else. 1 Corinthians 6:18 says, "Flee from sexual immorality. All other sins a person commits are outside the body, but whoever sins sexually, sins against their own body."

This is the only scripture that tells us to run from sin. We don't stand a chance if we try to stand and fight. Sexual sin will take you further than you want to go and cost you more than you want to pay. For those of you who are struggling, I implore you to reach out and get help before it costs you everything. I would love the opportunity to come alongside any of you men to help you walk this journey.

Make today count!

Day 340

The Jewish temple set up in the Old Testament is a detail that is easy to overlook, but carries great significance. There were essentially three areas. There was the outer court was called the court of women. The second layer of the corpus was called the hall of priests. Within the third level was the holy place, and the holy of holies. There was a curtain that divided the holy of holies place from the holy place. Only the high priest was allowed to enter the holy of holies. Once a year he would enter to make atonement for the people's sins.

Matthew 27:51 tells us, "At that moment the curtain of the temple was torn in two from top to bottom. The earth shook, the rocks split." It's easy to read right past this verse without understanding the context. This takes place right after Jesus took his last breath. The curtain it referred to is the curtain that divided the holy place from the holy of holies. It is significant that the curtain was torn from the top to the bottom indicating that it was done by divine hands. The separation between these rooms shows that Jesus made a way for us to access God without a priest. The separation also showed that sin was paid in full. Remember the priest made sacrifices to atone for the sins of man. When Jesus died, it was finished.

Scripture reminds us multiple times that Jesus is seated at the right hand of God. Jesus is seated because his work is done. His sacrifice satisfied the punishment for sin and removed our separation from a holy God. Can you imagine what Jesus' disciples were feeling that day as they saw the Lord hanging from a cross just a day before. It must have been significant confusion on their end. We are preparing now for the greatest comeback of all time. Sunday is coming!

Make today count!

Day 341

Last week Abi Kate had her first dentist appointment. She had a nervous excitement about her first time seeing the dentist. Cade had gotten her pretty excited about the toy chest at the end of the visit and that was enough to get her to comply with the dental hygienist as she cleaned and checked her teeth. A few short minutes into the cleaning, the dental hygienist looked up at me and said, "Dad, how often are you flossing her teeth?" This was not so much a question as it was a statement of, "Hey dummy, you need to floss her teeth." They showed me a couple x-rays of a small cavity in the back corner in between two of her teeth. She linked this cavity directly to the lack of flossing.

Small hidden cavities remind me of hidden sin. Eventually the cavity will grow and pain and discomfort will come with it. As humans, we tend to believe that if no one knows what's going on in the hidden areas of our lives, we will be able to continue in this sin without any consequences. Luke makes it quite clear in chapter 8 verse 17 that this is not the case: "For there is nothing hidden that will not be disclosed, and nothing concealed that will not be known or brought out into the open." Our sins will be found out sooner or later. It's not a matter of *if*—it's a matter of *when.*

My challenge for you today is to confess what's really going on in your life to your accountability partner. If you don't have someone who is walking life with you, that's your first step and my challenge for you today. Regular *spiritual flossing* helps fight spiritual decay.

Make today count!

Day 342

My kids love hopping on one leg. In fact, I think most kids enjoy it. Yesterday with my ankle injury, I found myself hopping around the house if I needed to navigate a short distance. The kids thought it looked like a lot of fun, and of course wanted to join in.

Hopping on one foot is fine I suppose for a short period of time, but I can tell you that over an extensive period of time, it begins to make your other leg very tired. The fun quickly fades.

Hebrews 11:25 says, "Choosing rather to be mistreated with the people of God than to enjoy the fleeting pleasures of sin." See sin, like hopping on one leg, is fun for a short period of time. The pain shows up later. It thrills, then it kills. My challenge for you today is not to be enticed by the lure of hopping on one leg. Know that eventually the pain will come.

Make today count!

Day 343

A few mornings ago, I was getting the kids' breakfast ready before school. Cade had asked me for a bowl of Cheerios and milk. I got his Cheerios ready and then Holly called him into the bathroom to fix his hair. Around the same time, Abi Kate asked for Cheerios and milk as well.

I handed Abi Kate the bowl of Cheerios I had poured for Cade. As I was pouring another bowl of cereal for Cade, he came back into the kitchen and asked me where his Cheerios were. He got very upset because he felt like I was taking something from him. However, my mindset was to give him Cheerios that would not be soggy. I was giving him something better.

I know, there have been times when I have felt like God has taken something away from me. In those moments, I feel frustrated and confused. Eventually, God fills the void with something far better than what I originally had imagined. Psalms 9:10 reminds us, "Those who know your name trust in you, for you, LORD, have never forsaken those who seek you." How encouraging is it to know that God will never forsake those that seek Him? My challenge for you today is to continue to seek Him, even when you can't see that he is working things out for your best.

Make today count!

Day 344

Every morning I make a breakfast smoothie. This morning both of my kids also wanted one. First, I made one for Cade and set it up on the counter. He found himself distracted looking at something on the refrigerator and accidentally bumped it off the counter spilling it everywhere. After talking him off the ledge, I made him a new one. Then as Abi Kate and I were preparing to leave this morning, she had her smoothie in her hand and somehow managed to pour it all over her pants. This, of course, required us to go back into the house and change clothes. See, sometimes your smoothie gets spilled twice.

Little annoyances and inconveniences are part of the reality of our lives. The question is, how do we let them affect the rest of our day? It would have been easy for me to get incredibly frustrated and allow these two little setbacks to alter the course of my day. Instead, I spent a few minutes after changing Abi Kate's clothes for the second time listening to her sing jingle bells with insatiable joy.

My challenge for you today is to find joy among the little annoyances that may come. Don't focus on them. Rather, focus on the joy ahead. "This is the day that the Lord has made, let us rejoice and be glad in it." (Psalms 118:24)

Make today count!

Day 345

The entry doors into the shower in my bathroom are made of glass. From a design standpoint, the glass doors look awesome. From a cleaning standpoint, not so much. Those of you who have glass shower doors know all too well how difficult it is to keep them clean. Water stains build up over time creating a dirty window. Shortly after moving into the house, Holly put a squeegee in the shower. The rule is that after you shower, you squeegee the glass. By doing this, any of the excess water that would sit and stain the glass is removed, ultimately making it much easier to keep the glass doors clean.

The concerns, troubles, and worries of life can easily build up on us. Just like with my shower, once buildup comes, it's much harder to remove. We can and should give these things up daily. Psalms 55:22 reminds us, "Cast your burden on the Lord, and He shall sustain you; He shall never permit the righteous to be moved." Your day, week, month, and year will be better if only you give these things up to God in prayer daily.

My challenge for you today is to "squeegee your glass." Relinquish control of your concerns, troubles, and worries. Give them to God daily and you might just be surprised at how your view through the window that you call life clears up!

Make today count!

Day 346

IF I asked you to make a list five people who have influenced you to be the person you are today, I bet you could easily produce this list. We are influenced every day by the people we surround ourselves with. Yes, there is the component of positive and negative influence, but there are also people we might see something in and choose to turn and go the opposite direction. Being an influencer and being influenced should not be activities that are done with little to no thought.

This morning I was reading James 1:3 and it served as a really good reminder for me. "Brothers and sisters, not many of you should become teachers. You know that we who teach will be judged more severely." It almost sounds harsh that God will judge people who are trying to teach his word at a higher level. Upon further review, we see that this judgment is fitting due to one word: influence. My goal as I communicate is to affectively line up typical truth with every-day life.

I know not all of you are in an official teaching capacity, and therefore this scripture does not necessarily pertain to you. My challenge for you today is to see the truth in it that reminds us to be aware of how we are influencing others and who we are allowing to influence us.

Make today count!

Day 347

Each of us have different resources available to us. We have differing amounts of education, income, and different circles of influence. The one resource we all have the same amount of is time. Each of us has been given 24 hours each day to use the way that we feel most beneficial. What I have found is if someone says they do not have time to do something, what they're really saying is it is not a priority for them. We will make time for the things we prioritize.

For me, there are things that I love to say I "don't have time for." The truth is, these are just things I don't want to do. Some of these things are things I know I should be doing. What are the things you have been putting off because you "don't have time for them?" It's interesting how when someone gets a devastating diagnosis that their time priorities can shift on a dime because of the news. Maybe there is someone who has a broken relationship with a family member and mending that relationship becomes a top priority when death is a near reality.

Proverbs 27:1 reminds us, "Do not boast about tomorrow, for you do not know what a day may bring." The time that we know we have is right now. Are you using your time for its absolute best return? My challenge for you today is to prioritize your time by taking care of something that you know you've been putting off.

Make today count!

Day 348

I absolutely love to mow my yard. The job is not complete, however, until I have pulled out the leaf blower. I'll use the leaf blower to get all the clippings off the driveway and sidewalk, but the most important thing I use the leaf blower for is to blow all of the debris from the past week out of the garage and into the grass. Cade is always more than willing to lend a hand. The last time I allowed him to use the leaf blower, he ended up blowing all the outside debris into the garage, creating a much bigger mess. See, the leaf blower can be used productively or destructively.

As with the leaf blower, our tongues can be used productively or destructively. James 3:4-5 warns us, "...take ships as an example. Although they are so large and are driven by strong winds, they are steered by a very small rudder wherever the pilot wants to go. Likewise, the tongue is a small part of the body, but it makes great boasts. Consider what a great forest is set on fire by a small spark." The tongue is a tool. It is one that can be used to speak life into people or to tear people down. My challenge for you today is to use your tongue as a productive tool.

Make today count!

Day 349

My six-year old son, Cade, seems to have a very natural ability to figure out how things go together. Any toy that comes with a manual and setup instructions is a task in which he excels. On the other hand, things like this are not my strong suit. I'm not the kind of guy who can look at an instruction book and understand exactly how things need to be arranged to make them work. When Cade has the option of a free-time activity, he is likely to choose something similar to building Legos. If Holly and I were to make a guess at what his vocational career will be, our guess right now would be an architect.

As parents, we have dreams and ambitions for our children. However, if we are not careful, we can try to live vicariously through them. We try to plant our unreached dreams, desires, and goals into their lives. Proverbs 22:6 tells us that we should "Train up a child in the way he should go, and when he is old he will not depart from it." What this verse is getting to is the natural bents and talents that God has placed within our children. God has given your kids certain skills and abilities that might differ from yours. This verse calls us as parents to encourage and challenge our children in the design God has placed within them.

My challenge for you today is to recognize the strengths and talents God has given your child and encourage them in that direction. Maybe your child is gifted in music and you can't carry a tune in a bucket. Or maybe your child is an amazing artist and you can't tell the difference between a pistachio and a Picasso. Your role as parent is to encourage and equip them in the best way possible. The largest part of this is showing them how they can use their natural gifting to bring glory to God.

Make today count!

Day 350

Lately, when Abi Kate and I are in the car at a stoplight, she starts yelling for me to go. This is not something that happens every so often. It's happens at every single light. She becomes increasingly frustrated with me when I tell her we cannot go. I believe she sees all the other cars around us going and can't understand it is not our lane's turn to move ahead. She doesn't understand that if I were to grant her request, it would cause us to have an accident.

I think we can be the same way with God. We know the path we want to travel, and we know when we want to travel. We see other people around us making progress, and we can't understand why we are not being allowed to move forward as we desire. All the while, we might be missing the fact that if we were to go, it could lead to our detriment. I don't think a single person would fault my wisdom over Abi Kate when it comes to making the correct decision about when to proceed while driving. In the same way, maybe we are the three-year-old in the backseat telling God it's time to go when the light is clearly red.

My challenge for you today is to trust that God sees the bigger picture. Proverbs 3:5-6 reminds us, "Trust in the LORD with all your heart and lean not on your own understanding; in all your ways submit to him, and he will make your paths straight."

Make today count!

Day 351

I have recently purchased a "new to me" bow and arrow set. I really enjoy shooting target practice at my house, but over the last few months, I have broken three of the arrows. This required me to look for some replacements. I found some that looked like a great choice online and purchased them. I was really excited to give them a try. I loaded the first arrow onto my bow and fired a shot. It missed far left. I repeated this process six more times but the arrow went significantly left of the bullseye with each shot. I then pulled out one of my old arrows and fired the same shot at the bullseye. I couldn't figure out what was making these arrows go to the left. Upon further investigation, I noticed a small piece of clear tape wrapped at the base where the feathers are glued onto the arrow. I removed this small piece of tape from each arrow and attempted the same shots again. After the tape was removed, each shot found went where I was aiming. This tiny piece of tape which was meant to secure the feathers on the arrow in transit resulted in the arrows drastically missing the target. It is incredible how something so small can have such a big effect.

This reminded me of a verse I read in Song of Solomon 2:15 which says, "Catch for us the foxes, the little foxes that ruin the vineyards, our vineyards that are in bloom." The phrase "little foxes" is a reference to the small things on the surface—issues we are aware of, but when we neglect to deal with them will create havoc. It's easy for these "foxes" to pop up in our marriages. When we choose to neglect dealing with these concerns, sooner or later they will cause bigger problems. These small foxes lead to the saying, "It was the straw that broke the camel's back."

What are the "little foxes" that have arisen in your relationships that could cause great damage? My challenge for you today is not to allow the little things to become big things.

Make today count!

Day 352

This week I have found myself having a similar conversation with three different men. Each of them essentially asked the same thing but they each had their own twist on it. In essence, the question was this: "What does God want me to do with my life?" The second part of the question stated by one of them was: "Is my vocational career path the one God wants for me?"

This is a hard question and one I definitely wrestled with while I was at the YMCA. This is the conclusion that I have come to. God calls in Matthew 28:19-20 "Go and make disciples of all nations, baptizing them in the name of the Father and of the Son and of the Holy Spirit, and teaching them to obey everything I have commanded you. And surely I am with you always, to the very end of the age." I believe each of us has been uniquely suited for our vocational career and because of that, we have an opportunity to share Christ within our circle of influence. Your unique skill set has given you a seat at a table I do not have access to.

My challenge for you today is to use your seat, your influence, and your skill set to go and make disciples.

Make today count!

Day 353

Cade is in first grade now and is learning to read and spell. As you all know, the English language can be quite difficult. Some of the phonograms and rules we use can be quite tricky. Cade tends to want to spell words phonetically, or by the way the word sounds. For example, to spell the word "phone" phonetically, he might spell it "fone." In his mind, if it sounds like an F, it must be an F. He has to remember the different phonograms and rules. He cannot spell by what he hears.

The same is true for us. We can't always trust what we hear. "For the time will come when people will not put up with sound doctrine. Instead, to suit their own desires, they will gather around them a great number of teachers to say what their itching ears want to hear. They will turn their ears away from the truth and turn aside to myths." (2 Timothy 4:3-4) I don't know about you, but I believe we are in this day. When we hear different speakers, online evangelists, and even people within our circles on Facebook, we should do our due diligence to see if their claims line up with what Scripture says. Ultimately, we should allow scripture to inform our understanding and opinions.

My challenge for you today is not to be deceived by what you hear. See if the things you are hearing and learning line up with what God's Word says. You are ultimately responsible for what you allow into your heart. Guard it carefully.

Make today count!

Day 354

One of my favorite parts about my job is getting to do premarital counseling with couples who are close to getting married. One of the common themes we frequently have to work through is conflict resolution and communication. These are incredibly normal and reoccurring themes that I see from couple to couple.

It's easy to let our emotions get the best of us when conflict arises. When these times come, we tend to speak from a place of emotion and before we have really thought about what we are saying. A few good indicators that you might have gone out of bounds would include using the word "you." This automatically puts the other person in a defensive mindset, so they are not listening to what you're saying. Also, the use of words like "always" and "never" are harmful. These words make the other person try to think of the one time that they did or did not do whatever it is that you're talking about. When dealing with conflict, try to use "I" statements and speak from a place of "we" and "us."

Proverbs 16:24 says, "Gracious words are like a honeycomb, sweetness to the soul and health to the body." My challenge for you today is to remember that when dealing with conflict, the problem is the problem. The problem is not the other person.

Make today count!

Day 355

Do you ever find yourself critiquing a problem you see somewhere? For me, a real-life scenario of this often occurs when I'm somewhere where food is being served. I find myself often leaning over to Holly and saying something to the effect of, "You know they really could have two lines going instead of just one." This is definitely an attribute that was passed on genetically through Jeff White (my dad).

God has gifted me in a way that allows me to see a process and see a way to improve and make that process flow more efficiently. I have no doubt that there are other people who were in the same line waiting for the food that gave little to no thought to this "brilliant" idea of scooting the food table off the wall to create lines on both sides of the table.

You are intended to be the solution to the problems that you see in the world. God has gifted you in a unique way. Your gifting comes through in the problems you see. You recognize them as problems because internally you recognize a solution. Take the opportunity today to start being the solution. Anybody can critique.

For we are God's handiwork, created in Christ Jesus to do good works, which God prepared in advance for us to do. (Ephesians 2:10)

Make today count!

Day 356

I have always considered myself to be a do-it-yourselfer, or a DYI kind of person. Well, that is until recently. I have begun to have a shift in this thinking because what I've come to realize is that I often make things much more difficult, time consuming, and expensive by trying to do them myself instead of hiring a professional on the front end.

Holly recently said she would love for us to redo our bathroom. She wasn't requesting anything major. She simply wanted to replace the giant mirror that was installed when the house was built with two smaller mirrors. Her other request was to repaint the bathroom. After watching several videos on the process of properly removing the mirror, I decided to seek out a professional. Then once I started looking at all of the small intricacies of trimming out the areas in the bathroom, I decided to call a painter. When I understood that my gifting is geared more towards vision and administration and put that to use and I found others who were gifted in the areas needed, the end product turned out fantastic.

Scripture is clear that each of us have different gifts and talents table. This is what makes up an effective body. Ephesians 4:11-12 says, "And He gave some as apostles, and some as prophets, and some as evangelists, and some as pastors and teachers, for the equipping of the saints for the work of service, to the building up of the body of Christ..." My old habits of trying to be a DIY guy are similar to someone saying they don't need the church. In essence they are saying they possess all the gifts needed. No one person possesses all of these gifts at the highest level. This is why it's so important for us to know what our gifts are and how they can tie into a local body of believers to advance God's kingdom.

Today as you investigate Ephesians 4, I hope this helps you further understand why you need to be connected to a local body of believers. My challenge for you today is to identify your spiritual gifts. If you have never taken a spiritual gifts inventory, you can do so by finding a gift inventory online. (You can do a simple Google search to locate one of these assessments.) Then pray that God will lead you to a place where you can get plugged in and serve.

Make today count!

Day 357

Christmas Eve is probably my favorite day of the year going as far back as my childhood. In fact, thinking about my childhood is probably the reason I am so fond of Christmas Eve. I can remember every year the traditional Bailey family Christmas party. Multiple families would come together at the Bailey's house, the kids upstairs and the adults downstairs. Thinking about this soirée now as an adult, it's amazing that the Baileys are still married. Upon returning from the party each year, my older brother and I would find a gift waiting for us. This gift was always something we could both enjoy together. The top gifts that come to mind were our indoor Michael Jordan basketball goal and our three-in-one tournament table. This night was filled with such excitement, such anticipation and such joy.

As I was reflecting on that this morning, a thought that crossed my mind. The first Christmas Eve was a far cry from what I experience today. No doubt there was anticipation as Mary was nine months pregnant with Jesus. However, I can imagine that there was a great deal of stress, anxiety, and fear. Many of us have read the Christmas narrative so many times that we don't allow the information to really penetrate our minds.

Luke 2:1-6 says, "In those days Caesar Augustus issued a decree that a census should be taken of the entire Roman world. (This was the first census that took place while Quirinius was governor of Syria.) And everyone went to their own town to register. So Joseph also went up from the town of Nazareth in Galilee to Judea, to Bethlehem the town of David, because he belonged to the house and line of David. He went there to register with Mary, who was pledged to be married to him and was expecting a child. While they were there, the time came for the baby to be born." Mary and Joseph had just finished traveling a significantly long journey. Mary was nine months pregnant and riding on a donkey. Have you ever been to Best Buy on Black Friday? That busyness and craziness wouldn't even have come close to all these people gathering for the census. Worst of all, there was no room. Mary and Joseph found themselves in a stable. Amidst all the fear, doubt and worry, Jesus was about to make his entrance.

He came to be a rescuer. He came to take away all the fear. He came to take away all the doubt, and He came to take away all of our worries.

Make today count!

Day 358

After many weeks of anticipation, the kids were more than excited to tear into their gifts today. Seeing their excitement and their joy is what makes the day for me. Seeing the fulfillment in their faces when they receive something they have been patiently anticipating is magical.

The excitement over the new gifts will fade over time and eventually these items will end up in a yard sale or thrown out. The joy they bring is temporary and fleeting. It is so easy to get wrapped up in the commercialization of the season and forget the true meaning.

Christmas is about a gift. The greatest gift ever given. The son of God coming to earth to pay the penalty for our sin. I love the way John tells the Christmas story in John 1:14. "The Word became flesh and made his dwelling among us. We have seen his glory, the glory of the one and only Son, who came from the Father, full of grace and truth." The Word is referring to Christ. Jesus came to give you a gift. Romans 6:23 describes the gift. "For the wages of sin is death, but the gift of God is eternal life in Christ Jesus our Lord." Just like any gift, you have to open it or receive it. This gift is one that brings complete joy.

Cherish the time today with your friends and family. Merry Christmas!

Make today count!

Day 359

After all of the Christmas present unwrapping subsided yesterday, I found myself putting together all of the new toys for the kids to play with. Cade received a really neat hot wheels track. The directions on how to put this thing together, in my opinion, were subpar. Amidst my struggles to get this thing put together, Cade shouted out to Holly's dad, "We need some help over here." This, of course, only spurred me on to make sure I got it completed. I was not going to let Cade see that something like this was too hard for me. After a few more minutes, I finally had the track together, only to realize it required two D batteries, which we did not have.

Early in the book of Genesis Abraham is told that he and his wife Sarah will have a child. When Sarah hears this, she laughs because she is 100 years old. I love the response here in Genesis 18:14: "Is anything too hard for the Lord? At the appointed time I will return to you, about this time next year, and Sarah shall have a son."

This is the same God we serve. So we can ask the same question: Is anything too hard for the Lord? No matter where you find yourself today, no matter how hard the situation, no matter how insurmountable the odds, nothing is too hard for God. My challenge for you today is to view your situation through the lens of God's ability to provide in it!

Make today count!

Day 360

Through the years I have attempted to master a number of disciplines only to find myself giving up on them after a very short time. For example, I wanted to learn to play the guitar and also to learn to speak fluent Spanish. My attempts failed because they primarily focused on me. However, I have started and been successful sticking with other disciplines. These included things like prioritizing time in scripture and prayer each morning, tithing, and a few others. I was successful in these because these disciplines were connected to something bigger than myself.

I believe when our goals align with God's calling, our chances for sticking with a discipline are much greater. We can draw significant wisdom from the life of Nehemiah. Nehemiah 6:15 tells us he was able to rebuild the walls of Jerusalem in just 52 days. I believe Nehemiah was successful because he had clear direction from God and the discipline to see it through.

What are the disciplines you need to put into practice today? My suggestion would be to start with a small commitment today and see it through for the next 30 days. As you have success, increase your commitment. Pray that God would reveal his purpose and blessing into the discipline you are trying to develop.

Make today count!

Day 361

It has been an incredible journey over the past year to write these devotional thoughts each morning. My purpose behind writing them has been to encourage, challenge, and hopefully inspire you. I don't believe there is any power in my thoughts, but I do believe there is power in the Word of God. Isaiah 55:11 says it well, "So shall My word be that goes forth from My mouth, it shall not return to Me void, But it shall accomplish what I please, and it shall prosper in the thing for which I sent it." My prayer is that this verse has resounded truth in your heart and mind.

Some questions for you to ponder: "What changes will you make in light of what you have processed? How do you look different because of interacting with God's word this year? What are the things you can begin to do each day to "make today count" regardless of the circumstances surrounding your day?

My challenge for you today is to live for a calling larger than one that is self-serving. Look for ways to impact the lives of those around you as you are uniquely positioned to do so. Use your gifts and talents to bring glory and honor to God.

Make today count!

Day 362

I would assume that many of you are like me in that on the rare occasion when you think about the time when your life will come to an end, you imagine yourself to be in your late 80s or early 90s, sitting up in bed with your friends and family gathered around you as you walk from this life into the next. This, for me at least, is the only way that I can make sense of death. When someone young passes away unexpectedly, it is almost as if every belief that we have is shaken to the core. It's so difficult to comprehend, it's difficult to process, and it's difficult to understand why.

For me, sudden tragedies have a way of realigning me to my purpose. My purpose in life is the same as yours, to make disciples as Jesus instructed us to do in the Great Commission. Matthew 28:16-20 says, "Then the eleven disciples went to Galilee, to the mountain where Jesus had told them to go. When they saw him, they worshiped him; but some doubted. Then Jesus came to them and said, "All authority in heaven and on earth has been given to me. Therefore, go and make disciples of all nations, baptizing them in the name of the Father and of the Son and of the Holy Spirit, and teaching them to obey everything I have commanded you. And surely I am with you always, to the very end of the age."

Tragedies create a sense of urgency within us, as none of us are guaranteed tomorrow. Time is not guaranteed. Eternity hangs in the balance. The question today for you is will you allow this urgency to invade your calling?

Make today count!

Day 363

Almost 10 years ago when I was fairly new in my position as the aquatics coordinator at the YMCA, I was asked to help open the outdoor pool of another YMCA. It was just four days before the pool was to open, and due to a multitude of circumstances, the pool was green and filled with leaves. For the next three days, I worked sun up to sundown doing everything in my power to make sure this pool passed the health inspection and was ready to be opened to the members on time. There was a great sense of urgency within the work.

When the need is clear, it is easy to keep urgency high. Craig Groeschel says what can happen is our "urgency can lead to complacency." Once we have completed the specific task we have set out to accomplish, we can become complacent. If you have been given a calling in which you feel a sense of urgency, you should always be pushing forward towards the next thing.

In Luke 12:16-20, Jesus tells a parable that speaks directly to complacency. "And he told them this parable: "The ground of a certain rich man yielded an abundant harvest. He thought to himself, 'What shall I do? I have no place to store my crops.' "Then he said, 'This is what I'll do. I will tear down my barns and build bigger ones, and there I will store my surplus grain. And I'll say to myself, "You have plenty of grain laid up for many years. Take life easy; eat, drink and be merry."'

"But God said to him, 'You fool! This very night your life will be demanded from you. Then who will get what you have prepared for yourself?"

My challenge for you today is to keep urgency at the forefront of your work. We, like the rich farmer, are not guaranteed tomorrow, so we should work with passion and purpose and an uncompromising sense of urgency.

Make today count!

Day 364

Each of these devotions have ended with the phrase, "make today count." I can't point to the exact time or event that took place, but several years ago I heard someone say that you and only you are in control of how your day goes. Regardless of our circumstances, we are responsible for our response to them. If we were to say we had no ability to determine how we respond based on the circumstance, then we have given up our right to choose. Each day God offers us the right to make the choice of how we will use our day.

I think King David had a great understanding about what it really means to make each day count. Psalm 118:24, "This is the day the Lord has made; We will rejoice and be glad in it." This verse reminds us that we should rejoice each day. It doesn't say rejoicing should only happen when things go the way you want them to go. You must choose to rejoice each day, and you and only you can choose to make today count.

So, make today count!

Day 365

Today is a cool day for me. As of today, for 365 days straight, I have tried to use my social media platform as a way to encourage and to point others towards Christ through a daily devotional thought based on scripture. I clearly remember last year being so tired of seeing so much divisiveness and negativity being spread. I was about to delete my social media accounts, but then the thought hit me that I can control what I post. I could use my posts for good. After a full year, I can tell you it has been pretty amazing to see how God has used this. The fact that God can use a person with dyslexia in this capacity is just another thing that shows his greatness.

It reminds me of when God called Moses, Moses gave God every reason in the world why he was unfit and unable to communicate clearly. God responded to Moses by asking him in Exodus 4:11, "Who has made man's mouth? or who makes the dumb, or deaf, or the seeing, or the blind? have not I the LORD?" We have a tendency to tell God the things we can and cannot do based on our perceived skill sets. God wants to use us despite our lack of certain abilities. This assures that God gets all the glory.

My question for you today is what are you doing to make an impact with your life? You have influences in circles you run in where you may be the only light of Christ they will ever interact with. How have you been telling God you are incapable of serving him? My challenge for you today is to turn your weaknesses to him and allow his strength to come out of them.

Make today count!